The Contemporary American Crime Novel

The Contemporary American Crime Novel

Race, Ethnicity, Gender, Class

Andrew Pepper

Edinburgh University Press

© Andrew Pepper, 2000

Edinburgh University Press Ltd
22 George Square, Edinburgh

Typeset in Garamond
by Textype, Cambridge, and
printed and bound in Great Britain by
MPG Books Ltd, Bodmin

A CIP Record for this book is available from the British Library

ISBN 0 7486 1340 4 (paperback)

The right of Andrew Pepper
to be identified as author of this work
has been asserted in accordance with
the Copyright, Designs and Patents Act 1988.

Contents

Acknowledgements

Many thanks to Clive Bloom, Paul Cobley, Geoff Hempstead, Andreas Hess, Peter Messent, Ralph Willett, Carol Smith and John Whitley for the helpful comments and advice on how to approach the subject, and to Nicola Carr at Edinburgh University Press for her editorial insights and professionalism. Special thanks also to my parents and Pauline Hoffman for their continuing support while writing and researching the book. Above all, the book is dedicated to Claire, without whose love and encouragement it would not have been started, let alone finished.

Portions of this book have been published in different forms as 'Taking the Black out of Noir: Deconstructing Blackness in Walter Mosley's Fiction', in *Borderlines: Studies in American Culture*, 27, 3 (Summer 1997), pp. 251–66; 'Bridges and Boundaries: Race, Ethnicity and the Contemporary American Crime Novel', in Kathleen G. Klein (ed.), *Diversity and Detective Fiction* (Bowling Green: Popular Press, 1999), pp. 240–59; 'Seriously Lurid: The Pitfalls of Publishing American Hard-Boiled Fiction in the UK', in John Gabilliet and John Dean (eds), *European Readings of American Popular Culture* (Westport, CT: Greenwood, 1996), pp. 51–8.

Introduction:
'Multiculturalism is Dead! Long Live Multiculturalism!'

Diversity and Division in the Contemporary United States

Diversity in America is everywhere. Ride the subways and buses, walk the streets, turn on the television, listen to the radio, and it is hard not to notice it staring back at you in the faces and voices of the country's ethnically diverse people. Division, too, is ever-present. Ride the subways and buses, walk the streets, turn on the television, listen to the radio, and it is hard not to notice the various axes of difference and division criss-crossing the American landscape. Diversity implies choice, plurality and strength through difference. Division implies separation, segregation and conflict. Diversity calls attention to America's glorious past as a 'teeming of nations' and to its golden future as a multicultural Babylon. Division looks back at a bloody history of racial segregation and hostility towards immigrants and forward to a nightmarish apocalypse where individuals are set against individuals, ethnic groups against ethnic groups, men, women, straights and gays against each other. Diversity is advertised by glossy corporate brochures featuring not-so-random groups of happy, smiling, multi-ethnic faces. Division is writ large in the words and images percolating into the media from the inner-city ghettoes and radical printing presses.

Popular culture, by and large, has willingly embraced diversity and division as shaping visions for its productions, packaging them to carefully demarcated audiences, or more tantalisingly to the same audiences, appealing to different sides of the same audience. Thus films like *Grand Canyon or How to Make an American Quilt*, with their avowed optimistic and remorselessly upbeat vision of harmonious pluralism, play at multiplexes or sit on video racks alongside *Blade Runner* and *Boyz 'n the Hood*, where suspicion and violent conflict tends to characterise relations between individuals and groups. This is a book about diversity and division in the contemporary American crime novel, how the attendant baggage of both terms, the hopeful longings implicit in the former term and the divisive anxieties implicit in the latter term, are simultaneously given voice in a form or genre whose internal features are themselves racked by tensions and contradictions. It is a book about the resulting complications, what happens when the diversity and divisions that characterise the contemporary United States are written into a genre whose cultural politics have always been ambiguous and problematic, a popular form made unpopular by its willingness to embrace a darker vision of humanity and, indeed, of America.

The question of whether America is better conceived of and understood in terms of its enabling diversity or its crippling divisions has, in turn, fed into and energised debates about the nature and depth of racial, ethnic, class and gender differences. Indeed focus on race, ethnicity, class and gender have recast the terrain of identity politics to such an extent that the term 'American' itself now seems too cumbersome and unwieldy, an identity that conceals as much as it reveals. If the practice of modern history, as David Thelan argues, was born a couple of centuries ago 'to invent narratives and persuade peoples to interpret their personal experiences within national terms and narratives'[1] then contemporary cultural studies and modern historiography, has sought with more than a little justification to challenge this assumption and expose the extent to which people's identifications and hence their identities have always been more complex, more problematic. The mask of nationhood may then have crumbled, though not entirely so, to reveal a snake pit of competing and overlapping subject-positions but to merely acknowledge this situation, like some kind of avid cultural trainspotter, is not sufficient. The United States, without a doubt, is a diverse or multicultural society but to characterise this multiculturalism merely by pointing to the full range of racial, ethnic, class, gender, religious and regional identities, so to speak, 'on offer', essentially reveals very little. As Ella Shohat and Robert Stam astutely remark, 'For us, the word "multiculturalism" has no essence; it points to a debate'.[2]

In many ways the intensity of this debate, which has raged voraciously not just in the academy but also in the public domain, in newspapers, magazines and on television and radio talk shows, has started to abate but in so doing has assumed a more thoughtful, intelligent complexion. Throughout the 1990s indignant neo-conservatives lined up across the trenches from exasperated liberals. The former conceived of multiculturalism in much the same way as they had done the Soviet threat in the previous decade, as a kind of mutant biochemical strain whose very presence could pollute the ideological and bodily purity of a sanctified and largely mythic America.[3] The latter, meanwhile, opted to describe the 'new' diversity by employing upbeat culinary metaphors such as 'salad bowl' or 'stir fry' or 'smorgasbord experience', to emphasise the distinctive contribution that each ingredient had to make and to underline their commitment to a 'different-but-equal' vision of America where no single culture or group took precedence over the other.[4] Yet firing potshots at one another from opposite wings of a rapidly narrowing political spectrum could only conceal their similarities for so long. In essence, both liberals and neo-conservatives were arguing for a definition of America that acknowledged the ethnic and racial diversity of its population (for who could do otherwise?) but which, implicitly or explicitly, advocated the maintenance of a common culture and interpreted it as 'a declaration of democratic faith in a plural, diverse society'.[5] Drawing both positions together, Thomas Sowell, neo-conservative critic dressed up as liberal or vice versa, positively enthused, 'The size and cohesion of American society is all the more remarkable because of the diverse origins of the people who make it up'.[6] In doing so, however, Sowell and others suggested where the terms of the future debate would lie because, implicitly, this kind of assertion, as Homi K. Bhabha would later point out, failed to interrogate the link between ideology and national unity fully enough, and thus papered over material inequalities and contradictions that lay at the heart of American life:

> Like all myths of the nation's 'unity,' the common culture is a profoundly conflicted ideological strategy. It is a declaration of democratic faith in a plural diverse society and, at the same time, a defense against the real, subversive demands that the articulation of cultural difference – the empowering of minorities – makes upon democratic pluralism.[7]

If a gap has opened up between the rhetoric and what might tentatively be termed 'reality', between the ideological posturing of liberals and neo-conservatives alike and the 'lived' experiences of those who either do not want to blend into a common culture that remains white Euro-American in orientation or have not been permitted to do so, and between the upbeat, public pronouncements of corporations and university brochures with their glossy images of happy, smiling, multi-ethnic faces and the more revealing, private anxieties about racial and ethnic difference that only get articulated behind closed doors, then it is merely an acknowledgement that the terms of the debate need to be reconstituted. Bhabha's remarks, which point to the willingness of those with social, economic and political power to embrace cultural pluralism without embracing what would seem to be the next step, the diffusion of that power from centre to margin, also indicate how the terms of the debate have changed. Increasingly critics like West, Marable, McLaren and Shohat and Stam have jettisoned the more ethereal question of what multiculturalism means, to focus on how it can lead to what Marable calls 'the radical democratic restructuring of the system of cultural and political power itself'.[8]

This shift, from the theoretical to the material or, if you like, from 'text' to 'world', is significant because, as Peter McLaren argues, it speaks about the importance of thinking about American 'difference' in the context of a long history of social, political and economic inequality and particularly racial discrimination, and anticipates attempts to 'change the material conditions that allow relations of domination to prevail over relations of equality and social justice'.[9] With it comes the implicit understanding that not all people and groups are oppressed in the same way, and that relations of domination and subordination cut across systems of race, ethnicity, class, gender, age, region and sexuality. On the one hand, this makes redundant old-fashioned models founded upon over-simplistic 'them' and 'us' formulas (for a black woman suffering at the hands of her white boss and black husband, who, after all, is to be classified as 'them'?). On the other hand, in the context of the United States, it allows for the re-inscription of race as perhaps the most significant axes of difference and, more pertinently, system of oppression. Patriarchy and capitalism have, of course, left manifestly visible scars but Cornel West makes the telling point that white supremacy and the enslavement of Africans, more so than other forms of domination, have been fundamental to the creation of 'democracy' in the United States. It is worth quoting West's thoughts on this subject at some length:

> Needless to sat, this fragile experiment began by taking for granted the ugly conquest of Amerindians and Mexicans, the exclusion of women, the subordination of European working-class men and the closeting of homosexuals . . . Yet the enslavement of Africans – over 20 percent of the population – served as the linchpin of American democracy; that is, the much-heralded stability and continuity of American democracy was predicated upon black oppression and degradation. Without the presence of black people in America, European-Americans would not be 'white' – they would be only Irish, Italians, Poles, Welsh, and others engaged in class, ethnic and gender struggles over resources and identity. What made America distinctly American for them was not simply the presence of unprecedented opportunities, but the struggle for seizing these opportunities in a new land in which black slavery and racial caste served as the floor upon which class, ethnic and gender struggles could be diffused and diverted.[10]

Given the depth and longevity of black/white fault-lines in American society, it is hardly surprising that West should argue for the centrality of race in determining cultural identity in the contemporary United States. Yet West's conception of 'race' is not static and one-dimensional, a fixed and unyielding trope distinguishing 'black' from 'white' with clinical, pseudo-scientific rationality. Quite the opposite, in fact. As science explodes the myth of racial purity and immigrants particularly from Latin America, the Caribbean and Asia further problematise the binary caste system, race is being transformed. Or rather as Manning Marable argues, '"race" continues to be central to American politics [and culture] but its definition, utilization and social construction are being readily transformed'.[11] In this context, I argue that multiculturalism, and indeed the American crime novel, needs to be viewed through the prism of race but only in so far as the transformation of race involves the acknowledgement of its interconnectedness with other axes of difference and systems of domination. Different cultures and races are fundamentally implicated in one another and the connections and divergences need to be documented, but this does not necessarily put America 'beyond' race. As Howard Wincant argues, 'The ongoing transformation and the increasingly complex construction of racial identities in the contemporary United States is an accomplished fact. The big question is how this perception is to be interpreted'.[12] It is a question, too, that looms large in this book.

Diversity and Division in the Contemporary American Crime Novel

The same kind of problems which have dogged social scientists attempting to conceive of a usable multiculturalism have also affected critics of the contemporary American crime novel. Too often the latter have surveyed the transformed ethnic and racial character of the American landscape like delighted tourists on safari, gazing out at the exotic panorama and marvelling at the full range of species on view, and using the same motif, have sought to learn or understand more about the different cultures themselves with the detective or protagonist as tour-guide. To this end, Gina and Andrew MacDonald argue that 'non-mainstream detectives explore cultural difference and act as links between cultures, interpreting each to each'.[13] Publishers, too, tout difference with evangelical zeal, pointing excitedly to the range of geographical settings and the myriad of racial, ethnic, class and gender identities at play in the contemporary crime novel; how the apparently unitary figure of the white, male, hard-boiled detective has been reconstituted in every possible guise and persona. Indeed a recent summary of genre's ethnic diversity revealed such intriguingly obtuse categories as 'Armenian-American', 'Basque-American', 'Irish-Puerto Rican-American', 'Mexican-Indian Anglo' and 'Slovenic-American'.[14]

The problem with this type of reading of the crime novel as barometer of social and cultural change is also the problem with a liberal pluralist vision of America. Both, in a word, are far too nice, or present a vision of America that is far too nice. Such problems are not entirely intertwined. Those who conceive of the hard-boiled detective as a kind of cultural mediator or tour-guide fundamentally misread the historical implications of the genre. Thus when the Macdonalds argue that just as the traditional hard-boiled detective mediates between haves and have-nots, interpreting each for each, 'so the ethnic detective mediates between the culturally assimilated and the culturally unassimilated, interpreting each for each',[15] they fail to acknowledge that American crime fiction has been characterised from its inception by violent tensions and often irreconcilable contradictions, and fail to acknowledge the extent to which the harder-boiled detectives, whatever their race, ethnicity or gender, struggle and usually fail to marry their antipathy towards their paymasters and established notions of justice to their function as 'equilibrium restorers'. In others words, most detectives are not, and have never been, polite cultural mediators, but rather usually violent, always conflicted figures who operate out of selfish as well selfless motivations.[16] Moreover while a diversity of voices and viewpoints is an inexorable feature of contemporary American crime novels and contemporary American life, to conceive of this diversity in harmonious, mannered terms is, at best, naive and, at worst, dishonest. After all, everyone has a voice or viewpoints but what about the same access to jobs and places to live, the same economic opportunities, or even the same representations in local and federal politics?

Still accusations of 'niceness' levelled at this type of criticism and at a liberal pluralist conception of America as 'gorgeous mosaic', constitute a usable common denominator because in both, any conception of pain, suffering, violence, discrimination or exploitation is ruthlessly expunged to the margins. Shohat and Stam make the point that a radical, substantive multiculturalism cannot simply be 'nice' but rather 'has to recognize the existential realities of pain, anger and resentment, since the multiple cultures invoked by the term . . . have not historically coexisted in relations of equality and mutual respect'.[17] From its inception, American crime fiction, particularly the raw, often brutal crime fiction practised by writers like Dashiell Hammett, has not shied away from portraying urban America and the problems and anxieties to be found there in a harsh, uncompromising light. Much of this book is concerned with the question of how contemporary American crime writers have responded to the kind of situation that Shohat and Stam describe. Consequently the book considers the emergence of African-American, female, gay and lesbian, Latino, Jewish and Asian writers alongside contemporary developments in white, male traditions in order to ask whether, or indeed how, the crime novel has been able to register the 'existential realities of pain, anger and resentment' experienced by different individuals and communities, and more significantly, relate these conditions to the oppressive character of an American society founded upon deep-rooted and at times all-pervasive relations of domination and subordination.

It is perhaps dangerous to conflate American crime fiction and a radical, transformative multiculturalism too closely. After all, the latter, as Shohat and Stam acknowledge, has less to do with culture *per se* – and cultural artifacts like the crime novel – than with the communities 'behind' the artifacts, and requires 'a profound restructuring and reconceptualization of the power relations behind cultural communities'.[18] Furthermore, as we shall see, the crime novel and the figure of the detective are, to some extent, implicated in the hegemonic ambitions of those who have benefited from the unequal distribution of power. Still, in so far as the detective is not entirely implicated in these ambitions and strives to assert his or her opposition, often through violence, to the dominant culture, the genre has much subversive potential, not least because the detective's function is arguably less a palliative one – to provide insights into social and cultural problems or to mediate between individuals and groups in order to reconcile differences – than an overtly aggressive one based on a desire to expose state-sponsored corruption and dismantle the hierarchies that spawned it layer by layer, piece by piece. Complications of course abound. State-sponsored corruption is both visible and invisible, easy to identify and yet hard to actually locate. Power is centralised in the hands of a few and yet dispersed throughout society. Detection is a means of social control as well as social revolution. The detective is opposed to dominant values and yet part of machinery through which those values are affirmed. He or she undercuts but also reinscribes relations of domination and subordination.

The contention of this book is that the crime novel offers no easy, clear-cut answers; it neither advocates revolution nor the *status quo*. Certainly its multiple forms, its traditional codes and conventions and the reinvention of these codes and conventions not just by an emerging collection of African-American, female, gay, Latino and Asian writers but also by straight white males, defy straightforward categorisation. Yet precisely because of these ruptures, these complications, the properties and ambitions of the crime novel anticipate and reflect those of a radical, substantive multiculturalism, at least in so far as both reject a kind of moralistic, preachy, austere homogeneity in favour of a fractured, hot-blooded, transgressive heterogeneity. Moving beyond the kind of bland, politically correct assumptions that have tended to underwrite this kind of project – that, for example, a crime novel by a black female writer will automatically be more radical than one by a white male writer – this book intends to explore the complex social landscape of the contemporary United States using the crime novel, with all its glorious inconsistencies and contradictions writ large, as cultural barometer. What emerges is neither a portrait of, to use REM's words, 'shiny happy people' nor a post-apocalyptic vision of America on the verge of civil war, but rather an America beset by bitter racial, ethnic, class and gender conflict nonetheless able to contemplate a present and future where 'difference' can be acknowledged and where relations of domination and subordination can be if not overturned then at least unsettled.

Notes

1. David Thelan, 'Making History and Making the United States', *Journal of American Studies*, 32, 3, December, 1998, p. 373.
2. Ella Shohat and Robert Stam, *Unthinking Eurocentrism: Multiculturalism and the Media* (London and New York: Routledge, 1994), p. 47.
3. See, for example, Arthur M. Schlesinger, *The Disuniting of America* (New York: Norton, 1992).
4. See, for example, Lawrence Fuchs, *The Ethnic Kaleidoscope: Race, Ethnicity and Civic Culture* (Hanover: University of New England Press, 1990).
5. See Peter McLaren, 'White Terror and Oppositional Agency: Towards a Critical Multiculturalism', in David Theo Goldberg (ed.), *Multiculturalism: A Reader* (Oxford and Cambridge, MA: Blackwells, 1994), p. 54.
6. Thomas Sowell, *Ethnic America: A History* (New York: Basic Books, 1981), p. 4.
7. See McLaren, *Multiculturalism*, p. 54.
8. Manning Marable, *Beyond Black and White: Rethinking Race in American Politics and Society* (London and New York: Verso, 1995), p. 124.
9. McLaren, *Multiculturalism*, p. 58.
10. Cornel West, *Race Matters* (Boston: Beacon Press, 1993), p. 156.
11. Marable, *Beyond Black and White*, p. xviii.
12. Howard Wincant, 'Dictatorship, Democracy and Difference: The Historical Construction of Racial Identity', in Michael Peter Smith and Joe R. Feagin (eds), *The Bubbling Cauldron: Race, Ethnicity and the Urban Crisis* (Minneapolis: University of Minnesota Press, 1995), p. 46.
13. Gina Macdonald and Andrew Macdonald, 'Ethnic Detectives in Popular

Fiction: New Directions for an American Genre', in Kathleen G. Klein (ed.), *Diversity and Detective Fiction* (Bowling Green: Popular Press, 1999), p. 60.

14. See Macdonald and Macdonald, *Diversity and Detective Fiction*, pp. 96–113.
15. Macdonald and Macdonald, *Diversity and Detective Fiction*, p. 79.
16. Ideas explored more fully in next chapter.
17. Shohat and Stam, *Unthinking Eurocentrism*, pp. 358–9.
18. Shohat and Stam, *Unthinking Eurocentrism*, p. 47.

CHAPTER 1

Making and Re-Making the American Crime Novel

One of the most significant generic transformations ushered in by the emerging American hard-boiled school of crime writers in the interwar years was a dramatic shift in the perception and representation of crime and its currency as social barometer. Crime was no longer seen as it had been in the 'classic' detective fiction of Christie and Sayers as the product of occasional and atypical tears in the otherwise secure moral fabric of genteel English society, but rather as bastard offspring of an urban-fuelled modernity. Using the fast-expanding metropolitan sprawls particularly of West-coast America, hard-boiled writers conceived and represented this emerging urbanity in grim, distopian terms. Seen through their eyes, crime was not only endemic, a connective tissue which could sour and soil relations between all social groups, but perhaps more disturbingly, it was shown to be an inevitable part of the institutional superstructure of American life. Their novels were littered with shady businessmen, conniving politicians, corrupt police departments and morally bankrupt judges. So dense was the foliage of criminal conspiracy, the figure and agency of the detective was transformed; no longer could he hope to exercise a near-total Holmesian control over his world. Instead his interventions were partial and limited; individual transgressions were often exposed and punished but the macro-environment responsible for nurturing deviancy remained untouched.

Yet to metaphorise 'crime' in hard-boiled crime fiction as some kind of endlessly replicating hydra, bloating itself on the unchecked degeneracy of American capitalist urban modernity is perhaps disingenuous. Critics have fiercely debated the nature and indeed the extent of the apparent schism between the hard-boiled school of crime fiction and its generic antecedents, and argued over the status and appeal of the genre or sub-genre; whether or not it has been, or indeed still is, able to give voice to a radical, oppositional political perspective. Furthermore critics have been unable to agree upon whether this hard-boiled school actually constitutes a single, homogeneous entity, or whether it is best theorised in stylistic rather than political terms, as a loosely aligned collection of sometimes overlapping, sometimes conflicting voices.

A cluster of critics working at the start of the 1980s, with Marxist sympathies – Stephen Knight, Dennis Porter, Franco Moretti and Ernest Mandel[1] – have identified the crime novel, whether English or American, as an essentially conservative form predicated on the goal of what Porter refers to as 'perceptual re-familiarization'[2] whereby the trajectory of the narrative leads inexorably to a restoration of the *status quo* and thus, a re-affirmation of the existing social order. Porter and Mandel acknowledge that significant differences do exist between 'classic' and 'hard-boiled' forms, at least in so far as the latter focus on the prevalence of social and economic corruption in American society, but argue that even as hard-boiled writers reveal this corruption, they offer a remedy or at least a tonic in the form of the individualist detective, whose not necessarily moral interventions make the necessary corrections. Knight expands upon this definition, to propose that the largely middle-class readership of crime fiction actually informs and validates the genre's inherent conservatism, and vice versa. To this extent, crime fiction not only creates 'an idea (or a hope or dream)' about controlling crime, but also realises 'a whole view of the world, one shared by the people who become the central audience to buy, read, and find comfort in a particular variety of crime fiction'.[3] Moretti and Porter, meanwhile, map these discussions on to a wider cultural canvas, to consider the relationship between 'low' and 'high' forms, between 'mass' culture whose function is to expel the 'strange' and reaffirm the normal and 'art' or 'literature' whose function is the opposite, to the expel the normal and reaffirm the 'strange'. Hence Moretti argues: 'The fabula narrated by the detective in his reconstruction of the facts brings us back to the beginning; that is, it abolishes narration . . . In this sense, detective fiction is anti-literary. It declares narration as a mere deviation'.[4]

Informed, in part, by the work of the Frankfurt School, these critics draw back from representing crime fiction in the uniformly negative manner in which Adorno and Horkheimer dismiss mass culture in general – standardised products, spewed out by an all-powering 'culture industry' and force-fed to a passive audience in order to reinforce the cultural values of consumer capitalist society – but in their view, the genre's oppositional potential is strictly limited. More recently, though, other critics, notably Jim Collins, Ralph Willett, and Woody Haut[5] have challenged the assumptions that underwrite these related position, arguing as Willett has done that hard-boiled crime fiction can be 'used deconstructively to display the fragmentation and complexity of modern life and to undermine the tendency of narrative to achieve control and closure'. The liminal, socially alienated status of the detective, the absence of clear-cut resolution, and the failure of the 'official' law to make the necessary corrections, Jim Collins argues, are significant component parts of a destabilising, socially radical discourse which 'forces contradictions rather than compromises; that is disruptive rather integrative, because "justice" is characterised as provisional, incomplete and virtually unenforceable by a State incapable of understanding its complexity'.[7] Or as Haut points out, the hard-boiled crime novel has always been characterised by 'uncertainty, deviancy, moral ambiguity, iconoclasm and a narrative suggesting cultural and psychological fragmentation'.[8]

Peter Messent makes some attempt to bring these positions together, arguing that the complexities and contradictions bound up within the codes and conventions of the detective novel, most significantly that the detective has to reaffirm a dominant social order that he or she knows to be repressive and unjust, make it difficult to classify it as either 'integrative' or 'disruptive,' 'conservative' or 'radical'. Ultimately, however, Messent draws back from this position to side with Porter and Moretti, arguing that 'in the final analysis [the detective] serves the interests of the dominant social order'.[9] In the final analysis, one could also argue that what links all of these criticisms, the crime novel's celebrants and detractors, is a tendency to ignore the role played by the reader in the construction of meaning and a tendency to overlook both the formal and thematic ambiguities prevalent in individual texts and the bewildering diversity that characterises the overarching category of crime fiction, with all of its genres, sub-genres and styles, and also the specific field of hard-boiled crime fiction; a field spanning seventy-odd years and comprising authors with not necessarily overlapping political, economic and social perspectives on what the hard-boiled crime novel actually is.

A recent manifestation of this shortcoming has been a tangential tendency of some critics, particularly those exploring the gendered and ethnic diversity that now characterises the genre in the United States, to offer a far too narrow definition of the hard-boiled tradition, as though a genre as diverse and complex as one comprising not just Hammett, Chandler and latterly Ross MacDonald, but also Paul Cain, James M. Cain, Horace McCoy, Cornell Woolrich, Mickey Spillane, David Goodis, Jim Thompson and John Franklin Bardin could be summarised and dismissed in the space of a few lines. Shuker-Haines and Umphrey, for example, seeking to differentiate the male hard-boiled 'hero' from his contemporary female counterpart, describe him simply as someone possessing a 'strict code of honour and renunciation' and embodying 'a vision of righteousness and justice',[10] while Kathleen Gregory Klein refers to the male model of the detective[11] as though the overlapping but also radically different identities of Hammett's Sam Spade and Chandler's Phillip Marlowe could somehow be unproblematically conflated. Neither of these descriptions come even close to doing justice to a figure as complex and contradictory as Spade or Hammett's other detective, the Continental Op. Featured in *Red Harvest* (1929), the Op is simultaneously a lone operator and state-sponsored henchman, someone who is attractive in so far as he is able to exercise his will and repulsive in so far as he is complicit in the bloodbath that follows his arrival in Personville. The Op is strong and yet without an identity, an independent agent yet completely in the grips of forces beyond his control, and a peacemaker whose tactics are overtly violent. He successfully cleans up the town, ridding it of its criminal element but in doing so re-inscribes the authority of its not-so-benign capitalist patriarch. One could perhaps add, as a kind of postscript, that the practice of denying or glossing over this complexity with an almost rude haste serves the purpose of these critics very well in so far as it makes the points of comparison between the so-called 'radical' new and 'reactionary' old that much easier to identify.

Much of this criticism may well pay lip-service to definitions of 'genre' which acknowledge its fluid constitution and constantly shifting parameters, but the conflation in their analysis of a whole spectrum of crime fictions and authors, whether to emphasise its reactionary or transgressive qualities, works in the end to deny this fluidity, to posit the crime novel, whether Hammett's *The Maltese Falcon*, or even Christie's *The Murder of Roger Ackroyd*, as belonging to essentially the same category and possessing the same kind of features. Bell and Daldry speak about exactly these concerns when they argue that such criticism 'covertly devalues the work it articulates, turning them into versions of some recurrent ideal, and leaving the critic with little to do other than survey the range of variations available'.[12] Their suggestion, that so much crime writing 'responds to, parodies and explores its own conventions' (not simply reiterating previous forms but reconfiguring them and exploring 'their congruities and incongruities')[13] informs much of what follows, because this kind of genuinely elastic conception of genre acknowledges the existence of difference; that, for example the fictions of Hammett and Chandler are not interchangeable simply on the grounds of their belonging to the same genre.

This kind of elasticity, moreover, allows for a definition of hard-boiled crime fiction that embraces, rather than closes off, its inherent ambiguities and contradictions. Instead of arguing for the genre either as exclusively 'conservative' or 'subversive', 'reactionary' or 'progressive', 'left' or 'right', 'hegemonic' or 'counter-hegemonic', much of what follows seeks to map out how and to what effect particular crime novels and writers combine these contradictory elements. The cultural politics of the hard-boiled detective, for example, have always been deeply ambivalent. At once an alienated loner or maverick whose interventions are necessary because the law is shown to be corrupt or inadequate, he or she is outside of the dominant social order and yet is a crucial part of the machinery by which social control is maintained and existing hierarchies, policed. In much hard-boiled American crime fiction, then, we see a complex set of overlapping and yet conflicting forces at play, some conservative, others radical. This book is interested in exploring how particular contemporary practitioners either open up or close off these tensions, as the detective or protagonist moves in and out of various positions and roles, making and re-making the genre in the process. It is also interested in examining how these particular disjunctures or ruptures are further complicated when the narrative or authorial focus shifts from male to female, from white to non-white, from straight to gay. Which is not to blithely suggest that the resultant situation is inevitably 'utopian' or 'transgressive'; just that such shifts further reconfigure the boundaries and assumptions of an already fluid genre and thus need to be investigated.

This kind of elasticity also foregrounds the role played by the reader in the construction of meaning; that is, meanings, and indeed genres, are not fixed within texts, as most criticism seems to assume, or secured through the interaction of text and critic, but are constantly being made and remade by readers. As Cobley notes, 'Texts may be shown to possess the internal textual organization that genre theorists have discerned . . . but repeatedly, reception theory has shown that textual meaning derives in large part from what the reader has imported him/herself'.[14] Only Knight, of those already discussed, has paid significant attention to the role played by crime fiction's readership in determining what the genre means, but rather dismissively he presumes a unity of opinion or thought that arguably does not exist; namely, that major examples of crime fiction create a hope about controlling crime which realises and validates a view of the world shared by its predominantly middle-class readership.[15] One could ask not only why Knight is so sure that major examples of crime fiction do create such a hope but also whether this hope is indeed shared by its readership, particularly since in a later essay he acknowledges that crime novels can also be 'radical' – that is, 'set out to construct a left hegemony within a form that most have assumed to be inherently complicit with bourgeois culture'.[16] Most critics maybe, but not most readers. In fact this apparent 'about-turn' and the co-existence of an often conflicting range of critical opinions about the same texts[17] is perhaps the best evidence one could put forward to support the claim that meanings are not fixed within texts but constructed by critics and readers (who are critics themselves).

The idea that readers of popular fiction construct politically or culturally transgressive meanings by way of their own interaction with the text and the world is pursued by McCracken's *Pulp* (1998). In sharp contrast, not just to Knight, Porter and Mandel but also to the contemporary disciples of Adorno and Horkheimer, McCracken argues that 'the negotiation between world, reader and text does not simply smooth over contradictions and conflicts. [Rather] it may well do the opposite and provoke a feeling of dissatisfaction, a sense that something is missing'.[18] Refusing to conceive of mass culture as an irresistible force, creating standard products for standard consumers, McCracken argues for mass culture as a contradictory phenomenon, 'open to intervention and affording the opportunity for critical engagement by its audience'.[19] Within the realm of detective fiction, McCracken is aware of the criticisms of Porter and Moretti, that the shock of the murder in detective fiction is diffused by the investigation and ultimately by the resolution, but suggests that detective fiction is read as much for the uncertainties provoked by the unknown (or the still to-be-revealed) as for the security given by the conclusion, and that 'more questions are raised in the narrative than are answered by formal closure'.[20]

There are, however, dangers associated with this kind of critical approach, too; dangers to which McCracken only alludes when he suggests that in the end, 'it is a matter of debate whether the narrative of detection confirms or disrupts the social boundaries transgressed'.[21] One could read this remark in one of two ways. Either he is suggesting that it is a matter of debate whether detective fiction in general confirms or disrupts social boundaries, or that it is a matter of debate which detective novels confirm or disrupt social boundaries. The difference is significant. The former position suggests that textual differences are less important than those constructed by the reader, that all novels and acts of popular consumption are potentially subversive, and that the creation of meaning at the level of popular consumption somehow flattens out or negates any textual differences that might exist. The latter position suggests that certain texts have 'built-in' meanings that are sympathetic to particular interpretations. McCracken's focus on a genre-bending author like Walter Mosley in a chapter entitled 'Transgression and Utopianism' indicates that particular texts and authors are better able to accommodate transgressive meanings; that said, his use in an earlier chapter of the arguably more conservative (generically and politically) Colin Dexter for the same purpose would tend to suggest otherwise. In any case the question of whether critical discrimination matters is carefully and, I would argue deliberately, circumnavigated.

The problem, then, at least is clear-cut. To ignore the role played by readers in the construction of textual meanings is to re-centre the text as an object of study – if you like, to do people's discriminating for them. But to ignore the fact that questions of value and discrimination matter is to flirt with the idea that all cultural products have equal value and reproduce the logic that underwrites Meaghan Morris's conception of 'banality' in cultural studies; that since 'people in modern mediatized societies are complex and contradictory, mass cultural texts are complex and contradictory [and] . . . people using them produce complex and contradictory culture'.[22] The solution is to tread some kind of uneasy middle way between both positions, between the cheerleaders and prophets of doom, to conceive of and interpret popular texts neither as standardised objects produced in order to make money and re-inscribe the ideological control of an all-powering consumer capitalist culture nor as unproblematic objects of empowerment whose redeeming features lie only in the act of consumption and whose value is somehow 'equated with the value of groups consuming them'.[23] As Morris concludes:

> The critical vocabulary available to people wanting to theorize the discriminations that they make in relation to their own experiences of popular culture – without debating the 'validity' of that experience, even less that culture as a whole – is still, today, extraordinarily depleted. It seems to me, therefore, that the worst thing one can do in this context is to accuse people trying to develop a critique of popular culture of succumbing to 'elitism' or pessimism.[24]

Simon Frith makes a significant attempt to do exactly this; to develop a critique of popular culture that addresses issues of value and discrimination head-on. Frith does not deny that it is a vexed issue – who, after all, has the authority to say that something is better than something else? Better for whom? Better according to whose criteria? But he argues that to deny that popular taste hierarchies exist, to deny the significance of value judgements in popular culture, is hypocritical and self-defeating. 'To gloss over the continuous exercise of taste by the pop cultural audience is, in effect, to do their discrimination for them, while refusing to engage in the arguments which produce cultural values in the first place'. Frith concludes, 'This is, in the end, to reduce people to a faceless mass or market every bit as effectively as the mass cultural theorists against whom the populists are supposedly arguing'.[25] This is not an unproblematic return to a Leavisite position, arguing for a restrictive, elitist canon promoting works of literature capable of influencing 'the moral sensibility of the reader'.[26] Rather it is an acknowledgement that the 'redeeming' features of pop cultural texts do not necessarily have to reside externally – that is, in the opportunities they afford for 'reading against the grain' – but can also be internal to their structures, or aesthetic. Frith argues that the traditional high/low culture dichotomy whereby the value of 'low' culture, unlike 'high' art, was thought to reside not in its internal features but in its usage, needs to be revised. Addressing the aesthetics of popular culture is a necessary critical practice because 'people bring similar questions to high art and low art, that their pleasures and satisfactions are rooted in similar analytic issues [whether something is beautiful or moving or repulsive], similar ways of relating what they see or hear to how they think or feel'.[27]

Of course, the question of what actually constitutes something as 'popular', indeed how one should judge whether something is popular or not, is not at all clear. If sales alone were used as a yardstick, then much hard-boiled fiction, with its hard-edged, contradictory politics, its ambiguous morality and ambivalent attitude towards violence, would not meet the necessary requirements.[28] Nor should we forget that crime fiction emerged as consumerism's bastard offspring, a commercial literature whose ambitions were nonetheless instinctively distopian, a body of writing not afraid to roll up its sleeves and get its hands dirty, to revel in the city at its seediest. Perhaps, though, this is exactly the point. Perhaps we need to distinguish between different types of popular culture and different ways of using it, or at the very least acknowledge that in so far as certain crime writers challenge experience, push against prescribed boundaries, upset conventional tropes of detection and morality, and bring the genre's constitutive parts into fresh, problematic configurations that cannot be easily resolved, they inevitably steer their work into the realm of the 'unpopular popular' and in doing so suggest that the appeal of certain kinds of popular culture relates to its utopian *and* distopian impulses. Or as Frith argues, 'the "difficult" appeals through traces it carries of another world in which it would be "easy"'.[29]

Applying Frith's remarks to the American crime novel, one could argue that the genre as whole is read more for the uncertainties it provokes than the securities it provides. But one could also point out that the aesthetics and politics of individual crime novels differ radically, that particular crime novels and novelists, more than others, significantly reshape the genre's formal structures and its contradictory politics to further disrupt the hegemonic ambitions of the dominant culture, or rather marshal competing forces and ideologies into violent, unruly configurations that cannot be easily brought under control. The issue at stake is not just a discursive one but one relating to power, authority and meaning. The term 'hegemony' has been picked up by cultural critics to describe 'the complex, interlocking political, social and cultural forces that maintain power in society'.[30] Crucially the concept of hegemony, applied to the United States, does not assume that the domination of one group by another is total; rather it describes the processes by which opposition to particular individuals, communities and classes is '"contained and channeled into ideologically safe harbours" not through imposition but through negotiation'.[31]

Cultural hegemony affords marginal groups a place within the so-called dominant culture, though without necessarily guaranteeing their subordination. Therefore, to talk about a 'dominant' culture is something of a misnomer, given that the kind of struggle between individuals, communities and classes, as Jim Collins argues, works 'to destabilize the very category of the "dominant" by asserting multiple, competing hierarchies'.[32] My point is not that cultural, political or economic domination is an apparition; the detective, as we shall see, can play a role in securing its aims. Rather, it is that strategies of domination do not inevitably reduce subjects or agents to powerless ciphers. To this end, my interest is directed towards those novelists who deliberately steer their texts into rough, open waters, not ideologically safe harbours, and those detectives whose interventions transgress boundaries, disrupt hierarchies, question traditions and traditional assumptions and provoke contradictions. Lest we forget that the 'best' American crime fiction is messy, disturbing, ambiguous, violent, shocking. Moreover, though the 'crime' in crime fiction inevitably produces a 'corrective' force whose job it is to neutralise this disruption, these measures are provisional and limited, opening up and exposing tensions at play in society as a whole. Lévi-Strauss once remarked that, 'mythical thought always progresses from the awareness of oppositions towards their resolution'.[33] The trajectory of at least some American crime novels would seem to be in precisely the opposite direction.

Alternative Canons, Future Directions: Dashiell Hammett, Jim Thompson, Marc Behm, James Ellroy

If Paul Lauter's statement, that making the literary canon is 'a means by which culture validates social power' is true,[34] then it follows that un-making the literary canon is a means by which social power is diffused. In recent years, the centrality of a white male tradition of writing has come under sustained attack in the United States and elsewhere, with increasing numbers of non-white, un-straight, and non-male writers coming to the fore and forcing a reassessment of what actually constitutes American literature, thereby undermining the racist and

sexist ideologies that underwrote their exclusion in the first place.[35]
Within the realm of crime fiction, similar trends have been noted, and
whereas the tradition particularly of American hard-boiled writing has
in the past been 'frequently viewed as if it was the gift of its "brand
leaders", Hammett, Chandler and Macdonald',[36] nowadays the growing
presence of generically 'important' crime writers like Sara Paretsky, Sue
Grafton, Barbara Wilson and Walter Mosley, signals a significant social
and cultural shift.

As questions of culture, representation and identity increasingly
become interlaced with ones of power and ideology, it is perhaps
unsurprising that the white male detective, urban cousin to the Western
outlaw, should be implicated in the hegemonic ambitions of the
dominant white, male, heterosexual culture.[37] But just as the Western
outlaw, in revisionist Westerns at least, was not merely uncomfortable
with this role but violently rebelled against it, so too must the status of
the hard-boiled detective as willing talisman for a heroic white,
Christian/patriarchal order be called into question. Similarly, just as the
inclusion and exclusion of particular writers and texts from literary
canons has been, and still is, a reflection of prejudice and power, one
needs to be careful about consigning texts and writers to the proverbial
rubbish bin simply on the grounds of their established or marginal
status. In the rush to jettison or at least to push to one side significant
figures within the 'canon' of American crime fiction, one might heed
Clive Bush's warning that anti-canonicalness can be 'pure iconoclasm
and [obliterate] the need for judgement. It may even lead to the
ludicrous supposition that all art is of equal value'.[38]

My point, then, picking up on debates and arguments outlined in the
previous section, is not that canons either do not exist or have no
detrimental impact. It is simply to suggest that in our increasingly
fragmented society, it is no longer clear, to borrow Umberto Eco's
phrase, where the message is coming from;[39] that is, we can no longer
be certain of exactly who or what determines the constitution of literary
canons, whether they are part of what might be termed the 'dominant'
culture and indeed what this term actually means. If canons are defined
simply as 'preferred' collections of texts and authors, then we could say
that crime fiction canons are constructed not just by 'elitist' critics and
academics; readers, too, make distinctions, form and re-form canons
based on personal tastes and opinions, that very often do not coincide
with those being legitimised within the academy. One only has to look at
a recent list of the 'All-Time Ten Best American Crime Novels' voted for
by customers of a London bookstore, a list that included Elmore
Leonard's *City Primeval*, Walter Mosley's *Devil in a Blue Dress*, Jim
Thompson's *The Killer Inside Me* and Charles Willeford's *Miami Blues*

but nothing by Hammett, Chandler or Macdonald. One could also point to the large amount of criticism currently being devoted to the 'feminist' crime novel as evidence that Sara Paretsky, Sue Grafton and Patricia Cornwell may now constitute a new dominant crime fiction canon.

Readers, then, as much as critics and authors, are reconfiguring the social and cultural landscape of the United States, making and un-making genres and canons in the process, seeking out and unearthing new connections between dissident voices, dissolving and recon-structing themselves in the spaces 'in-between' traditional axes of nationality, race, class, gender, and sexuality. This is more than just postmodern playfulness. As we shall see, interest in different kinds of crime fiction produced by writers whose marginality is defined in terms of their class, gender, race, region, sexuality or even by general feelings of disaffection and dislocation, relates in part to these writers' subtle examinations of power, to their questioning of traditional assumptions about identity, justice, law, morality and crime, and to their willingness to embrace a dark, often disturbing portrait of a contemporary America where, in Hammett's terms, beams can fall on anyone and at any time. To this extent, the following is not intended to be a definitive account of the development of the American crime novel but rather an example of the way in which alternative canons or traditions are continually being made and remade by readers, writers and critics.

Hammett's *Red Harvest* is not only the first hard-boiled crime novel; it is also one of the toughest, most innovative, radical and violent. It describes what happens when an unnamed detective from the Continental Detective Agency, the Continental Op, arrives in Personville from San Francisco to discover a grim, foreboding town despoiled by brick-stacked smelters belching out yellow smoke and by a general dirtiness caused by its principle industry – mining. The Op arrives to discover that Donald Willsson, a newspaper editor who has contracted his services, has been assassinated. Feeling some compunction to find out why, or who was responsible, he approaches the dead man's father, Elihu Willsson, President of the Personville Mining Corporation and First National Bank, who appears to place the blame at the door of the town's criminal gangs; gangs that he himself brought to Personville in order to break up costly labour strikes in his mines. Aggrieved that the gangs have usurped his power, Willsson hires the Op for a fee of ten thousand dollars to clear up the town or at least curtail the influence of the gangs. The Op agrees, but only so long as he is given complete autonomy to do the job as he sees fit, remarking:

> These people you want taken to the cleaners were friends of yours yesterday. Maybe they will be friends of yours next week. I don't care

about that. But I'm not playing politics for you. I'm not hiring out to help you kick them back in line – with the job being called off then. If you want the job done you'll plank down enough money to pay for a complete job. Any that's left over will be returned to you. But you're going to get a complete job or nothing. That's the way it'll have to be. Take it or leave it.[40]

The Continental Op's remit – to investigate crime and political corruption in Personville – means that he must work alone, since the town's police department is implicated in the corruption. But in so far as he has also been contracted by a capitalist megalomaniac in order to reinscribe that person's authority, the Op's professed autonomy is called into question. Operating in a field of tension between independent private eye and state-sponsored henchman, his claim to agency is affirmed by his status as detective and undercut by his relationship to Willsson. In the final analysis, the Op is neither a right-wing vigilante purging enemies of the industrial-capitalist state with wanton and ruthless abandon, nor is he a pro-union sympathiser, a champion of the people or as Porter puts it, an embodiment of 'an idealised average American-ness'.[41] Rather he is a disconcerting cocktail of 'right' and 'left' politics, an enforcer and liberator whose contradictory nature is best summarised when he declares:

It's this damned berg. You can't go straight here. I got myself tangled at the beginning. When old Elihu ran out on me there was nothing I could do but try to set the boys against each other. I had to swing the job the best I could. How could I help it if the best way was bound to lead to a lot of killing? The job couldn't be handled any other way without Elihu's backing. (p. 139)

The startling complexity of this statement and its implications for understanding the Op's function as detective need further unpacking. In order to do the job which he has been hired to perform and clean up Personville, the Op has no choice but to set gang members against one another in the hope that they will kill each other. One could argue that in so far as his ambitions are realised, the Op is ultimately 'successful'. But at what cost and in whose terms? One could just as easily argue that the Op's lack of agency forced him to adopt this strategy in the first place, pushed him unwillingly into a compromising, violent situation over which he had little or no control. The Op is certainly not comfortable about what he has done and his uneasiness is confirmed when he 'returns' the town to Elihu Willsson at the end of the novel, 'all nice and clean and ready to go to the dogs again' (p. 181). The ending is simultaneously utopian, because the Op has done what he set out to do, and distopian because, in the final analysis, little has changed, apart from the fact that Willsson's power has increased. As James Ellroy summarises, the Op 'succeeds in restoring order at a great cost. In the end marshal law is imposed, the little guy gets fucked and the mining company takes over stronger than ever. It's a dark view'.[42]

Despite Hammett's own radical politics, *Red Harvest* is neither an unequivocal assault on the evils of industrial capitalism nor a celebration of the democratic possibilities implicit in a frontier-derived individualism. In this 'damned berg' both individualism (the ability to act according to one's own attitudes and ambitions) and collectivism (the ability to function collectively to pursue commonly shared goals) are irrelevant, and the best that the Op can do is what he is hired to do and no more. Defined in terms of his function as detective and employee of the Continental Agency, the Op's willingness to return to the company fold at the end of the novel is matched only by his willingness to transgress company rules during his time in Personville and act out his violent frustrations on those around him. Seen in this light, his final action of restoring law and order, or at least paving the way for the National Guard to take over from a hopelessly inefficient and corrupt police department, is not conservative, at least in so far as it constitutes 'a reaffirmation of national self-worth',[43] nor can it be framed in terms of Bakhtin's 'undisciplined life-force', a carnivalesque celebration of the ability of the 'low' or 'folk' to overturn and debunk 'official' discourses and social hierarchies. The further consolidation of state power might somehow be inevitable, but as the events of the narrative demonstrate, particularly the Op's willingness to challenge Willsson's authority, it is no guarantee of order. In such a world, power is not merely elusive – it is everywhere and nowhere – and while there are identifiable figureheads like Willsson who embody or represent the wider capitalist system, his frailty, petulance and ultimate unwillingness to take on the gangs suggest a disturbing void right at the heart of the state. 'The rule of nobody', Hannah Arendt once wrote, characterises the nature of bureaucratic capitalist society, alluding to exactly this kind of indeterminacy, concluding that in such a world, there is a 'dangerous tendency for things to get out of control and run amok',[44] Arendt could not have described the unfolding situation in Hammett's *Red Harvest* any more succinctly.

Lou Ford, the deputy sheriff of a small west Texan town in Jim Thompson's *The Killer Inside Me* (1952), is similarly aware of the disturbing indeterminacy which characterises his world, casually remarking to a suspect in a murder investigation:

'How can a man ever really know anything? We're living in a funny world, kid, a peculiar civilization. The police are playing crooks in it, and the crooks are doing police duty . . . It's a screwed up, bitched up world, and I'm afraid it's going to stay that way.'[45]

The cornerstones of knowledge, order, morality and rationality which defined the parameters of the 'classical' detective novel are visibly absent in Thompson's dark tale of psychosis and murder. The good-natured, corny *bonhomie* which appears to distinguish Lou Ford's behaviour and first-person narrative in the opening pages of the novel dissolves, almost at once, to reveal a more disturbing side to his personality, one alluded to through apparently uncharacteristic acts like grinding a cigarette into the wrist of a street 'bum' and by oblique references to 'the sickness'. Ford's schizophrenia and psychosis, induced or at least brought to the boil by a teenage sado-masochistic relationship with his father's maid, are re-awakened by similar feelings for Joyce Conway and manifest themselves in her bloody, brutal murder, which Ford describes with typically laid-back detachment. 'I wiped my gloves on her body; it was her blood and it belonged there. I took the gun from the dresser, turned off the light and closed the door' (p. 50). Though Ford admits to having genuine feelings for Joyce, acknowledging after he has killed her that 'she was the only person I could have talked to, who'd have understood what I was talking about' (p. 102), he can do little to prevent himself from killing her and later, from 'splitting . . . right down the middle' (p. 119). Locked into an ever-widening cycle of violence and recrimination, he kills again, to cover his tracks, and finally turns on his sweet, good-natured girlfriend, Amy Stanton. The assault begins as standard pulp violence, but as James Sallis argues, 'suddenly becomes something else, something reptilian, the narrator's abruptness and paralysis emphasized by the precision of description and by the discontinuities of thought and action'.[46] During the scene, as Michael McCauley, observes, 'One feels every punch and kick to Amy Stanton's body . . . not in the service of some over the top lurid exercise in pulp writing, but because Thompson imparts exactly what it must be like to kill and be killed'.[47]

Thompson's Lou Ford is a generic cousin to Hammett's the Continental Op in more ways than one. While Hammett's detective is not the victim of a mental illness, his mask-as-identity barely conceals the traces of a personality predisposed towards violence, and like Ford's blankness and put-on charm, this mask cannot quite disguise the horror of what lurks beneath the surface. Drawn into their worlds through the use of first-person narratives, readers are encouraged, if not compelled, to identify with Ford and the Continental Op, until that is, the violence escalates and the bodies pile up. Yet in so far as Ford and the Op remain sympathetic even, or especially, while they commit acts of violence, consensus over what this violence means, who these characters are and indeed what they represent, inevitably breaks down. 'Good' and 'evil', 'right' and 'wrong' bleed into one another in the same way that Ford's laid-back charm mutates without forewarning into murderous rage. As Sallis argues, 'Perhaps Thompson's greatest gift is luring the reader into the cave of the protagonist's consciousness . . . [thereby] making the reader identify with his monsters . . . [bringing] us almost to sympathy with their helplessness and mangled innocence'.[48] In the end, denied or lacking a 'true' or 'essential' self, Ford and the Continental Op are physical or rather fictional manifestations of a disaffected contemporary American society that, somewhere along the way, had turned rotten, consigning the damaged, the poor, the socially alienated to a life of misery and suffering over which they appear to have little and no control. And before he is shot dead by his fellow police officers at the end of the novel, Ford delivers an appropriately downbeat epitaph:

> Yeah, I reckon that's all unless our kind gets another chance in the Next Place. Our kind. Us people.
> All of us that started the game with a crooked cue, that wanted so much and got so little, that meant so good and did so bad. All us folks. Me and Joyce Lakeland, and Johnnie Pappas and Bob Maples and big ol' Elmer Conway and little ol' Amy Stanton. All of us.
> All of us.
>
> (p. 244)

A similar kind of 'sickness' affects the protagonist of Marc Behm's 1980 novel *The Eye of the Beholder*, an anonymous private detective known simply as the Eye. The Eye knows his daughter only as one of fifteen young girls in an old school photograph and is consumed by sexually tinged fantasies of one day bumping into her or following her on a case. Anxious to suppress what may well be paedophilic tendencies, tendencies that manifest themselves on a case when he 'unzips' in front of two little girls, 'exposing himself in broad daylight next to a fucking playground',[49] the Eye follows an attractive young woman who has murdered his client's son as she zigzags back and forth across the United States, slipping in and out of different identities, using various disguises and aliases and killing for money along the way. Remarkably efficient at blending anonymously into the background, the Eye's interest in the woman (whose 'real' name turns out to be Joanne Eris) escalates from mild curiosity into full-blown obsession until his entire identity is defined in terms of watching her, everything else, his job, his former life and eventually even his daughter, dissolving into the background. As the body count over a number of years continues to mount and the police threaten to close in on Eris and her various alter egos, the Eye takes on a more active, though still anonymous role, intervening to protect her from would-be attackers, tipping her off when the police get too close and aiding her financially, even to the point of setting himself up as one of her potential victims. Not knowing that the Eye has been following her for so many years, Eris shoots him in his motel room, as he predicts she will, and takes off with his money. When she, later, dies in a perhaps self-inflicted car accident, the Eye, whose own injuries are not fatal, arranges to have her buried and for the rest of his own life remains close to the grave.

Like *The Killer Inside Me*, Behm's novel is more intimately focused than either Hammett's *Red Harvest* or, as we shall see, Ellroy's LA Quartet, choosing to identify individual sickness as a manifestation of a genealogical dysfunction and general malaise in American society rather than explicitly linking it to the workings of the political and economic superstructures in the United States. 'Crime' in *The Eye of the Beholder* and *The Killer Inside Me* is refracted through the lens of a Gothic-noir tradition whereby psychosis and mental instability, rather than state corruption, feed and further impair the distopian and paranoid American landscape (though in much of Thompson's work the two are tentatively connected).

Yet there are also important areas of overlap between these works, particularly relating to the agency (or lack of agency) of the detective-protagonist. Remembering Frith's assertion that 'the "difficult" appeals through the traces it carries of another world in which it would be "easy"'[50] one could argue that the appeal of *The Eye of the Beholder*, like *Red Harvest* and *The Killer Inside Me*, lies in the way in which Behm appropriates but also subverts the conventional tropes of the genre and of the detective. Popularly, the detective might be characterised as someone who watches, listens and, above all, intervenes to either expose or punish the actions of others, but as part of what might be considered as 'unpopular-popular', Behm's detective may appear to be adept, watchful, careful, at ease in all surroundings, and prepared to use violence where necessary, but all too quickly these 'traces' begin to dissolve and the reader is thrust into a world where the familiar is at once made unfamiliar, where agency (or agency as it is traditionally understood, at least in relation to detective fiction) mutates into something more disturbing, where rage or insanity or voyeuristic obsession undermines or rather exposes the detective's pretence of control, where the detective is either powerless to halt or even check the mounting chaos or more likely is deeply implicated in its proliferation, to the point where it becomes impossible to distinguish between the 'detective-as-hero' and 'detective-as-killer/voyeur'. In the end, whether these detectives act on their own or as part of a collective, the result is the same; inevitable descent into a nightmarish abyss of their own making. One could also argue that the deep-seated indeterminacy that characterises these novels, their lack of fixed moral guiding posts, and their counter-hegemonic dissection of the functioning of 'power' (whether it related to politics and economics or not), goes some way to explaining the appeal of 'unpopular-popular' crime writers who have found new and expanded audiences in the contemporary world. Or, as James Ellroy says, trying to explain his now phenomenal popularity in the United States and also in Europe, 'I suppose in the end, readers love this kind of perverted . . . shit'.[51]

Ellroy's LA Quartet, a four-volume narrative of the city's secret history from the mid 1940s to the late 1950s comprising *The Black Dahlia* (1986), *The Big Nowhere* (1988), *LA Confidential* (1990) and *White Jazz* (1992), successfully fuses these various dysfunctions, contradictions and disruptions into perhaps the quintessential expression of 'noir' crime fiction, replete with labyrinthine plots, multiple protagonists and emphasis on the confluence of political and economic corruption and psycho-sexual obsession. If Hammett's *Red Harvest* alluded to the terrifying consequences of a world so completely satiated in the logic of political and economic corruption that the erosion of collective or individual agency became a kind of grim inevitability, and Thompson's *The Killer Inside Me* and Behm's *The Eye of the Beholder* made much the same point by slowly revealing their protagonists' implicit moral and mental degeneracy, Ellroy's LA Quartet reshapes 'noir' into social history or at least focuses on the ways in which psycho-sexual obsession and forms of mental and physical sickness inform and shape the nature of public life.

At the heart of *The Black Dahlia*, the Quartet's first instalment, lies the brutally mutilated, dismembered corpse of Betty Short, a hopeful starlet for whom the Hollywood dream of wealth and celebrity has run up dead against the realities of a sexually exploitative system in which male violence against females is commonplace, a dream which ultimately withers under a frenzy of razor-wounds and blows inflicted by her enraged attacker. Short's murder is picked up upon and exploited by a salacious mass media eager to boost circulation by pouring over every gruesome detail of her assault. In doing so, Ellroy is suggesting that the spectacle of her disembowelled corpse, once commodified by this mass media, becomes part of the spectacle of the city, of a booming post-war Los Angeles landscape dominated by signifiers of a rapidly emerging consumerism – 'giant billboards advertising department stores, jumbo shopping centers, kiddie parks and movie theatres'.[52] As Josh Cohen argues, the link between different forms of spectacle (visual culture, land development and Short's murder) is affirmed towards the end of the novel when the central protagonist, Bucky Bleichert, discovers that the murder took place on a building site belonging to wealthy property tycoon Emmett Sprague, located in the Hollywood Hills, just beneath the Hollywood sign:

> Bleichert is confronted by a doubled image of urban development. On the one hand, he sees the phantasmagoric mass spectacle of the sign, accompanied by a band striking up 'Hooray for Hollywood' . . . On the other, he witnesses its secret and blood-drenched underside . . . Crucially, both the abstracted spectacle of the Hollywood sign and its unpalatably visceral negative looming beneath are tied to the same economic force, namely Emmett Sprague's development interests.[33]

This thematic alignment of state and individual corruption, of public spectacle and private nightmare, is further developed in the remaining novels of the Quartet. The sustained and often vicious public assault on apparent Communist infiltration of the Hollywood unions in *The Big Nowhere*, and police clampdowns on Chicano immigrant activities and protests, bleed into a hidden narrative involving police collusion in blackmail, murder, incest and heroin trafficking, climaxing in a series of brutal murders where homosexual victims are targeted and then mutilated by a man fixated by wolves and wearing wolverine teeth. Similarly in *LA Confidential*, the construction of a Disney-style theme park and an ambitious road-building project conceal the complicity of its founders in a public bribery and extortion scandal, and their involvement in covering up a twenty-year-old familial massacre. This juxtaposition of public spectacle and a darker, bloodier version of history lurking somewhere beneath is replicated elsewhere in the novel where official rhetoric about bringing the perpetrators of a shotgun attack in a Hollywood coffee shop to justice dissolves to reveal the involvement of certain high-ranking police officers not just in the shooting itself but also in a pornography racket and heroin trafficking scheme. In fact the trajectory of the Quartet in general mirrors this shift, with Ellroy's focus increasingly directed inwards at his police officers and the struggle between and among them for power and position. In *White Jazz*, the final instalment of the Quartet, conflict between two senior police detectives over who should assume control of the department, between various units in the Los Angeles police department, and between the LAPD, the District Attorney and the US Attorney, informs and feeds a spiralling 'turf' war which rips apart the city and claims more than fifty lives.

The politics that underwrite a shift of this nature presuppose the increasing co-option of the detective by the state or rather the loss of independent, autonomous agency in the face of mounting pressure from the competing but also interlocking institutions that comprise the power elite or 'dominant' culture. Seen in this context, a figure like Danny Upshaw, a young maverick deputy in the LA County sheriff's department, whose interventions in *The Big Nowhere* threaten to expose the complicity of police officers and politicians in the violent subjugation of Mexican immigrants and union leaders, is reconfigured in *LA Confidential* as Ed Exley, an ambitious, authoritarian young detective in the LAPD whose actions are satiated in the logic of an uneasy combination of competitive individualism and bureaucratic rationality, both important tenets of a rapidly emerging capitalist culture.

Yet whether this means that Ellroy's protagonists, even those like Exley, and indeed his crime novels in general, necessarily serve the interests of the dominant social order or re-inscribe its pre-eminent social and economic position, is open to question. Given the stranglehold of particular individuals and agencies on political and economic power, it is tempting to conceptualise power relations in the LA Quartet in terms laid out by Foucault in *Discipline and Punish* – as a network of omnipresent relations of subjugating power that seem to preclude the possibility of meaningful individual freedom.[54] But who or what is subjugating who, and what exactly is this 'centralised' power? Because as soon as one tries to define the State or 'centralised power' in unproblematic terms, difficulties and contradictions mount up. Rivalries and tensions between agencies and individuals shatter any pretence of unity and the nakedly self-serving ambitions of Exley and others undercut the idea that the state can tame and subjugate individuals. Despite the tone of rhetoric in *Discipline and Punish*, Foucault understood the complexity of this dilemma, and in a later essay argued that power had to be defined in terms that presupposed rather than annulled people's capacity as agents, that power in society was 'an endless and open strategic game' in which individuals were 'always in the position of simultaneously undergoing and exercising their power'.[55] Or, as Jim Collins argues:

> To abandon the 'dominant culture' as an archaic concept does not mean that cultural domination is not still at work or that dominant classes do not 'really' exist . . . It simply means that domination is conducted by a multiplicity of agencies and the dominant social class has no monopoly over that process, that it has far less to do with the production of meaning than it has been given credit for in the past.[56]

Critics who conceive of and understand the genre's formal and thematic properties as necessarily conservative, at least in so far as they end up defending 'the established social system even as it reveals widespread corruption both in leading citizens and public officialdom'[57] or perpetuating 'a mildly revisionist status quo' so that the detective 'is complicit with its continuing hegemony'[58] fail to identify the complexities of Ellroy's crime fiction. Rather than framing the LA Quartet as either conservative or radical, we need to explore the way in which divergent traditions and narratives are brought into violent confrontation and consider how the 'excess' of meaning produced by such confrontations inevitably resists or undermines the genre's prevailing tendency to perpetuate the *status quo*. After all, Bucky Bleichert's investigative abilities may, in the end, resolve the enigma of *The Black Dahlia* and expose, if only to the reader, those responsible for the dissection and disembowelment of Betty Short, but can we necessarily assume that the 'excessive' nature of the attack is easily contained by this resolution? Likewise the 'excessively' mutilated corpses that litter the pages of *The Big Nowhere* and the graphically described suicide of Danny Upshaw, who 'slashed himself ear to ear, down to the windpipe in one clean stroke' (p. 369) two-thirds of the way through the narrative, disrupt and unnerve as much as the resolution itself satisfies and reassures.

The idea or hope that 'crime' can be controlled is wilfully abandoned in Ellroy's fiction, not least because every aspect of the dominant social order and those who occupy positions of power and privilege is satiated with an oppositional logic; that individuals do not really know themselves, do not understand the tangled mess of repressed neuroses (usually of a sexual nature) which compel them to perform acts which might otherwise be seen as 'disgusting', 'perverse' or 'sick'. To this end, the LA Quartet is perhaps best understood not as four individual novels but as a continuous, overlapping narrative where resolutions are, at best, partial and incomplete, where moments of 'excess' disrupt and overturn the formulaic constraints of the genre, where 'shitbird cops out to fuck the disenfranchised'[59] are neither contained nor censured at the end of each novel but rather allowed to play out their ambitions in the next instalment. The trajectory of the Quartet is characterised by an increasing focus on the ambitions of Dudley Smith, a high-ranking officer in the LAPD whose plans to wrest control of the drug trade from familiar underworld figures and flood the city's poor black neighbourhoods with cheap heroin for personal profit and to formulate 'a means to keep the nigger filth sedated'[60] bleeds from *The Big Nowhere* into *LA Confidential* and ultimately *White Jazz* where the tableau of violence and recriminations unleashed by these plans reach bloody climax.[61]

Given that Dudley Smith's actions, and those of Ellroy's various 'shitbirds' or 'dirty white cops' inevitably work towards re-inscribing the dominant social position of the straight, white male and reaffirming the logic of a capitalist ethos, Ellroy himself has tended to be pigeon-holed as a right-wing author. The contempt that many of his characters seem to display towards liberal politics or rather the equation of liberalism with compromise, weakness and the erosion of white, male power further cements this perception. Yet Ellroy's fiction could just as easily be read as a left-wing critique of right-wing politics; attempts to dress up the nakedly self-serving actions of his 'dirty white cops' as ideologically motivated inevitably crumble to reveal a dog-eat-dog world where conservative values count for little.

Haut identifies this political ambiguity – that Ellroy characterises himself as right-wing but writes about the Hollywood witch hunts from what could be called a left-wing perspective – in terms of the increasing pressures of commercialisation and a willingness on the part of author and publisher to accede to the demands of the market:

> After all, the business of crime fiction, like any such enterprise, is based on hype, which in turn functions as the conceptual engine of a consumer culture. Appealing to all ideologies simultaneously, corporate publishing absorbs contradictions, while encouraging – though never at the expense of profit – the depoliticisation of that which it produces.[62]

Yet rather than appealing to all ideologies simultaneously, in a cynical move to attract a wider readership, Ellroy's fiction, like that of Thompson, Behm and particularly Hammett, who could after all be described as a left-winger writing from a right-wing perspective, rejects or at least questions the effectiveness of 'right' and 'left' ideologies to make a difference in the kind of deterministic, dog-eat-dog world where power is exercised though a combination of state and individual channels. In Ellroy's world, there is very little that individuals can do to 'buck' existing trends or overturn 'dominant' hierarchies and power structures, just as there is very little that those presiding at the head of power structures can do to prevent those underneath them from tearing their organisations apart at the seams and putting their own ambitions and agendas ahead of those they work for and with. Rather than being popular because his work is populist, Ellroy's work has struck a chord with readers precisely because its bleakness and cynicism are somehow in tune with contemporary attitudes and cannot be easily rendered harmless by a corporate publishing industry. As we shall see, the destabilisation of traditional boundaries between 'high' and 'low' or 'left' and 'right' that lies at the heart of Ellroy's work is part of a wider phenomenon whereby the efforts of social and economic power 'elites' to uphold the validity of such distinctions and hierarchies meet head-on with challenges seeking to expose and overturn the strategies that underwrite them.

Dismantling the 'Dominant': Reconfiguring the American Crime Novel

The startling growth in the genre's popularity over the past twenty years, both for writers and readers, has been hard, if not impossible, to ignore. A significant upturn in the number of titles and authors in print has been precipitated and also reflected by the genre's higher profile in bookstores, in the media, with authors like James Ellroy, Sara Paretsky and Walter Mosley fast becoming celebrity figures, and in academia, with increasing numbers of university courses now focusing on American crime fiction and more scholarly material being produced than ever before, both in the United States and elsewhere. Of much fiercer debate have been the underlying reasons for this new found popularity. Otto Penzler, founder of the Mysterious Press and owner of New York's Mysterious Bookstore, points to the genre's emerging prominence at a time marked by a philosophical and political shift to the right and argues that the conservative mood that underwrote the Reagan–Bush years helped to generate renewed interest in what he perceives to be an inherently conservative genre.[63] Woody Haut, though, explains the growing commercial appeal of American crime fiction in altogether different terms, arguing that a new breed of 'neon' noir writers, by shamelessly plumbing the depths of taste and decorum, confirmed what their hip but increasingly depoliticised middle-class readership instinctively knew and wanted to hear; that the violent, fragmented and morally impaired landscape of contemporary America was a bankable commodity precisely because it was violent, fragmented and morally impaired; hence *The New Republic's* claim neo-noir constituted 'the moral phenomenology of the ruined middle classes'.[64]

Yet neither explanation acknowledges the dizzying range of texts that constitute the genre of American crime fiction, or the sheer multiplicity of possible meanings thrown up by a type of fiction which deliberately embraces contradiction. To this end, one could just as easily classify the kind of 'alternative' tradition outlined above as a 'dominant' tradition since *Red Harvest*, *The Killer Inside Me* and *The Eye of the Beholder* and the LA Quartet could all be described as misogynistic, at least in so far as they feature male violence directed against women. On the other hand, the idea that crime novels whose protagonists are so clearly unable to control or determine what they do, and whose violence is represented in such a deliberately problematic manner as reflecting and even re-inscribing 'dominant' values is less than satisfactory. My point, then, is that these novels deliberately embrace anxieties and discontinuities in order to open up and draw attention to wider social, economic and political tensions in American society as a whole, and force readers into an active, interpretative role, since meanings are not secured or legitimised within texts themselves. Rather than shying away from this challenge, furthermore, there has been a marked and growing interest among contemporary audiences in crime novels that challenge and disrupt conventional ways of reading and understanding popular fiction, that draw attention both to their status as artifice and their claim to verisimilitude, that display palpable dissatisfaction with boundaries between 'high' and 'low' or 'left' and 'right' or 'popular' and 'serious'. Ion Mills, founder of a specialist crime fiction press in the United Kingdom, acknowledges that his interest in hard-boiled fiction derives, in part, from a desire to 'safely escape' into another altogether more visceral world – 'hoping to God that what happens in the books never happens to me'. But he also accepts that comfort derived from the apparent distance between text and reader evaporates in so far as the violent complexities which characterise these novels reflect contemporary mores, attitudes and landscapes. 'Crime fiction is not like historical romances, which are pure escapism and very safe', Mills concludes. 'It's real, it's on the cutting edge'.[65]

Inevitably the growth in the genre's popularity over the past twenty years has seen a corresponding increase in the number of non-white, un-straight, female crime writers and of course readers – a reflection of changing social patterns and demographics and an acknowledgement of important shifts in the social status of women, gays, lesbians and ethnic minorities. More significantly, though, this shift is part of a sustained and proliferating contemporary interest in writing which calls into question traditional boundaries not just between 'high' and 'low' but also between 'centre' and 'margin'. One might also add that to account for this higher profile within the genre in terms of a Reagan-sponsored political and philosophical shift to the right would seem to be more than a little short-sighted, given that Reagan and his cohorts actively sought to re-inscribe the centrality of the straight, white, male. I do not wish to suggest that writers like Hammett, Thompson and Behm somehow paved the way for the emergence of their un-straight, non-white, female counterparts, but rather that renewed interest in their fiction on the part of contemporary audiences is linked to a growing interest in writing which usurps and overturns traditional social and racial hierarchies. This is not an excuse to equate the experiences of protagonists, writers or indeed readers, whatever their social, racial or economic situations. Nor is it intended to promote the absurdly dogmatic idea that a crime novel by a straight, white male writer will automatically be satiated in the logic of the 'dominant' culture or by the same reasoning that one by an un-straight, non-white, female writer will be alive with oppositional possibilities. Rather it is to propose that as cultural spaces and identities in the United States become more unfixed, more unsettled, as the social and racial landscape undergoes unprecedented transformation, as discussions of culture become increasingly linked to the question of power, we need to conceive of and understand the uneasy relationship between American crime novels and the 'dominant' culture in terms that do sufficient justice both to the novels themselves and the complexity of power structures and relations in the United States.

To claim that the detective, white or otherwise, is somehow automatically synonymous with the state and the functioning of state power is clearly a misnomer, but to entirely ignore the ability of a centralised power formation, whether we call it the state or the 'dominant' culture, to enforce relations of class, gender, racial and ethnic domination-subordination is just as problematic. As Smith and Feagin point out, the logic of such relations, pitting white European settlers against native populations, African slaves and later against immigrants of Asian and Latin American extraction, underwrote the foundation of the United States and affected the pattern of its subsequent development:

> In the American case, the archetypal foundation for centuries of subsequent racial-ethnic incorporation, negotiation, and conflict began with the early colonial struggles between European settlers and Native Americans and between the settlers and their imported African slaves. State policies of genocide and exclusion from white spaces were developed for the native population, while a policy of highly ideologized, labor-oriented oppression within white communities was developed for Africans.[66]

More recently the interplay between race and other axes of social difference, notably ethnicity, class, gender and sexuality, has complicated this scenario considerably and while hierarchies of power based on the subordination of non-whites by whites is still very much a feature of the contemporary United States, the relationship between 'centre' and 'margin' is, as Mike Hill puts it, 'a mutable arrangement' at least in so far as there is no longer 'an all-purpose category' of the oppressed. 'Nobody likes to think so', Hill maintains, 'but one could, for example, be black, rich and sexist, a working class racist, or a feminist with classist or racist dispositions'.[67]

When one maps these difficulties on to the already ambivalent terrain of the American crime novel and considers that the detective, white or black, male or female, straight or gay, has always been a liminal, contrary figure, one gets some idea of the complexities of the task in hand; what, after all, can we do with a genre so riven with ambiguities and contradictions, so amenable to antithetical readings and so satiated in a logic that is simultaneously reactionary and progressive? This book is an attempt to at least address and hopefully answer some of these questions, though inevitably the answers offered will be provisional and tentative ones. In doing so it looks at the complex set of overlapping and yet conflicting voices and forces at play in particular American crime novels, and how various writers explore and open up the tensions such arrangements produce as their characters move in and out of the shadows of the 'dominant' culture.

Notes

1. See Stephen Knight, *Form and Ideology in Crime Fiction* (London: Macmillan, 1980); Dennis Porter, *The Pursuit of Crime: Art and Ideology in Detective Fiction* (New Haven, CT: Yale University Press, 1981); Franco Moretti, *Signs Taken for Wonders: Essays in the Sociology of Literary Forms* (London: Verso, 1983); Ernest Mandel, *Delightful Murder: A Social History of the Crime Novel* (London: Pluto, 1999).
2. Porter, *The Pursuit of Crime*, p. 3.
3. Knight, *Form and Ideology in Crime Fiction*, p. 2.
4. See Scott McCracken, *Pulp: Reading Popular Fiction* (Manchester and New York: Manchester University Press, 1998), p. 56.
5. See Jim Collins, *Uncommon Cultures: Popular Culture and Post-modernism* (London and New York: Routledge, 1989); Ralph Willett, *The Naked City: Urban Crime Fiction in the USA* (Manchester and New York: Manchester University Press, 1996); Woody Haut, *Neon Noir: Contemporary American Crime Fiction* (London: Serpent's Tail, 1999).
6. Willett, *The Naked City*, p. 8.
7. Collins, *Uncommon Cultures*, p. 34.
8. Haut, *Neon Noir*, pp. 8–9.
9. Peter Messent (ed.), *Criminal Proceedings: The Contemporary American Crime Novel* (London: Pluto, 1997), p. 8.
10. Timothy Shuker-Haines and Martha M. Umphrey, 'Gender

(De)Mystified: Resistance and Recuperation in Hard-Boiled Female Detective Fiction', in Jerome H. Delamater and Ruth Prigozy (eds), *The Detective in American Film, Fiction and Television* (Westport, CT: Greenwood Press, 1998), p. 71.

11. See Kathleen G. Klein, *The Woman Detective: Gender and Genre* (Urbana and Chicago, IL: University of Illinois Press, 1988).

12. Ian A. Bell and Graham Daldry, *Watching the Detectives: Essays on Crime Fiction* (New York: St Martin's Press, 1990), p. x.

13. Bell and Daldry, *Watching the Detectives*, p. x.

14. Paul Cobley, *The American Thriller: Generic Innovation and Social Change in the 1970s* (London: Macmillan, 2000), p. 19.

15. See Knight, *Form and Ideology in Crime Fiction*, p. 2.

16. Stephen Knight, 'Radical Thrillers', in Bell and Daldry, *Watching the Detectives*, p. 172.

17. See, for example, the divergent positions taken up by Collins, *Uncommon Cultures*, pp. 55–60 and Knight, *Form and Ideology in Crime Fiction*, pp. 135–68, over Raymond Chandler's Phillip Marlowe novels.

18. McCracken, *Pulp*, p. 13.

19. Ibid., p. 19.

20. Ibid., p. 50.

21. Ibid., p. 63.

22. Meaghan Morris, 'Banality in Cultural Studies', in John Storey (ed.), *What is Cultural Studies?: A Reader* (London: Arnold, 1996), p. 159.

23. Simon Frith, *Performing Rites: Evaluating Popular Music* (Oxford and New York: Oxford University Press, 1998), p. 13.

24. Morris, *What is Cultural Studies?*, p. 165.

25. Frith, *Performing Rites*, p. 16.

26. See Simon During, 'Introduction', in During (ed.), *The Cultural Studies Reader* (London and New York: Routledge, 1993), p. 2.

27. Frith, Performing Rites, p. 19.

28. For a more detailed picture of sales and readership figures in the US and the UK, see Andrew Pepper, 'The Pitfalls of Publishing American Hard-Boiled Crime Fiction in the UK', in John Dean and Jean-Paul Gabillet (eds), *European Readings of American Popular Culture* (Westport, CT: Greenwood Press, 1996), pp 109–15.

29. Frith, *Performing Rites*, p. 20.

30. See McCracken, *Pulp*, p. 29.

31. Neil Campbell and Alasdair Kean, *American Cultural Studies* (London and New York: Routledge, 1997), p. 15.

32. Collins, *Uncommon Cultures*, p. 25.

33. Campbell and Kean, *American Cultural Studies*, p. 9.

34. See Peter Messent, *New Readings of the American Novel: Narrative*

Theory and its Applications (London: Macmillan, 1990), p. 4.

35. See Paul Lauter, 'Race and Gender in the Shaping of the American Literary Canon: A Case Study from the Twenties', *Feminist Studies*, 9, Fall, 1983, 3, p. 435; John G. Cawelti, 'Canonization, Modern Literature and the Detective Story', in Jerome H. Delamater and Ruth Prigogy (eds), *Theory and Practice of Classic Detective Fiction* (Westport, CT: Greenwood Press, 1997), pp. 5–16.

36. Cobley, *The American Thriller: Generic Innovation and Social Change in the 1970s*, p. 55.

37. See particularly Bethany Ogden, 'Hard-boiled Ideology', *American Quarterly*, Spring, 1992, 34, 1, pp. 71–85.

38. Clive Bush, 'Eric Mottram, America and Cultural Studies', in Robert A. Lee (ed.), *A Permanent Etcetera: Cross-Cultural Perspectives on Post-War America* (London: Pluto Press, 1993), p. 153.

39. Umberto Eco, 'The Multiplication of the Media', in *Travels in Hyperreality* (London: Picador, 1986), p. 149.

40. Dashiell Hammett, *Red Harvest*, in *The Four Great Novels* (London: Picador, 1982), p. 43.

41. Porter, *The Pursuit of Crime*, pp. 171–2.

42. See Charles P. Silet, 'Mad Dog and Glory: A Conversation with James Ellroy', *The Armchair Detective*, 28, 8, Summer, 1995, p. 238.

43. Porter, *The Pursuit of Crime*, p. 216.

44. See Hannah Arendt, *Crisis in the Republic* (London: Faber, 1963).

45. Jim Thompson, *The Killer Inside Me* (New York: Black Lizard), p. 118.

46. James Sallis, *Difficult Lives: Jim Thompson, David Goodis, Chester Himes* (New York: Gryphon, 1993), p. 21.

47. Michael McCauley, *Sleep with the Devil: A Biography of Jim Thompson* (New York: Mysterious Press, 1991), p. 52.

48. Sallis, *Difficult Lives*, p. 26.

49. Marc Behm, *The Eye of the Beholder* (first published 1980) (Harpenden: No Exit Press, 1999), p. 17.

50. Frith, *Performing Rites*, p. 20.

51. See Pepper, *European Readings of American Popular Culture*, p. 109.

52. James Ellroy, *The Black Dahlia* (London: Arrow, 1991), p. 77.

53. Josh Cohen, 'James Ellroy, Los Angeles and the Spectacular Crisis of Masculinity' in Messent (ed.), *Criminal Proceedings*, p. 181.

54. Colin Gordon (ed.), *The Foucault Effect: Studies in Governmentality* (London: Harvester Wheatsheaf, 1991), p. 4.

55. Ibid., p. 5.

56. Collins, *Uncommon Cultures*, p. 39.

57. Messent (ed.), *Criminal Proceedings*, p. 8.

58. Sally Munt, *Murder by the Book: Feminism and the Crime Novel* (London and New York: Routledge, 1994), p. 45.

59. James Ellroy, *My Dark Places* (London: Random House, 1998), p. 209.

60. James Ellroy, *LA Confidential* (New York: Mysterious Press, 1990), p. 400.

61. Ellroy's novels, particularly *White Jazz*, are also characterised by stylistic 'excesses' including truncated sentences, elliptical references, paired-down descriptions, frequent use of profanities.

62. Haut, *Neon Noir*, p. 9.

63. Otto Penzler, Owner, Mysterious Bookshop, New York; interview with A. Pepper at the Mysterious Bookshop, New York (9 November 1995).

64. See, for example, Stanley Kauffmann, 'Pulp', *The New Republic*, 24 November 1994, pp. 26–7.

65. Ion Mills, Editor, *No Exit Press*; interview with A. Pepper at Harpenden, Herts, 29 April 1994.

66. Michael Peter Smith and Joe R. Feagin (eds), *The Bubbling Cauldron: Race, Ethnicity and Urban Crisis* (Minneapolis, MN: University of Minnesota Press, 1995), p. 6.

67. Mike Hill, 'Introduction: Vipers in Shangri-La', in Hill (ed.), *Whiteness: A Critical Reader* (New York: New York University Press), p. 7.

CHAPTER 2

'The Unbearable Whiteness of Being': White Crime Fiction in the Contemporary US

I haven't the faintest notion what possible revolutionary role white heterosexual men could fulfill since they are the very embodiment of reactionary-vested-interest-power.[1]

(Robin Morgan, *Sisterhood is Powerful*)

White power . . . reproduces itself regardless of intention, power differences and goodwill, and overwhelmingly because it is not seen as whiteness, but as normal.[2]

(Richard Dyer, *White*)

'How did I become the enemy here?'

(D-Fens [Michael Douglas], *Falling Down*)

As the transformation of America's ethnic and racial landscape continues to accelerate, fuelled by changing immigration patterns and increasingly frequent border crossings between and among individuals from different communities and cultures, attention has begun to focus on the matter or substance of whiteness; how whiteness, at least traditionally, has operated to conceal itself, to pass itself off as a universal marker of cultural worth, and how this and other strategies of domination, the various ways in which white power is secured and legitimised, have been exposed and even dismantled as the centrality and invisibility of white culture is called into question. In the brave new world of multi-ethnic America, Robin Morgan is perhaps right that the white, heterosexual male is necessarily satiated in the logic of 'reactionary-vested-interest-power' and Nat Turner or Sitting Bull may now be more appropriate 'revolutionary' figures than Davy Crockett or Daniel Boone. Certainly with the rising profile of white paramilitaries and white supremacist groups and even the growing predilection for terms like 'white trash', the unproblematic identification of whiteness with notions of innocence, civilisation, cleanliness and virtue has been broken once and for all; or rather as Mike Hill puts it, what Frantz

Fanon called the 'octogenic' crisis of whiteness has forever snapped 'the "seal" of self-perceived (white) neutrality'.[3] This break, unsurprisingly, has not been without serious consequences. The question posed by D-Fens at the end of the 1992 film *Falling Down* – 'How did I become the enemy here?' – has, in a sense, become a self-fulfilling prophesy, with white militia groups angrily reacting to their perceived marginalisation in this brave new world by taking up arms. Thus D-Fens' rampage through an alien, multi-ethnic Los Angeles becomes the Branch Davidians taking on the FBI at Waco, Timothy McVeigh venting his fury at the Federal Government in Oklahoma City, and the still-to-be-identified pipe-bomber causing havoc at the 1996 Summer Olympics in Atlanta.

The actions of McVeigh and the Branch Davidians are without doubt extreme manifestations of what might be termed a white backlash and anyway, if one is to believe glossy university brochures and corporate America's advertising billboards featuring not-so-random collections of smiling mixed-race individuals, America is already a genuinely multicultural nation and the white paramilitaries and religious cults represent just a 'lunatic' fringe. But while the situation has evolved and the kind of overt racism which has tended to characterise white relations with non-whites has mutated, strategies of subjugation practised by (white, heterosexual, male) power elites have not simply fallen by the wayside. It may no longer be possible to secure or legitimise white identity as superior through a straightforward process of silencing or erasing racial others but then again, as Henry Giroux argues, we may well be entering into an era marked by forms of 'friendly' colonialism:

> Cultural difference has descended on America like a fog. Dominant groups are now driving very carefully through a cultural terrain in which whiteness can no longer remain invisible as a racial, political and historical construction. The privileges and practices of domination that underscore being white in America can no longer remain invisible through either an appeal to a universal norm or a refusal to explore how whiteness works to produce forms of 'friendly' colonialism.[4]

Within this context some attention has already been paid to American crime fiction. Building upon work already undertaken by Toni Morrison and Kenneth Warren,[5] Liam Kennedy has noted how 'race' operates as a structuring absence in the hard-boiled fiction of Hammett and particularly Chandler, or rather how blackness functions as a kind of ghost in the machine – 'as exegate or interpreter of the ethnic traces inscribed everywhere (but nowhere) in the American topography'[6] – an unseen but nonetheless determining force in the process of identity formation. Hence Marlowe's identity, a conflation of frontier-individualism and bourgeois pragmatism, is held up as a paradigm of 'Americanness' because it is defined in relation to an invisible 'Africanist' presence that is mediated through a white lens as savage. Meanwhile Fred Pfiel has reconfigured Giroux's terms to argue that the increased number of writers working in the contemporary genre illustrates and reflects the basic premise of his exegesis; namely:

> that of the smashing and diffusion of the conventions and definition of a normative straight white Fordist masculinity in our day, like a single atom hitting the wall at the end of a particle accelerator, and the proliferation, transformation and eccentric recombination of the subatomic particles released.[7]

Pfiel goes on to suggest that this diffusion has tinkered with but not entirely dismantled the genre's hegemonic attitudes, describing Jonathan Kellerman's Alex Delaware and Robert B. Parker Spenser as 'soft-boiled dicks' – characters whose gentler and to some extent feminised qualities do not quite conceal a more traditional constitution.

Of the two, Pfiel's analysis comes closest to acknowledging the complexities and contradictions of hard-boiled crime fiction, or at least the bewildering range of disparate texts that comprise the genre. This is not to suggest that the binary set up by Kennedy is necessarily problematic. Certainly the persona of the straight, white male detective in much hard-boiled fiction, traditionally, has been constructed by silently demonising all those things which he is not – not a woman, not gay, not black, not working class. Chandler's Phillip Marlowe may well be witty, humane and above all 'normal', rather than a serial rapist and Klan-apologist, but as Julien Isaac remarks, culturally dominant identities, like Marlowe's, secure universal consent to their hegemony as the norm 'by masking their coercive force with the invisibility that marks off the Other (the pathologized, the disempowered, the dehumanized) as all too visible'.[8] With its basis in Said's orientalism – how 'the Occident defines the Oriental in order to define itself against the Other'[9] – this kind of analysis, when applied to the hard-boiled crime novel, is useful to a point, but implicit in Pfiel's talk of 'proliferation and transformation' is an acknowledgement that it fails to sufficiently account for the genre's multiplicity of forms, tones and styles (even in white, male hands) or the ideological complexity of the figure of the detective.

Robin Morgan may be correct that the white heterosexual male can fulfil no revolutionary role, but then again, neither can we unproblematically posit the straight, white male detective as unreconstructed state-sponsored henchman. And what of white female or female-lesbian detectives? Do we assume that they have no revolutionary potential or that this potential is eroded by their racial identity, since subjects socialised as white, according to Spivak and others, 'almost inevitably reproduce Orientalist orderlings'?[10] Or that non-white, non-straight and non-male detectives are automatically revolutionary on account of their marginal status in relation to the 'dominant' culture? Part of the problem with these kinds of assumptions is that they ignore the politics of the hard-boiled detective, and genre, which have always been ambiguous and contradictory. Of far more significance than any spurious efforts to consign the detective, whatever his or her racial or ethnic or gendered identity, as either 'revolutionary' or 'reactionary' is an examination and assessment of the way in which particular writers organise these contradictory elements in order to open up tensions which cannot be easily resolved and thus disrupt the genre's narrative or structural tendency towards neat, clear-cut closure.

This tension, arguably the genre's key disjuncture, has always suggested the limitations of detection as a means of social control and exposed significant cracks in traditional configurations of white, heterosexual, male power. Which is not to pretend that hegemonic tendencies never surface in hard-boiled crime fiction, never manifest themselves, for example, in overdetermined anxieties about the white, male detective's 'nervous masculinity'[11] or fear of racial others; just that these tendencies almost always co-exist with ones underwritten by an oppositional politics and a marked and tangible distrust of the state, in all its various guises. What follows, then, is not intended to be a revisionist attempt to deny the colonising, hegemonic properties of whiteness, nor is it proposing the white detective, male or female, as some kind of angelic, politically correct presence, worn down by recriminatory guilt and driven by an ambition to fight previous wrongs. Instead much of this chapter will argue that some recent examples of the form seem to be underwritten by a desire to de-colonise and reconstitute whiteness (and related blackness) in altogether more problematic configurations. And while this new situation may not be exactly 'unbearable' at least for the various white protagonists and authors discussed here, as the admittedly blithe title for this particular chapter suggests, it does imply the need for a good deal of further investigation.

The anxieties, ellipses and contradictions that surface in much contemporary American crime fiction can be mapped on to the broader landscape of a multi-ethnic nation rapidly undergoing major transformation and compelling writers to reposition themselves, personally and politically. In the context of the fast-changing landscape of a multicultural, multiracial America, a growing number of white writers have made tentative, awkward steps towards renegotiating the 'ideological, discursive and material structures that form the centred (though never complete and stable) sources of power and knowledge'.[12] This is an admittedly fine and to some extent dangerous tightrope to walk because separated from the larger context that informs the rest of this book, this type of project runs the risk of promoting what Mike Phillips suspects might be a 'new assertiveness . . . amounting to a statement of "white ethnicity", the acceptable face of white nationalism'.[13] But while old habits do, in some cases, die hard and racist attitudes are, in other cases, simply repackaged in slicker 'friendly' forms, the genre, with its structuring tension between the detective's hegemonic and counter-hegemonic tendencies, is an appropriate vehicle for assessing the matter and nature of whiteness not least because the authority of the detective (and his or her whiteness) is always under threat.

Rather than conceiving of and representing 'dominant' identities in homogeneous terms, these writers also explore how and to what effect modalities of exclusion based upon gender, class, region, ethnicity and sexuality intersect with 'race' to contest and problematise notions of white hegemony. To this end, Cultural Studies, as an academic discipline, has been seeking to explain why the kind of secure and whole identities that might have once (and perhaps still do) seem attractive – not coincidentally the kind of identity traditionally associated with the white frontiersman and his urban cousin, the hard-boiled detective – are no longer possible. Homi Bhabha suggests that what is theoretically innovative and politically crucial is:

> to think beyond [these] narratives of originary and initial subjectivities and to focus on those moments or processes that are produced in the articulation of cultural differences . . . These 'in-between' spaces provide the terrain for elaborating strategies of selfhood – singular or communal – that initiate new signs of identity, and innovative sites of collaboration, and contestation, in the act of defining the idea of society itself.[14]

The trajectory of this chapter follows this logic, demonstrating how a focus on 'difference' as historical and social construction, and a commitment to exposing the complex network of power relations that characterise social and economic relations, can offer a way of thinking about identity which undermines traditional hierarchies of power and material structures of inequality.

Policing the 'Ghetto' – Negotiations across the Racial Divide: James Ellroy, Peter Blauner, Richard Price, Jack O'Connell

Denouncing the romanticised private-eye figure personified most famously by Raymond Chandler's Phillip Marlowe as 'essentially bullshit',[15] James Ellroy has set out to create a series of violent, reactionary white, male cop-protagonists whose identities are constructed upon a need to metaphorise gays, sexually promiscuous women and African-Americans, irrespective of class or gender, as polluting influences. Unlike earlier hard-boiled novels, race in Ellroy's LA Quartet no longer operates as a 'structuring absence' but rather constitutes perhaps the crucial axis of social division, a method of categorisation that affirms and reinforces existing social and economic inequalities because 'white' is always privileged over 'black'. In this environment, blackness becomes what Kennedy has termed 'a symbolic repository of white fears and fantasies'[16] a signifier of mindless savagery and ultimate worthlessness which operates within 'official' linguistic structures to secure and legitimise white hegemony. The issue of institutionalised racism lies at the heart of this particular practice. David Klein, a typically racist, misogynistic police detective and narrator of the final instalment of the Quartet, *White Jazz*, may express private feelings about African-Americans as 'porch-loafing jigs' with 'voodoo eyes'[17] but his language is nonetheless satiated in the logic of official departmental rhetoric. The description of three African-American suspects in *LA Confidential* as 'stark raving mad beasts'[18] by another of Ellroy's white 'shitbird cops' during an official departmental briefing is passed over without reaction or comment by others in the room.

The 'Africanist' presence – a barely visible ghost in the machine in traditional hard-boiled fiction – is magnified through the demonological lens of Ellroy's protagonists and becomes a voracious, polluting gargoyle. Concerns about race underpin and motivate the Quartet's conspiratorial machinations, even, or perhaps especially, when these conspiracies are the product of institutional strategies pursued by the Los Angeles Police Department. The latter instalments of the Quartet feature an unravelling scheme propagated by a select group of like-minded officers to gain control of the city's heroin trade and flood poor black neighbourhoods with cheap product both for personal profit and to pacify or even annihilate its residents. Such plans have institutional legitimacy in so far as 'only selling to Negroes' is 'the way that Chief Parker likes things'.[19] Meanwhile a 'turf' war whose epicentre is the city's poor black neighbourhoods and whose victims are predominantly African-American is used as additional justification for intensifying the coercive strategies that enforce relations of racial domination-subordination. Threats posed by Federal agents investigating alleged corruption and the LAPD's complicity in the escalating violence are dismissed by senior officers within the department on the grounds that the FBI is 'not conversant with the realities of maintaining order in Negro-inhabited sectors'.[20]

Representing blackness in terms of rampaging deviants whose propensity for violence is essentialised in their pathology reflects prevailing attitudes within dominant discourses at the time that Ellroy is writing about and foreshadows what Peter McLaren calls the 'postmodern' image which many white people now entertain of the African-American underclass – 'a population spawning mutant youths with steel pipes who, in the throes of bloodlust, roam the perimeter of the urban landscape high on angel dust, randomly hunting whites'.[21] The production and circulation of such images, however, needs to be understood primarily as a vehicle for white self-exploration and identity construction; in Orientalist terms, the negative classification of the non-white 'them' allows the white 'us' category to be silently filled with all the desirable traits which 'they' do not possess. So far, so good. But what makes Ellroy's work so original, and from my point of view interesting, is that this process is far from invisible. If the effectiveness of this kind of strategy depends upon its invisibility – after all Richard Dyer's thesis on whiteness is predicated on the argument that white power is secured by the fact that whiteness is made hard to see[22] – Ellroy's overdetermined illumination of relations of racial domination-subordination has far-reaching consequences.

If white identities, in Orientalist analysis, are constructed primarily by listing the deviant traits of the racial other in order to silently secure whiteness as a benchmark of humanity and civilisation, the misogynistic, luridly bigoted tendencies which characterise the actions of his white-cop protagonists, together with the conflation of economic and political power and psycho-sexual degeneracy, shake up, if not entirely shatter, the logic underwriting this process. The debased sexuality of the wealthy, politically influential Sprague family in *The Black Dahlia*, the incestuous relationship between Emmett Sprague, the family patriarch, and his eldest daughter, and in the brutal mutilation and dismembering of Betty Short by Emmett's wife Ramona and her lover, George Tilden, is not an aberrant blot on an otherwise unsullied landscape, but rather an albeit more extreme manifestation of the kind of degenerate behaviour which characterises Ellroy's white-cop protagonists throughout the Quartet. Official discourse may cite *The Black Dahlia's* twin protagonists, Bucky Bleichert and Lee Blanchard, as 'good wholesome white boys',[23] particularly given their iconic status in the department following their involvement in a boxing match that generates favourable publicity, but in so far as that Blanchard is revealed to be a bank robber, drug addict, blackmailer and hired assassin and Bleichert, a compulsive-obsessive whose fixation with Betty Short propels him into a destructive relationship with Sprague's daughter who bears an uncanny resemblance to the murdered woman, one could be forgiven for interpreting this description with some degree of irony.

In the light of overwhelming evidence to the contrary, attempts by LAPD officers to nominate a deviant blackness as the root cause of criminal activities and societal problems ring hollow. Instead what Ellroy's LA Quartet illuminates is the constructed nature of whiteness, its parasitic dependency on blackness or a blackness represented as morally monstrous. Strategies of domination implicit in the crime fiction of, say, Raymond Chandler, strategies that manifest themselves, for example, in Marlowe's fear of the contaminating racial other, are made explicit in the revisionist grotesqueries of Ellroy's fiction. Yet by making these strategies explicit, by intensifying the racist rhetoric of his various white-cop protagonists almost to the point of parody, Ellroy shatters any pretence that what he is representing is somehow either invisible or natural. The distorting influence of social power is omnipresent in the often overblown rhetoric of his protagonists and cut free from its secure moorings, whiteness becomes a free-floating signifier, a Janus-like, schizophrenic figure whose efforts to convince as a beacon of civility and democratic freedom are undercut by an ill-concealed propensity for barbarism and a neo-colonial desire to control or even annihilate dissenting voices.

A prevailing white fear of black crime is brought into sharp, unequivocal focus by Peter Blauner's *Slow Motion Riot* (1991). The novel's opening line – 'Now that the baby was two months old, she seemed to be waking up at least twice a night'[24] – engenders immediate sympathy for the scene's focaliser, Frankie Page, a white New York police officer with a wife and newborn child, a narrative strategy that makes his subsequent and entirely indiscriminate murder at the hands of Darryl King seem that much more heinous and unnecessary. Shorn of compassion and without a moral compass to guide his actions, King, a black adolescent with a lengthy arrest record, is presented from the outset as white America's worst nightmare. Acutely aware of the image he is projecting, replete with Kangol hat, ropes of gold chains dangling around his neck and a hyper-aggressive attitude, King has appropriated the racist stereotype conceived of by white middle-class imaginations and turned it back on its creators as 'the ultimate "fuck you"' (p. 60). King's move from petty crime to organised drug dealing and crack addiction is monitored by Steve Baum, a white probation officer of Eastern European Jewish extraction. Though nominally a liberal,

Baum's efforts to redeem his client are jettisoned once he senses that King is beyond rehabilitation, setting protagonist and antagonist on a collision course which perhaps unsurprisingly ends in King's shooting and death.

Magnified through a distorting white lens, King is not merely emblematic of a nightmarish vision of disenfranchised black adolescence. In other words, Blauner has not simply chosen to represent King in this manner in order to secure and legitimise Baum's white identity as normal. Rather, by narrating the story from the twin perspectives of Baum *and* King, his is an attempt to understand King, to place his actions in some kind of social and cultural context. The endless, self-replicating logic of the ghetto is effectively articulated through Blauner's intricate portrait of inter-generational family relations within the King household. In this context, Darryl King's descent into crime is no great surprise, given his family background; an absent father and a mother who is a prostitute and heroin addict facing a pending indictment for dealing drugs and having already served prison-time on manslaughter charges. Nor is King's alienation and disaffection a shock, given the decrepit state of his family's apartment, its peeling walls, flaking paint-work, damp patches, dry rot and floors covered in rat-pellets and urine stains, or the free availability of crack or the issue of police brutality towards African-Americans and other racial minorities which further stoke his feelings of anger and frustration. Underwriting the novel is a fascinating set of competing values and ideologies and Blauner skilfully brings them into disruptive and violent confrontation. Liberal values are suggested in so far as black crime is not simply consigned to the realm of the morally monstrous; reactionary ones, by the vigilante-style ending in which the problem is 'solved' by Baum's assassination of King after an aborted hostage-taking incident. Ultimately one does not cancel out the other and readers are left to question the value or even the relevance of either position.

Reflecting this ambivalence, the novel's structure in which King and Baum are placed on a collision course may foreground racial divisions, but clear-cut oppositions are muddled by the presence in New York of a myriad of ethnic groups and individuals for whom 'black' and 'white' do not constitute appropriate classifications. Baum is 'white' but he is also Jewish and imagines that when clients look at him, they see not just a white face but a 'skinny Jew with curly hair and glasses' (p. 6). In the light of his father's lived memories of the Nazi death camps in Poland, the conflation of Baum's identity as white and Jewish is never seamless or unproblematic. In other words, his whiteness may intersect with his Jewishness but does not entirely subsume it. Nor, though, does his identity as Jewish entirely undermine deep-rooted 'black'/'white' divisions. Baum's claim to marginal status via his Jewish ancestry – he tells King, 'I know what it's like to be on the outside looking in' (p. 51) – is categorically rejected by King who makes reference to his 'white' skin. Later in the novel, Baum's coupling with Andrea Frame, a mixed-race DA, is itself a partial erosion of racial boundaries and Blauner does not entirely preclude the possibility of realignments to conventional hierarchies and power relations. Though the personal may well be political, their relationship is not emblematic of seismic shifts in the tone and substance of race relations in larger institutions and the fact that their initial coupling takes place against a backdrop of race riots on New York's Lower East Side is perhaps the clearest indication that individual attempts to transgress socially constructed racial boundaries cannot hope to significantly alter deeply entrenched relations of domination and subordination with their own logic and history.

The intractability of this division and the anxiety it produces conspire to severely problematise the agency of Blauner's surrogate detective. If one of the more self-evident tropes of detective fiction has been the need for the detective to assume what John G. Cawelti calls the 'functions of exposure, protection, judgement and execution',[25] given that the law and its 'official' enforcers are usually too weak or selfish to make the necessary interventions, *Slow Motion Riot* both re-inscribes and undermines this logic. In one sense, Baum does assume the function of judgement and execution because his interventions lead directly to King's assassination, but as in much hard-boiled fiction, exactly what terms like 'justice' and 'morality' mean, and whether Baum has actually done the right thing, is much less clear. Given that King's earlier execution of two white police officers have earned him the support of many disaffected African-Americans, who conceive of his actions as entirely justifiable, one could ask how his eventual death serves their interests or whether 'justice' can said to have been done when deep-seated anxieties about the ability of police officers to serve black interests remain. Collective action – that is, action taken by the wider community – to address the problem emblematised by the conflict between King and Baum is futile in so far as different communities, split by gendered, class as well as racial affiliations, have starkly opposed views not just over what should be done but also about the nature of the problem in the first place. Individual action – the responsibility of the hard-boiled detective – is similarly problematic because though Baum may successfully reinvent himself as a Field Service agent and play his part in King's termination, his final decision to leave not just the Probation Service but also New York City itself is an implicit admission of failure. As he concludes, 'This city is a slow motion riot destroying itself piece by piece and I don't have a place in it anymore' (p. 370).

Ralph Willett describes the urban detective as someone who 'listens, searches and above all . . . sees and deciphers the signifiers of that labyrinth of populated spaces and buildings which forms the modern metropolis'.[26] Implicit in such a remark is the idea that the detective's power derives from an ability to be able not just to read and decipher signs but also to control them. Yet Willett only partly addresses what seems to be a far more interesting question; namely, what happens when the (watchful) male detective attempts to read signs and signifiers that he or she does not entirely understand, that do not relate to his or her own experiences and culture? What happens when these attempts result in ultimate 'failure' rather than 'success'? The idea of the detective not reading but *mis*-reading the situation unravelling in front of him is played out in Richard Price's *Clockers* (1992).

Called upon to look into the murder of a black drug dealer, Rocco Klein, an investigator for the Public Defender's Office, immediately identifies Strike, a rival dealer, as prime suspect. A veteran cop with an altruistic bent, Klein's liberal credentials – 'I wanted to be a cop', he declares, 'Why, to beat up on minorities? No, I wanted to help people . . . white, black, yellow, whatever'[27] – run up dead against his belief that Strike is guilty, that he has convinced his brother, Victor, to confess to the shooting because as a first-time offender pleading self-defence, he is likely to escape with a lesser or no punishment. Klein's assessment of the situation is based on his initial reading of Strike as the eponymous African-American drug dealer, someone who profits from other people's misery, and of Victor as a quiet, hard-working family man who holds down two jobs in order to provide for his children, one as the manager of a fast-food outlet and the other as a night watchman at a clothes boutique.

Klein's interpretative skills are openly called into question, though. Strike may appear to fit the mould of the stereotypical black criminal, a deviant whose propensity for violence is essentialised in his pathology, but Klein's reading is fatally undercut by the structure of the novel. By juxtaposing Klein's narrative with Strike's, Price is able to construct an alternative portrait of Strike as a cautious, nervous teenager, someone who is naive in relationships with women, modest-living and who sells crack only because it offers him a means of becoming economically self-sufficient. Meanwhile Klein's reading of Victor as honest and hard-working, a latter-day incarnation of Horatio Alger's working-class heroes, able to transcend difficult circumstances through dedication and perseverance, is incomplete because he cannot fully appreciate the strains of having to live and work in a hostile, white-controlled world. Victor longs to move his family out of the projects but his ability to do so is thwarted by institutional discrimination and racism. Safer, predominantly white middle-class neighbourhoods have established formal mechanisms for repelling aspiring black residents, even those with middle-class aspirations. In one case, a housing complex temporarily lifts a ban on African-American families – to try and scare white residents into settling outstanding rent bills – but the required deposit is still too much for Victor, despite his two jobs. His plea for a bank loan to cover the shortfall, furthermore, falls on deaf ears because as an African-American living on the projects he is dismissed as a poor investment. Trapped in a dying community, Victor's vents his frustrations by hitting out at its perceived wreckers – dealers or 'clockers' – and the shooting, as Klein is reluctantly forced to acknowledge, was little more than a 'capper on a bad day' (p. 587).

For Klein, racial difference is the spanner in the interpretative works. As someone who is white-identified and of Jewish, middle-class descent, he quite simply does not understand what could have driven Victor to do what he did, nor is he fully aware of the hopelessness and disaffection that characterises life for black residents on the projects. In so far as he ultimately arrives at the 'truth' one could argue that some kind of albeit fragile equilibrium is restored at the end of the novel but the fact that Strike evades punishment for his drug dealing and is encouraged to leave the projects with his life-savings intact, indicates significant ruptures in configurations of white power. In fact, one is continually struck by the disorganisation of not just the 'clockers' but also the police officers. Multiple fields of jurisdiction and competition between antagonistic agencies mean constant disruption to the smooth-running of police operations, while the survival tactics employed by the police and the 'clockers' mirror one another and position both groups within a particular kind of masculine, blue-collar culture where 'bullshitting' one another is a way of life: 'The cops bullshitted each other, the dealers bullshitted each other, the cops bullshitted the dealers, the dealers bullshitted the cops, the cops took bribes, the dealers ratted each other out. Nobody knew for sure which side anybody was on' (p. 23).

Which is not to suggest that racial differences or the relations of domination and subordination are mere illusions; just that *Clockers* seems to propose that the limitations of detection as a means of social control is not simply the product of the chaotic urban environment, but rather of the unresolvable tensions between Klein's liberal and reactionary politics, tensions whose origins can be traced back to confusion over racial identities and uncertainty over the precise nature of the relationship between race, poverty and criminality. 'The surface of this order', Michel de Certeau once said, of the modern city, 'is everywhere punched and torn open by ellipses, drifts and leaks of meaning'.[28]

Willett argues that the representation of the modern city as ordered and regimented draws in part on the work of theorists like de Certeau, 'whose baleful critiques postulate a world of regulated spaces, controlled supervision and manipulation'.[29] Yet de Certeau's version of the city as space controlled by state-sponsored surveillance technologies and by the geography of modern grid-like patterns, gives way to an alternative view whereby 'ordinary practitioners of the city' who walk its streets on a daily basis, often hidden from the panoptic gaze of such technologies, are afforded a degree of agency. De Certeau's vision of 'walkers', individuals 'whose bodies follow the thicks and thins on an urban text they write without being able to read'[30] is a utopian one but interpreted in distopian terms, it provides a useful entry point for thinking about the representation of race and urban space in Jack O'Connell's *Box Nine* (1992).

Set in the fictional, post-industrial city of Quinsigamond, located someone in the north-eastern United States within three hours drive of Boston, *Box Nine* draws a devastating picture of urban decay; Quinsigamond is literally choking from the polluting influences of drug-related crime. Centred around an area of the city called Bangkok Park, the rampant degeneration has spawned an underworld culture of drug cartels and addicts, transforming a once respectable blue-collar neighbourhood into a blighted war-zone where every kind of perversion was catered for and any atrocity was 'an ongoing possibility'.[31] Seen through O'Connell's dark lens, the city's traditional contours have all but disintegrated; factories have been abandoned, the airport disused and railway tracks and sidings have fallen into terminal disrepair. The ellipses, drifts and leaks of meaning to which de Certeau referred, have become gaping chasms.

The fog of urban chaos cannot quite conceal the power relations which structure Quinsigamond's fractured society, relations which inevitably place the city's Narcotics Squad into conflict with the principal drug traffickers who tend to be of Asian or Latin American extraction. The timing of the city's decline coincides with the arrival of huge numbers of Asian and Latin American immigrants and the Bangkok Park's not-unrelated fall from grace can be traced back to a decision taken by a shadowy alliance of city politicians and organised criminals to 'turn the whole place over to the Jamaicans, Cambodians and every other refugee party off the boat' (p. 205). At the pinnacle of Bangkok Park's criminal fraternity is Cortez, a European-born Argentinean immigrant who presides over a vast network of dealers, pimps and prostitutes and whose power and influence extends across the entire eastern seaboard. Cortez may be compared to an old-fashioned Yankee baron, someone 'with a sense for building solid and conservative foundations' (p. 102), but in other respects his tastes and pre-dispositions reveal a darker streak. Under his orders a formerly derelict hotel, the Penumbra, has been renovated, its Gothic exteriors internalised, metaphorically and literally, to countenance an interior space devoted to the commercially driven pursuit of recidivist pleasures.

Yet a straightforward Orientalist reading of O'Connell's dissolute environment, one that focuses upon the various ways in which Quinsigamond's white-dominated Narcotics Squad expels its collective anxieties on to a subaltern other, quickly collapses in the face of carefully drawn ambiguities and contradictions. Though white cops tend to square off against Asian or Latin American drug dealers, O'Connell moves to undermine, even overturn, the logic of such oppositions, emphasising instead the confusion and sense of indeterminacy that characterises relations between and among both communities. 'The Park's a different world', someone declares, 'Everything's painted even subtler shades of gray than the outside' (p. 207). In such a world, attempts to map racial divisions on to a cartoon-like landscape of 'white' and 'black' hats, overdetermined signifiers of a divinely transmitted morality, inevitably fail. Lenore Thomas, the novel's protagonist and a leading officer in the city's Narcotics Squad, dismisses attempts made by her peers and superiors to justify their project by metaphorising their targets as deviant others as naive, reductive and even facile. Attracted by Cortez's ruthlessness and existential detachment as much as she is repelled by her own superior's weakness and indecision, Thomas' attempt to construct herself in the image of the former is successful to a point. But even such clinical rationality cannot distil and bring into order the quickly unravelling situation which threatens to engulf and destroy her. All she can do is watch, helplessly, as everything around her – the case, her family, relationships – crumble.

For Jim Collins, the blunt, hard-edged, laconic language of the hard-boiled detective underwrites or even legitimises his or her narrative dominance, and whereas particular hard-boiled texts may showcase a bewildering polyphony of different voices, 'there can only be one "language of truth": the hard-boiled language of the detective'.[32] In Box Nine, however, Thomas' efforts to transform her hard-boiled rhetoric into actual dominance crumbles because the ability to communicate, like everything else in Quinsigamond, has been corrupted and debased. Despite a sophisticated inner life, revealed through a present-tense third-person narrative rich in detail and complexity, Thomas' personal interactions with colleagues and even her twin brother take place at the level of cliche and platitude, shared remarks about the weather and bland pop cultural references. Meanwhile attempts to address the problem manifest themselves in the manufacture of a synthetic drug nicknamed 'Lingo', so called because it induces phenomenal advances in one's linguistic ability by allowing people to converse at incredibly quick speeds. Yet Lingo accelerates the flow of words to such an extent that subsequent communications become unintelligible, reducing language to 'an awful, scratchy, buzzing sound, as if a high-speed motor has materialised in [people's] larynxes' (p. 143). Unable to exercise Marlowe-esque linguistic mastery, Thomas' response to her twin brother's plea to spend some time with her – just to talk – is to give him a Lingo pill, an act that renders his attempts his converse entirely meaningless. 'He keeps repeating the word why until its nonsensical', we are told, 'until it's just some awful, annoying sound, like nails down a blackboard or knuckles being cracked' (p. 279).

Lingo, or the condition it induces, is particularly significant in relation to *Box Nine's* multiracial environment. Seen in these terms, Quinsigamond is transformed from melting to boiling pot, a Babel-like city where meaningful communications are non-existent and different groups and individuals co-exist in a state of uneasy disharmony. Hope is manifested in the guise of Harry, a Cambodian immigrant, and Isabelle, his Puerto Rican wife, who run a cafe in the middle of the city. Rollie's Grill is a potentially utopian space in which people from different backgrounds and cultures can freely mix. As Thomas acknowledges, 'It's as if Isabelle has formed a tiny nation composed of artifacts from two very different worlds. And it's as if this minute, barrel-roofed nation immediately transcended its origins and wound up stronger and more peaceful than his forebears' (p. 79). Yet hope engendered by such a project is snuffed out when the cafe and its customers are attacked by an Uzi-wielding motorcyclist, who in the process of trying to assassinate Thomas, shoots dead Harry's cousin, Lon. Even a place like Rollie's, which appears to act as a billboard for the possibility of family and belonging, falls prey to the polluting influence of a drug-ridden, *fin-de-siècle* urban modernity, a reminder that O'Connell's canvas is a multiracial America where the breakdown of community and communication have produced a distopian individualism which is projected on to the city's alienated, closed-off subjects. Ultimately *Box Nine* is a compelling but undeniably dark portrait of a multiracial dis-United States that, quite simply, does not work.

'Somewhere Over the Rainbow (Coalition)': Sara Paretsky, Julie Smith, Barbara Wilson, Vicki Hendricks

If white heterosexual males, as Robin Morgan argues, are by their very nature unable to perform any kind of genuinely revolutionary function, because their actions are satiated in the logic of 'reactionary-vested-interest-power', then one must assume that to be revolutionary one has to be something other than white, male and heterosexual. In the realm of crime fiction, particularly hard-boiled crime fiction, critics have focused on the ways in which an emerging group of female novelists have gone about revising the hard-boiled crime novel in their own images. Revision, though, is not revolution; nor is this the apparent ambition of writers like Paretsky, Smith or Wilson. Rather their work, as interpreted by critics like Sabine Vanacker, selectively borrows from particular hard-boiled novelists, raiding them for those features which are considered to be attractive to their predominantly, though by no means exclusively, female readership (an emphasis on self-reliance and where applicable, on combating social injustices) and eschewing some of the perhaps more sinister, anti-feminist components of the male tradition, notably a predilection for violence and a rejection of communal values in favour of a solipsistic individualism.[33] Bethany Ogden, meanwhile, is more bold, declaring that Paretsky and others are only superficially 'hard-boiled' because although their detectives usually work alone, carry guns, talk tough and operate in dangerous urban settings, they do not share with their male counterparts a 'hard-boiled ideological orientation'; that is, a particular ways of seeing the world which by its very nature re-inscribes white, patriarchal values.[34]

Yet inherent within such critical approaches is a tendency to oversimplify what are more complex matters. For starters, as Peter Messent suggests, they presuppose an ideological unity and consistency among (white male) hard-boiled writers that arguably does not exist.[35] Much of the previous section sought to show that writers like Ellroy, Price and O'Connell are not the unreconstructed vanguard of a white, patriarchal order but rather critique and reconstitute aspects underwriting that order, creating ideologically complex and as a result formally innovative narratives that constantly defy and frustrate readerly expectations. Then there is the problematic tendency of attaching an overarching, catch-all 'feminist' tag to hard-boiled female crime novels.[36] As Sally Munt argues, feminism is a slippery term, at least in so far as there are different strands of feminism – 'liberal', 'socialist', 'Marxist' – and more tellingly 'the taxonomies which follow do not describe discreetly-bound philosophies'.[37] Munt suggests that the crime writers most often described as feminist – Paretsky, Grafton, Cornwell – embody a liberal feminist ideal, based around 'an optimistic belief in reform seen as extendable to all areas of social life',[38] but that in actuality other overlapping but also conflicting feminism(s) and writers co-exist alongside them. The idea that there is a unity of purpose and ambition among so-called liberal feminist crime writers is similarly suspect. As we shall see, a progressive gender politics motivated by an optimistic belief in reform does not necessarily inform a progressive racial politics. Certainly this is the case with some writers but just as often, as Munt notes, white women crime writers 'have fallen into exploiting the easy post-colonialist attitudes of functional racism, often by reproducing racial Others as criminal or exotic'.[39] And to talk about the 'feminist' or 'liberal feminist' school of hard-boiled crime fiction as a single group fails to conceive of and understand readers, and the way in which they go about interpreting what they read in appropriately diverse terms.

Munt makes an interesting connection between form and content, suggesting albeit tentatively that radical content in the crime fiction of, say, Sara Paretsky or Sue Grafton – their sustained assaults on the ills of white, patriarchal, capitalist culture – is often undermined by 'deep structures of conventionality'; that this act of containment is 'structurally imposed by the predetermination of the genre, which may well be working against the reformist aspirations of the authors'.[40] My point is merely this; reformist ambitions of particular writers may well be undermined by conventional generic structures but the idea that genre is something so fixed and unyielding as to imprison subversive ideas surely needs to be revised, particularly if form as well as content is determined by not just aesthetic but also political considerations.

Sara Paretsky has created perhaps the eponymous female private investigator of the era, VI Warshawski. A zealous and combative professional driven by a sometimes uneasy mixture of self-reliant individualism, sympathy for the socially marginalised and belief in collective responsibility, Warshawski wears her feminist credentials like a badge of honour. But so, too, does she recall in all but her gender the idealised figure sketched out and made famous by Raymond Chandler's often quoted passage, 'Down these mean streets must go a man who is not himself mean'.[41] Paretsky has been praised for her attempt to vocalise 'the liberal feminist idea of the liberated woman who is equal to the male role but still retains her femininity'[42] and criticised for unproblematically re-inscribing the primacy of direct action, even violence, as a valid *modus operandi* for the feminist detective. Yet in so far as the targets of Warshawski's investigations tend to be bastions of patriarchy and class or inherited privilege (multinational corporations, private law firms, defence contractors, insurance companies) Paretsky fuses anti-establishment and liberal feminist concerns without drawing too much attention to possible ruptures within this alliance, or to borrow Jesse Jackson's phrase, this rainbow coalition. *Bitter Medicine* (1987) sees Warshawski investigating the death of a poor Chicano woman during childbirth, unearthing a conspiratorial web that implicates a rogue's gallery of charmless white, male protagonists – hospital administrator, doctor, lawyer, civil servant and anti-abortionist – and ultimately marshalling a rearguard action to thwart their ambitions comprising like-minded friends and acquaintances drawn from across the ethnic, class and gender spectrum; Lotty Hershiel, chief doctor in a medical practice whose memories of a Nazi mob gathering outside her parents' home in Vienna are revived by anti-abortionists outside her clinic, Malcolm Tregiere and Carol Alvardo, her colleagues and, respectively, of Haitian and Mexican descent, Manny Diaz, a Chicano legal aid lawyer, Murray Ryeson, a muckraking reporter of Swedish extraction, Conrad Rawlins, an African-American police officer, and a trio of 'ethnic' white ex-union activists.

In later novels Paretsky manages to problematise the apparent seamlessness of this coalition, to varying effects. In *Tunnel Vision* (1995), Warshawski's suspicions are aroused when the patrons of a female-run charitable trust ask her to investigate malpractice in the awarding of building contracts by civic officials, then revoke their request when an award is made to them. Ultimately, though, the actions of the trust are self-serving rather than corrupt and at the heart of the novel is a scheme operated by a cartel of white male bankers, politicians and defence contractors to launder funds procured from illegal arms sales through a small, suburban bank; a scheme that has damaging implications for various women's groups and minority businesses, since the bank withdraws its support for these groups in its rush to embrace new, wealthier clients. More successful is *Burn Marks* (1992) in so far as tensions within this rainbow coalition that are glossed over in previous novels are brought out into the open. Warshawksi's investigations place her on to a collision course with many of Paretsky's usual suspects – corrupt police officers, building constructors and politicians – but implicated in the criminal transgressions are co-feminists like Rosaline Fuentes whose political ambitions and agenda dovetail with hers. Tensions produced by this disjuncture are not easily closed off, thereby enabling Paretsky to counter what has become an increasingly frequent criticism of her work – that her valorisation of Warshawski ends up re-inscribing exactly the kind of unified female identity that liberal and any other kind of feminism has sought to expose as a social construction. As Vanacker remarks, 'this mesh of relationships prevents Warshawski's belief in an illusion of wholeness . . . and highlights her feelings of frustration and incompleteness'.[43]

Still, critics of Paretsky's fiction remain unconvinced. Contrary to Vanacker's assertion, Umphrey argues that Paretsky's utopian vision is 'based on an uncritical acceptance of the concept of a unified "woman's" identity and community',[44] while Munt makes the point that liberal feminism's emphasis on individual equality can end up 'positioning "race" as a "prop" to the grand narrative structure of the myth of a coherent White identity'.[45] What links all of these comments, but what Paretsky's detractors and advocates only partially address, is the matter of form. Paretsky's fiction is less radical than it might initially appear to be not simply because it is underwritten by a soggy liberalism where equality rather than difference is foregrounded, but rather because by moving her detective too far to the 'left' she ends up extinguishing the structural tensions – between a 'left' and 'right' politics – upon which the genre's unruly, subversive potential usually depends. Warshawski's occasional recourses to violence are not so much an acknowledgement of the problems of having a feminist working within or just outside of the system without co-opting her principles, as they are an affirmation and indeed celebration of her ability 'to do what a (wo)man's gotta do'. *Burn Marks* aside, without such an acknowledgement, that working within the system will inevitably compromise Warshawski's principles and evoke anger, frustration, or guilt, Paretsky's detective, as Woody Haut observes, is 'too good to be true'.[46] One could perhaps say the same of her creator's racial politics, too.

Far more effective in exploring the fluid, indeterminate and indeed problematic nature of identities in contemporary America, and the impossibility of trying to conceive of and understand identity politics without due consideration of the deforming influence of unequal power relations, is Julie Smith's *New Orleans Mourning* (1990). Smith paints a rich and complex portrait of New Orleans society, one where racial and class boundaries are both disturbingly fixed and maddeningly elusive. Rather than expressing fixed or ontological essences, terms like 'black' and 'white' quickly give way to reveal a myriad of other differences lurking somewhere beneath. Racial divisions are, undoubtedly, significant but just as white society is organised according to a complex set of determinants so that Creoles and WASPs are distinct from Jews and the Irish, and old money from the *nouveau riche*, black society is similarly fragmented, with axes of race, ethnicity and class tropes criss-crossing with each other and conspiring to distinguish between people of colour based on their wealth and social status, something which is in turn determined by the relative darkness of their skin.[47] Trying to make sense of this landscape is Skip Langdon, a white, female beat officer with the New Orleans police department whose own background is decidedly middle, if not upper middle class. At play in the novel, and in Langdon's character, are a number of competing identities (as white, female, a police officer, from a privileged background); identities which simultaneously re-inscribe and undermine her status as part of what

might be called the 'dominant' culture. More than Paretsky, Smith seems
to be only too aware of the agency and lack of agency that result from
slippages between these positions; Langdon manages to exploit family
connections in order to gain access to elite circles not usually open to the
police, but almost at once finds herself marginalised within the police
department because she is a woman and excluded from social gatherings
involving her friends and family because she is a police officer.

A sophisticated identity politics informs a complex racial politics and
vice versa. Called upon to investigate the murder of Chauncey St. Amat,
a prominent figure in white New Orleans society, Langdon's
interventions reveal clues that implicitly foreground the extent of
miscegenation in Southern culture while simultaneously underlining the
depth and pervasiveness of racial boundaries. Amat's liberal social and
racial politics – politics that have driven a wedge between himself and
other more conservative figures in New Orleans society – are initially
cited as a possible factor in his murder. What Langdon's investigations
actually reveal, however, is the fraudulent nature of his liberalism. When
a nurse examines Amat's child during a routine medical check-up and
notices what she identifies to be a Mongolian spot, Amat is forced to
acknowledge what for a man in his prominent social position is
potentially devastating; that his status as adopted has concealed, from
others if not himself, his mixed-race ancestry and a tangled genealogy
that means he can appear to be 'white' but, as Langdon remarks, still 'be
"black" enough for the genes to come out in one of his children'.[48] In
doing so Smith cleverly re-inscribes and undermines race as a trope of
difference, drawing attention to the arbitrariness of racial boundaries, at
least in a strictly biological sense, while simultaneously underlining the
extent of the social and economic rewards available to those who can
pass as white, and the costs levied on those who cannot.

The unravelling logic of the situation has devastating consequences
for Amat and his family, in so far as a daughter he has previously given
up for adoption, someone whose blackness is signified not just by a
Mongolian spot but by the hue of her skin, returns to blackmail him.
Amat kills her in order to safeguard his secret but when his wife, Bitty,
learns of what he has done, discovers that the daughter she never wanted
to give up in the first place has been killed by the person who forced her
to do so, she arranges for him to be assassinated. Race and gender may
well be social constructions rather than markers of innate difference but
what Smith's emphasises is the extent to which racial and gendered
differences are not just arbitrary constructions but rather products of
material inequalities and relations of domination and subordination.
The fact that Bitty had been forcibly coerced into giving up her child for
adoption by her husband and her father (both fearful about the impact

that the child's racial identity could have on their social and economic positions) reaffirms the logic of white patriarchal power. This logic is, in part, challenged, even overturned, by Bitty's interventions, and also by Langdon's, at least in so far as it is her 'feminine' investigative skills (gossip, instinct etc.), which help to unravel the conspiratorial web. Yet this erosion of traditional hierarchies of power and patronage is only temporary because Langdon's efforts to expose and punish Bitty's culpability are short-circuited by Bitty's father who makes a deal with the District Attorney for the charges against his daughter to be dismissed. Power is possessed and exercised by men like Bitty's father but it never reduces those in its stare to impotent ciphers. In the same way, individual agency can disrupt or even overturn hierarchies of position and power, but good intent is not always a guarantor of desired effect. Ultimately Langdon's reaction to the political manoeuvring that conspires to free Bitty, a mixture of anger, bewilderment, cynicism and also relief, all point to the contradictory nature of sentiments and ideologies at play in the novel as a whole, sentiments and ideologies that, as other crime novels have revealed, cannot be easily reconciled despite the sheen of order that seems to characterise the act of closure.

If the traces of anxiety that remain are more pernicious in *New Orleans Mourning* than in Paretsky's *Bitter Medicine* or *Tunnel Vision*, they are nonetheless sanitised or made palatable by the formal mechanisms of the genre; it may well be a dirty, corrupt world but it is a dirty, corrupt world we understand, one in which Langdon's well-meaning interventions successfully explain what has happened, and apportion blame, if not 'justice'. Munt would argue that the formal conventions of the genre, here, are working against the progressive or 'reformist' ambitions of the author; in fact it may well be the other way around. To talk about the genre's formal structure is to talk about something that does not actually exist or rather it exists only in so far as it is constantly undergoing revision. Smith's novel buys into the basic premise of a type of hard-boiled crime fiction perfected by Raymond Chandler; that the detective, who is himself or herself 'good', if not exactly innocent, can hope to achieve limited success – exposing the murderer, apportioning blame – but the idea (or hope or dream) of him or her replicating this 'success' in a wider context or remaining untouched by the pervasive corruption that pollutes the very air he or she breathes is never realised. Yet this is by no means the only available generic blueprint, nor is Smith compelled to replicate its logic. Moreover, so long as this template is only tinkered with but never fully dismantled, attempts to dissemble whiteness, to make visible its contours, to foreground whiteness as a social construction, will only be partially realised.

Of course, it is easy to argue that inserting a female detective into what has traditionally been a male-dominated role and world is more than tinkering with the genre's template, but this is not automatically the case. The female detective may well be significantly different from her male counterpart, at least in terms of her investigative methods, her ambitions, her behaviour or character and her relationship to others; indeed much criticism has focused on exactly this issue.[49] Much less attention has been paid to the relationship between crime as a fictional construct in crime fiction and crime as a violent, messy, sordid, disruptive, damaging presence in the 'real' world. My point is this: until the effect of this presence on the detective, or his or her surrogate, is acknowledged, that is, until the damage that operating in this violent, messy, alienating milieu is fully registered, his or her identity will always be too good to be true – and ultimately too whole or too secure to draw attention to the fluid, unstable, artificial, contradictory properties of whiteness. In other words, the apparent ease with which some white detectives, male or female, shrug off the effects of exposure to crime ends up essentialising their identities, fixing them in a kind of asocial vacuum. It would be too glib to suggest that whereas Dave Klein slips into some kind of personal hell at the end of Ellroy's *White Jazz* as a result of his exposure to, and complicity in, the sordid events of the narrative, Smith's Skip Langdon goes home to have a shower – and very possibly the latter is a more appropriate and perhaps also 'realistic' response to the unsavoury nature of the world. It would be too glib because this is not necessarily a gender issue. At the same time, though, perhaps because there has been a burden of representation on female crime writers, more than male writers, to draw their protagonists in 'positive' terms, to make them sympathetic, accessible, likeable, even heroic, one cannot discount gender as a contributing factor.

Munt's point is that the structures of the genre works against the reformist aspirations of the female or feminist crime writer. My point is simply that these reformist ambitions can undermine the ability of the writer to reshape the genre's codes and conventions, or at least to properly acknowledge the extent to which 'crime' is not merely a problem to be tackled but a dirty, messy, corrupting force, one that alters the way people think, the way they act and react to the world. A brief look at two writers, Barbara Wilson and Vicki Hendricks, illustrates the point. The politics of Wilson's *Murder in the Collective* (1984) are deliciously subversive. The milieu in which the novel takes place, a radical printing collective in Seattle, enables Wilson to foreground what is its structuring opposition; in one corner, a global patriarchal capitalism and in the other, a disparate collection of left-wingers, women, lesbians, African-Americans and Filipinos. Not that the latter group are represented as a single, homogeneous mass. Though an important context for the novel is the plight endured by Filipinos under the Marcos regime and also as immigrants in America, and the damaging long-term economic and social impact of American imperialist policies, the members of the printing collective are by no means agreed on how to direct their energies, who to help, who to target, even what to do, just as their respective identities collide into one another as often as they merge or overlap.

Zenaida Oberon, a Filipino immigrant, finds common ground with the novel's protagonist, Pam Nilsen, a white, middle-class feminist, on the grounds that the problems facing Filipinos need to be understood in terms of gender as well as ethnicity (in so far as the worst victims of American imperialist policies, as she puts it, tend to be women – 'If they are not being used for their sex, they are pushed into factories and ruin their eyes looking through microscopes, making computer chips for Hewlett-Packard').[50] But she also distrusts Nilsen because she is a lesbian and from a middle-class background. Similarly Oberon has much in common with another member of the collective, Ray Hernandez, on the grounds of their shared non-white identity, and with Jeremy Plaice, because like her, he is from a working-class background. Plaice and Hernandez connect in terms of their status as male in a predominantly female working environment, though ethnicity and class constitute significant barriers for them to overcome. Meanwhile Nilsen enjoys a close relationship with Hernandez, because of their Marxist sympathies, with Oberon, because of shared feminist beliefs, and with members of a lesbian printing collective with whom they collaborate, on the grounds of her own sexual orientation, but also clashes with all of them because Hernandez is male, because Oberon is Filipino and heterosexual, because the lesbian printing collective will not focus on issues relating to class and ethnicity, a situation which not just splinters the collective but fragments its members, Nilsen included. Ethnicity, class, politics, gender and sexuality merge and jar with one another, a kaleidoscopic mosaic of conflicting and overlapping axes of difference that shatters the coherence and legitimacy of the 'self' – that is, the 'self' as whole and secure – and foreshadows the need to represent America's social landscape in appropriately sophisticated terms, one no longer predicated on a simplistic 'them' and 'us' model, an alliance of minority groups arranged around a homogeneous centre. Which is not to say that traditional relations of domination and subordination have simply fallen by the wayside; just that to brand, say, Nilsen in the role of oppressor because she is white, or Hernandez because he is male, fails to sufficiently acknowledge the complexity of their multiple identifications.

Without losing sight of the fact that imperialist policies in America and the Philippines have far reaching consequences, the novel's identity politics are satisfyingly complex, but can the same be said of its generic revisionism? Is it a 'good' crime novel? As I discussed in the previous chapter, the question of whether one novel is 'better' than another is a notoriously problematic area and one that is ultimately counter-productive; after all, on whose terms should such a judgement be made? That said, Pam Nilsen, the novel's protagonist, comes across as a strangely detached, even muted figure, someone for whose job or function, as her partner remarks, is merely 'to find out how it all links up, what it all means' (p. 74). A printer by profession, she assumes the mantle of detective only when a member of the printing collective is murdered, most likely by a colleague. The fact that Nilsen operates in a closed environment where there are a limited number of suspects – all known to her – recalls Christie as much as it does Chandler. To some extent such a comparison is unfair because whereas Christie's detectives carried out their investigations in a hermetically sealed world, untouched by the debased forces of a capitalist modernity, Wilson's novel illuminates their destructive capacity. But Wilson's depiction of the latter, what we might tentatively call 'global crime', is more fully realised than her portrayal of the personal, those infractions and jealousies that result in the murder itself, so that when Nilsen and her sidekick, Hadley, eventually reveal Zee Oberon to be the murderer, there is a palpable sense of 'so what?'. No one really wants to see Oberon punished, since she only did what she did because she was being blackmailed, and the ending, where Nilsen's anxiety about glossing over Oberon's complicity quickly dissolves in the face of greater anxieties provoked by her lesbian affair with Hadley, snuffs out the potentially fascinating tension between Nilsen's liberalism and the reactionary qualities also required to be a detective; that to be a detective involves not just finding out how things link together but also getting your hands dirty, compromising your principles and damaging your friendships. The global, not the local, is what damages and corrupts in Wilson's novel and though in the end Nilsen is let down by those closest to her, she is able to pick herself up because she knows that she has not compromised what is dearest to her; her feminist beliefs, her lesbian identity, her opposition to American cultural and economic imperialism. On the other hand, the more problematic and equally significant issue of whether she has failed, or indeed succeeded, in her function as a detective is not ultimately addressed.

Vicki Hendrick's *Miami Purity* (1997) veers off in almost exactly the opposite direction. Shunning what others have termed 'the burden of representation' – having to be a 'positive' role model – Hendrick's protagonist, Sherri Parlay, is a deliciously politically incorrect figure, someone whose concerns are not the injustices of capitalism or patriarchy but rather where to find a job, how to deal with her abusive husband, whether she should give into or hold out against her over-active libido. Compared to *Murder in the Collective*, some might see the politics of *Miami Purity* as potentially regressive. Sherri is not a feminist icon, even if she does crack her husband's head open with a 'boom-box' radio and kill him after he has 'slugged' her in a moment of drunken rage. Sherri just wants to have a good time, wants a man, wants to take risks, and all three converge when she accepts a job at a dry cleaners and sets her sights on Payne, the store's manager and someone whose 'mix of innocence and animal' starts her 'juices running'.[51]

Sherri is not a detective but undertakes an investigation of sorts when her libidinous advances on Payne are checked, particularly when the bulge in his jeans suggests an interest in her that is more than platonic. Frustrated by his apparent reticence to actually consummate their relationship, despite early indications to the contrary – as Sherri puts it, 'I ground my bone hard into him and I could feel him rock hard inside his pants' (p. 21) – she soon confronts him and learns that he is unwilling to get involved with anyone because of his overbearing mother. Payne tells Sherri that his mother Brenda owns the business, rules it with an iron-grip, and he doesn't want to rock the boat by getting involved with someone she wouldn't approve of. But when Brenda starts spending more time away from the store, to open up another shop somewhere else in Miami, their relationship blossoms. Still, Sherri cannot break down the barrier between them entirely, despite her considerable experience in servicing male needs. Her suspicions mount and her investigations into Payne's background and relationship with his mother deepens. Eventually she discovers that Brenda has been sexually abusing him since he was a child and as a punishment, Sherri kills her. But during the time that he has been sleeping with Sherri, Payne has also been having sex with Brenda and such action, such betrayal, in Sherri's eyes, also merits punishment. Despite his pleas for mercy, Sherri's final act is to order Payne into one of the shop's dry-cleaning machine at gunpoint and watch as his head clunks against the side of the machine as it starts to spin, 'picturing his mouth open and the powerful cleaning fluid filling his mouth, lungs, stomach – pooling in his ears, penetrating into his skin, burning through the tiny pipe of his cock, tearing its way like a knife up his asshole' (p. 223).

Whether this ending is meant to be gratuitously horrific or slyly amusing is not ultimately clear, though this ambiguity, I would suggest, is deliberate. Whereas Wilson seems to be unwilling to address the matter of how crime, and reactions to crime, at least on a personal level, affect their behaviour and warp their perspectives, Hendricks is not so circumspect. The politics of the novel may be regressive, even offensive to some, but the ending is formally satisfying because it provokes or opens up more questions than it answers. Is Sherri morally justified in taking this action? How should Brenda's 'crime' and Payne's infidelity – if it can be called that – be punished? Or is Sherri a twisted psychopath with an uncontrollable bloodlust? Does it matter that she professes to love Payne and vice versa? Should we celebrate Sherri's ingenuity and willingness to defend her honour and take matters into her own hands? Or do her actions lay bare her dysfunctional mindset? And perhaps more to the point, how should we, as readers, react to Payne's demise? If we find something darkly humorous or unremittingly grim or offensive about the manner in which he dies, and the way in which it is described, what does it say about us, about our own values and morality? Maybe what is satisfying about *Miami Purity* is its staunch refusal to answer any of these questions, its ambition to challenge, not reassure, to provoke rather than smooth over. Then again, maybe all that can be said is that Hendricks' novel is no better, or no worse, than *Murder in the Collective*, and that while the latter novel dislodges whiteness from its secure moorings by emphasising cracks and divisions in its constituency, *Miami Purity*, with its violent, subversive, psychotic, attractive 'white trash' heroine achieves the same end-result by illuminating whiteness to point where its connotations are so muddled, so confused, that one can no longer be sure what it means.

'A Stained White Radiance?' James Lee Burke's 'Old' World Order

If nothing else, the often bewildering range of texts discussed thus far and the dizzy complexities of their racial and cultural politics should be enough to convince even the most hard-nosed sceptic that to posit the white detective, and author, as either violently reactionary, figures so satiated in the logic of white supremacy and convinced of the 'value' and legitimacy of their claim to power that they are blind to the gaping imperfections of the system, or avowedly progressive, cultural mediators whose primary function is to smooth over differences between groups and individuals and like Coca-Cola, if we are to believe the advertisements, make the world a better place, is quite clearly a mistake. Though the manner and degree to which individual writers marshal these opposing values and ideologies differs considerably, what connects all of them is the similarly ruthless manner in which they interrogate and problematise the so-called 'centre' or 'dominant' culture as either homogeneous or omnipotent. In one sense there is nothing particularly startling about this practice – drawing attention both to significant fault-lines running through white culture and the failure of so-called agencies of white power to entirely subjugate dissenting voices. Yet by locating difference as the product of historically and culturally specific relations of domination and subordination, and by exploring the way in which other modalities of exclusion, based on gender, class, ethnicity, locality, intersect with race to successfully contest white hegemonic ambitions, these writers reveal not just the instability and fluidity of the dominant culture but also the degree to which different communities and individuals are increasingly bound to one another in a myriad of complex relationships.

Building upon the theoretical foundations of Foucault and de Certeau, John Fiske's *Power Plays, Power Works* provides a useful framework for understanding not just the diversity of contemporary America and the manner in which power is possessed and exercised but also the complex politics and aesthetics of James Lee Burke's Dave Robicheaux novels. Preferring de Certeau to Foucault, because the former 'gives far greater weight to the diversity and creativity of forms of resistance',[52] Fiske's synthesis of de Certeau's dynamic conception of power, of the ongoing conflict between 'weak' and 'strong' powers, where neither one assumes total dominance, offers a number of excellent entry points for thinking about Burke's series featuring Dave Robicheaux, a detective with the New Iberia police department, an agency policing the small south Louisianan town and outlying bayou community.[53]

De Certeau argues there are two types of power in operation in modern society – 'imperializing' power exercised from the top-down and 'localized' power exercised from the bottom-up.[54] Weak power, even powerlessness, would appear to aptly describe the situation of many of Burke's poor black characters, who occupy a twilight world on the fringes of white society servicing it as maids, butlers, chauffeurs, drug dealers and pimps. As if to reflect their subordinate social status, predominantly black neighbourhoods tend to be drawn in grimly foreboding terms. Rural communities, little more than makeshift shantytowns that have grown up around the edges of sugar and cotton plantations, tell their own story. The ramshackle dwelling occupied by the parents of a murdered prostitute in The *Neon Rain* is typical; it has no windows, no plumbed water, a hinged board flap that acts as a door and walls insulated by pages torn from an old Sears catalogue. Similarly blighted is a neighbourhood, described in A *Morning for Flamingos*, where 'chickens pecked in the dirt yards, the ditches were littered with garbage, [and] the air reeked of someone cooking cracklings outside in an iron kettle',[55] and, in an urban context, a crumbling New Orleans housing project, described in *Dixie City Jam*, where 'normal' conditions of life assume apocalyptic undertones and 'gang rape, child molestation, incest, terrorization of the elderly . . . and knivings'[56] are all commonplace.

More far-reaching is the 'imperializing' or top-down power of the so-called social, economic and political elites, a fragmented alliance of businessmen, politicians, civil servants and military officials, nonetheless identifiable in terms of their similar social status, usually as white and male. Anticipating the Iran-Contra scandal, which blew up in Ronald Reagan's second term as president, The *Neon Rain* features a conspiracy involving army generals and CIA agents to smuggle arms to the right-wing Contras in Nicaragua using profits accrued from the sale of illegally imported Colombian cocaine. Jerome Gaylan Abshire may be a semi-retired two-star general with a record of distinguished service in World War Two and Korea but his genteel ante-bellum home in New Orleans' elegant Garden District, replete with 'gold and silver grandfather clocks, deep purple divans with scrolled walnut frames . . . [and] oil portrait of a Southern military family that went back to the war of 1812' (p. 138), cannot conceal his culpability in a scheme that has devastating implications for Nicaragua's Indians. Robicheaux is told that weapons purchased by the Contras with Abshire's aid have been used to systematically brutalise and repress the Indian population and a number of them have been thrown out of US military helicopters at high altitudes by right-wing paramilitaries simply for 'kicks'.

Yet the cracks in such relations of domination and subordination are everywhere and just as Burke's poor black – and white – characters are not simply drawn as powerless ciphers, interpellated by a vast, intestate capitalist culture and shorn of any kind of ability to affect the direction of their lives, the political, economic and social dominance of figures like Jerome Abshire is never a '*fait accompli*', a situation guaranteed by wealth, privilege and connections. Given the pervasive links between ideology and the politics of representation, moreover, this dialectical relationship is not played out against a backdrop of an invisible whiteness and deviant, overdetermined blackness, where the connections between social power, cultural formations and historical processes are either consciously or unconsciously obscured. Burke's bayou landscapes are populated by a motley crew of all too visible, usually physically deformed white degenerates who wear their misogynism and racism like badges of honour and whose predilection for sadistic violence is not simply innate to their genealogy but rather is linked to the historical forces of racial hatred which have their roots in the institution of slavery. Though they might be extreme manifestations of white hegemonic ambitions, their extremity and visibility is important because it destabilises the ability of white culture to conceal the coercive strategy that underwrite its domination. Bobbie Joe Starkweather from *The Neon Rain*, Eddie Keats from *Heaven's Prisoners*, Murphy Doucet from *In the Electric Mist with Confederate Dead*, Jody Hatcher from *Dixie City Jam* and Aaron Crown from *Cadillac Jukebox* are all worthy examples of Burke's impressive gallery of white-trash recidivists but even more memorable are the singularly repugnant Eddie Raintree and Jewel Fluck from the appropriately titled A *Stained White Radiance*. It perhaps goes without saying that both Raintree and Fluck are physically repulsive; Raintree has a 'face full of bone', 'the kind you could break your fist on',[57] a visual signifier of a degenerate morality that manifests itself in terms of his long prison record for 'bigamy, check writing and sodomy with animals' (p. 62). Significantly, though, their deviancy has political and racial overtones since both were recruited in prison into a shadowy white supremacist organisation called the Aryan Brotherhood. Their vitriolic racism expressed in terms of their violent excesses, perhaps more disturbingly, is re-inscribed as quasi-respectable in the persona of Bobby Earl, an articulate, well-groomed demagogue in the mould of David Duke, but what is significant is that both versions of whiteness (the unobtrusive, invisible whiteness of Earl and the excessive, grotesque whiteness of Raintree and Fluck) are conceived of, and represented as, cultural constructions, at least in so far as relations of domination and subjugation are products of a long, brutal history that might date as far back as the arrival of African slaves in the region but still exercises an iron-clad grip over the present. As Robicheaux is forced to acknowledge in a later novel, *Burning Angel*:

> I wanted to believe that all those nameless people who may have lain buried in the field – African and West Indian slaves . . . Negro labourers whose lives were used up for someone else's profit – would rise up with the smoke and force us to acknowledge their humanity and its inextricable involvement and kinship with our own.
>
> But they were dead, their teeth scattered by plowshares, their bones grounded by harrow and dozer blades into detritus, and all the fury and mire that had constricted their hearts and tolled their days were now reduced to chips of vertebrae tangled in the roots of a sugarcane stalk.[58]

Nowhere, though, are the slippages or rather tensions between 'imperialising' or top-down and 'localised' or bottom-up power more apparent than in terms of the character, actions and ambitions of Burke's protagonist, Dave Robicheaux. As part of the official machinery of law enforcement, it is perhaps inevitable that Robicheaux's actions should, in part, underpin the *status quo* and consequently, the economic and political interests of the state, while his position as family breadwinner and traditional attitudes towards parenting and marriage seem to further reaffirm the authority of a white, patriarchal order. Yet Robicheaux is a far more complex figure than this suggests, an outsider whose anti-establishment sympathies have been fostered and stoked by his Cajun ancestry and status as a recovering alcoholic and disillusioned Vietnam veteran. This oppositional stance is, of course, integral to the persona of the detective; though not a private detective, self-definition for Robicheaux is achieved by exercising his own 'alternative' justice, often in conflict with the legalistic strictures of the department. However what distinguishes Burke's fiction and elevates Robicheaux above more traditional generic figures is that the tension this disjuncture produces manifests itself in outbursts of gratuitous, even shocking violence on the part of Robicheaux, thereby further calling into question the genre's already shaky moral foundations.

Throughout the series, Robicheaux constantly elides the constrictions imposed on him by his status as a police officer, first in New Orleans and then in New Iberia, a practice that allows him to vent his considerable fury against those who, for various reasons, look like they might escape legal punishment. But in doing so he undermines his agency as a detective and draws attention to his own destructive tendencies, or rather those tendencies become part of the supersaturation of violence emanating from society's every pore. His alcohol-induced interventions in *Heaven's Prisoners*, where he strikes a suspected assassin, Eddie Keats, with the metal-end of a pool cue, so hard that he actually felt 'the wood knock into bone and saw [Keats'] skin split open' (p. 110), may have a quasi-moral authority, given Keats' background and attitudes, but the excessive nature of the attack undercuts this legitimacy. As Fred Pfeil eloquently puts it:

> [Robicheaux] is openly riven by ambivalence, troubled by complicit desires and doubts and obsessed with its old, unhealable wounds . . . [he is] a man caught and constituted by the ceaseless tension between a Victorian paternalist-patriarchal idealism and its dialectical Other, the urge to get down with the rampaging monsters and go with the flow, and with the open acting-out of this tension in virtually every book.[59]

As a corollary, one could add that in so far as these tensions resurface again and again, disrupting the order and tranquillity that Robicheaux perversely hankers after, one of the genre's cornerstones, the need for closure, is further eroded. One could also point out that Robicheaux's multiple points of identification, not just as a man, as white, as a father or a police officer but also as a Cajun, as someone with working-class sympathies and a burning antipathy towards the exploitative practices of profit-motivated businesses, destabilise attempts to align him with the values and ambitions of the establishment he uneasily serves. His identity as white and male may not exactly position him on the margins of society but his Cajun ancestry and his sense of belonging to a fast-disappearing Creole-Cajun-Arcadian world, draw him into a head-on collision with various outside agencies (property developers, oil companies, organised crime) seeking to harness the region's natural resources and exploit the working poor for short-term economic gain. If 'imperializing' power, as Fiske suggests, is defined as 'a systematic set of operations upon people which works to ensure the maintenance of the social order',[60] Robicheaux's interventions, best understood as examples of 'localised' or bottom-up power, are most effective not in his official role as policing the *status quo* but rather as an advocate for and protector of the culture of his upbringing. In other words, his actions are most effective when directed against the various vested-interest powers that seek in vain to co-opt him. When a priest, in *Burning Angel*, asks Robicheaux to try and explain and rationalise the rage that, from time to time, threatens to consume him, asks what bothers him the most – his memories of Vietnam or the death of his first wife, Annie, or his ongoing battle against alcoholism – Robicheaux's answer is simple but revealing, 'It's what we've allowed them to do', he says, without hesitation. 'All of them, the dope traffickers, the industrialists, the politicians' (p. 244).

Robicheaux's sadness over the gradual disappearance of the way of life which had 'belonged to our people since the Arcadians first came to Louisiana in 1755'[61] is tempered in part by associations of that world with slavery and the subsequent forced separation of black and white worlds, tempered by his own memories of white boys 'who went nigger-knocking in the little black community of Sunset, who shot people of color with BB guns and marbles fired from slingshots, who threw M-80s onto the galleries of their pitiful homes'.[62] Yet rather than glossing over the material structures of inequality underwriting race relations in the contemporary or seeking to locate the plight of these same 'people of color' in a historical vacuum, Burke takes care to contextualise these inequalities in terms of institutional racism stretching back over generations. In *In the Electric Mist with Confederate Dead*, Robicheaux's discovery of the remains of a black man murdered in the 1950s, a murder he subsequently finds out was carried out by white vigilantes acting with the tacit approval of the town's sheriff, has important ramifications for black characters in the contemporary because, like the return of the repressed, it underlines the influence of past over present and the lack of progress in race relations made in subsequent years. As Robicheaux is forced to acknowledge:

We live in what people elect to call the New South. But racial fear, and certainly white guilt over racial unjustice, die hard. Hogman Patin, who probably feared very little in this world, had cautioned me because of my discovery of the lynched black man . . . To Hogman, those events of years ago were still alive today, still emblematic of an unforgiven and collective shame, to be spoken about as obliquely as possible.[63]

Yet while the so-called 'color line' in Burke's southern Louisiana certainly does not lack genuine substance, a binary system of classification clearly cannot account for the complexity of racial and ethnic identities that characterises the region. How, after all, can this kind of system make sense of a world where mixing or miscegenation is widespread, make sense of people like Robicheaux himself who enjoys the privileges of being identified as 'white' but whose father is described throughout the series as a 'dark' Cajun, or Cecil Aguillard, a deputy in the New Iberia police force, whose brick-coloured skin and 'redbone' heritage derive from his kaleidoscopic identity as Cajun, Negro and Chitimacha Indian, or a mixture of all three?

Racial divisions are pervasive but so too are class and cultural divisions; in fact the latter, on occasions, override, even erode, the former. *Sunset Limited* is littered with references to episodes from the region's inglorious past, manifestations of a vitriolic racial hatred directed towards people of colour not just by the Klan and other white supremacist organisations but also by the rich and powerful; two Klansmen shooting dead a fourteen-year-old black boy from Chicago for whistling at a white woman; a black man, executed for attacking a plantation overseer who had raped his wife; the Terrebones, one of New Iberia's wealthiest families, whose ancestors made their fortune from the slave trade in the pre-Civil War era. Such episodes are not merely confined to the past, either. The brutal rape of a young black woman, Sunshine Labiche, by two Klan sympathisers and the failure of the law to bring them to trial is a stark reminder of how little has changed. At the heart of the novel, though, is the forty-year-old murder of Jack Flynn, a white Union activist who was nailed upside-down to a barn door and left to die in 1956 for his part in trying to mobilise support for the working poor. Flynn's murder is compared to the shooting of the fourteen-year-old black boy by Klansmen and whereas the killers in the latter case, set free by a white jury for apparent lack of evidence, are ostracised by their Mississippi community after their release, no such action was ever taken against Flynn's murderers. Searching for an explanation of this discrepancy, Robicheaux realises that 'the killers in Mississippi were white trash and economically dispensable'[64] and such logic gives momentum to the trajectory of the narrative which, as it gather momentum, implicates wealthy patriarch Archer Terrebone in Flynn's murder and intensifies Robicheaux's own feelings of antipathy towards not just Terrebone but the capitalist class he represents. 'You don't like rich people', his boss, the town's sheriff, observes, even before Terrebone's guilt has been confirmed, 'You think we're in a class war' (p. 62).

At the heart of *Sunset Limited*, as in much of Burke's fiction, is an ongoing conflict between the haves and have-nots in which the domination of the former and the subordination of the latter is all but guaranteed by the complicity of government officials, businessmen and civic leaders in the novel's unravelling conspiratorial web:

> Archer Terrebone, who would murder in order to break unions, financed a movieabout the travail and privation of plantation workers in the 1940s. The production company helped launder money from the sale of China white. The FBI protected sociopaths like Harpo Scruggs and let his victims pay the tab. Harpo Scruggs worked for the state of Louisiana . . . The vested interest of government and criminals and respectable people was often the same. (p. 279)

Relations of domination and subordination, it goes without saying, are racially determined but not exclusively so, and Burke's fiction is perhaps at its strongest when focusing on the effects of shady business deals, political corruption, drug trafficking and self-interested policing on the working poor – black and white – 'those faceless working people whom historians and academics and liberals alike treat with indifference' (p. 310). The fact that Robicheaux represents, in part, the vested interests that he despises, to the detriment of exactly those 'faceless working people' he claims to identify with, affords Burke's work a degree of complexity and sophistication missing from much so-called 'politicized' crime fiction, and distances it from the kind of soggy liberalism whose racial politics is underscored by a belief that 'we just need to get to know one another'. Though Robicheaux is often right in pointing out that the interests of poor blacks and whites often converge, he has no answer when Batist Perry, a dark-skinned Creole who helps him run a boat rental business, remarks, '[Jack Flynn], the one got nailed to the barn? You know how many black men been killed and nobody ever been brought to cou't for it?' (p. 290).

Intransigence and hostility still characterise race relations in southern Louisiana but one also finds in Burke's novels brief glimpses of what it could be like to live in an environment and a culture that was committed to resolving differences and antagonisms through dialogue. This is not a naive, utopian fantasy but rather what Jonathan Rutherford calls 'living with incommensurability' and it is interesting to note his close description of this mirrors the contours of Burke's world:

> This means a culture and individual sensibility that pays attention to that old liberal adage that we must learn to live together – not attempting to construct oppositions based on hierarchies of value and power, not through the politics of polarity, but in the recognition of ourselves, through the transformation of relations of subordination and domination.[65]

Burke's world is not free of hierarchies of value and power, of course. The influence of social and economic interests is clearly visible and one could even argue that Burke's narrative technique constitutes a different kind of hierarchy, one in which Robicheaux's discourse is privileged over and above other characters. Seen through his controlling perspective, Batist, his friend but nevertheless his employee too, could be interpreted, given the Southern context, as a reconstituted servant-figure, the white ideal of a loyal and faithful black helper, prepared to spill blood to protect his master. Yet this kind of politically loaded reading is partial and inaccurate because it fails to take into account the warmth, understanding and mutual respect that underwrites their relationship, and while there might be something unsettlingly paternalistic, as Robicheaux is quick to concede, about a white Southern man talking about 'the loyalty of a black person'[66] their relationship offers hope that boundaries of race and class can be crossed, though not collapsed, that new affinities and connections can be forged across previously impenetrable frontiers. In a society where widespread miscegenation and the geographical proximity of black and white worlds cannot conceal the depth of divisions and animosities, it remains only a possibility. *Burning Angel* concludes with the double suicide of a wealthy white property developer and his poor black housemaid, a tragedy brought about by their despair over the impossibility of ever being able to formally acknowledge their relationship to the outside world. But even in this darkest of moments, Robicheaux finds some small grain of hope because their re-enactment of a centuries old Southern 'black-white confession of need and dependence' was, if nothing else 'a recognition of the simple fact of our brotherhood' (p. 339).

Conclusion: Towards a New Cultural Politics of 'Whiteness'

In 'The New Cultural Politics of Difference' Cornel West urges communities and individuals to 'look beyond the same elites and voices that recycle the older frameworks' to embrace 'a new language of empathy and compassion' able to better describe 'the contingent, provisional, variable, shifting nature of all identities'.[67] Since West's contention is that this new cultural politics of difference can only succeed with sufficient numbers of people of colour cultivating 'sensibilities and personal accountability',[68] to use either Burke or Wilson or Price as a paradigm would appear to be a, at best, dubious critical practice, one whose outcome, whether it was intended or not, threatens to once again marginalise non-white voices and reaffirm the authority and centrality of whiteness. Yet we move into an age where cultural space, as Giroux observes, is becoming unfixed and porous, and identities are being 'rewritten within new and shifting borders of . . . race and ethnicity'[69] whiteness needs to be de-colonised, shorn of its traditional associations with notions of power and domination. It would be churlish to maintain that social, racial or gendered hierarchies are entirely dismantled in the novels discussed in this chapter, but in so far as the crime novel has always been a vehicle for subversive or rather contradictory political ideas, contemporary white crime writers have taken significant and more than just cosmetic steps in this direction, de-stabilising white identities, refashioning whiteness as grotesque, exploring how and to what effect axes of gender, class and ethnicity intersect with race, exposing the social and economic foundations to relations of subordination and domination; in essence, laying down the foundations for a new cultural politics of whiteness, one that, in part, heeds Stuart Hall's call for 'the centred discourses of the West to be deconstructed'.[70]

Yet Cornel West's argument remains a valid one, and the implication that whiteness is being dismantled only from the inside is entirely erroneous. Arguably of greater significance is the pressure brought to bear from the outside, and certainly the fast-changing cultural landscape needs to be understood not merely in relation to shifting notions of whiteness but also to an entire spectrum of non-white ethnicities and identities. In the realm of the crime novel, this means exploring how, and indeed whether, changing the racial or ethnic identity of the detective or protagonist, who is anyway alienated from or opposed to 'dominant' values, reconfigures the genre's structures and ambitions, or rather how and to what extent this shift provides a new framework for thinking about the nature and meaning of multiculturalism in the United States. The focus of the rest of the book is resolutely aimed in this direction, exploring the racial, ethnic and gendered kaleidoscope of contemporary America, as seen through the eyes of its crime writers; not just white crime writers but also African-American, Caribbean, Chicano, Korean, Native American and Jewish crime writers. What emerges is a fascinating portrait of a society where traditional relations of domination and subordination are still pervasive but where singular visions of a national culture are being questioned and eroded; a heterogeneous society where new identities are being made and re-made on the borders between race, gender, ethnicity, class and sexuality.

Notes

1. See Mike Hill (ed.), *Whiteness: A Critical Reader* (New York: New York University Press, 1997), p. 4.
2. Richard Dyer, *White* (London and New York: Routledge, 1997), p. 10.
3. Hill, *Whiteness*, p. 2.
4. Henry A. Giroux, 'Living Dangerously: Identity Politics and the New Cultural Racism', in Henry A. Giroux and Peter McLaren (eds), *Between Borders: Pedagogy and the Politics of Cultural Studies* (London and New York: Routledge, 1994), p. 28.
5. See Toni Morrison, *Playing in the Dark: Whiteness and the Literary Imagination* (Cambridge, MA and London: Harvard University Press, 1992); Kenneth Warren, *Black and White Strangers: Race and American Literature* (Chicago, IL and London: University of Chicago Press, 1993).
6. Warren, *Black and White Strangers*, p. 11.
7. Fred Pfiel, *White Guys: Studies in Postmodern Domination and Difference* (London and New York: Verso, 1995), p. 121.
8. Isaac Julien, 'Introduction,' *Screen*, 29, 4, Autumn, 1988, p. 6.
9. See Sally Munt, *Murder by the Book: Feminism and the Crime Novel* (London and New York: Routledge, 1994), p. 85.
10. See Munt, *Murder by the Book*, p. 101.
11. Stephen Knight, *Form and Ideology in Crime Fiction* (London: Macmillan, 1980), p. 163.
12. Jonathan Rutherford, 'A Place Called Home: Identity and the Cultural Politics of Difference', in Rutherford (ed.), *Identity: Community, Culture*, Difference (London: Lawrence and Wishart, 1990), p. 12.
13. See Dyer, *White*, p. 10.
14. Homi K. Bhabha, *The Location of Culture* (London and New York: Routledge, 1994), pp. 1–2.
15. See John Williams, *Into the Badlands* (London: Paladin, 1991), p. 90.
16. Liam Kennedy, 'Black Noir: Race and Urban Space in Walter Mosley's Detective Fiction', in Peter Messent (ed.), *Criminal*

Proceedings: The Contemporary American Crime Novel (London: Pluto, 1997), p. 45.

17. James Ellroy, *White Jazz* (London: Random Century, 1992), p. 13.
18. James Ellroy, *LA Confidential* (New York: Mysterious Press, 1990), p. 111.
19. Ellroy, *White Jazz*, p. 50.
20. Ellroy, *White Jazz*, p. 120.
21. Peter McLaren, 'White Terror and Oppositional Agency: Towards a Critical Multiculturalism', in David Theo Goldberg (ed.), *Multiculturalism* (Oxford and Cambridge, MA: Blackwells, 1994), p. 46.
22. See Dyer, *Screen*, p. 45.
23. James Ellroy, *The Black Dahlia* (London: Arrow, 1991), p. 54.
24. Peter Blauner, *Slow Motion Riot* (first published 1991) (New York: Avon, 1992), p. 1.
25. John G. Cawelti, *Adventure, Mystery, Romance: Formula Stories as Art and Popular Culture* (Chicago, IL: University of Chicago Press, 1976), p. 152.
26. Ralph Willett, *The Naked City: Urban Crime Fiction in the USA* (Manchester and New York: Manchester University Press, 1996), p. 3.
27. Richard Price, *Clockers* (London: Bloomsbury, 1992), p. 95.
28. Marcel de Certeau, 'Walking in the City', in Simon During (ed.), *The Cultural Studies Reader* (London and New York: Routledge, 1993), p. 160.
29. Willett, *The Naked City*, p. 3.
30. De Certeau, *The Cultural Studies Reader*, p. 153.
31. Jack O'Connell, *Box Nine* (first published 1992) (London: Pan, 1994), p. 97.
32. Jim Collins, *Uncommon Cultures: Post-modernism and Popular Culture* (London and New York: Routledge, 1989), p. 68.
33. Sabine Vanacker, 'VI Warshawski, Kinsey Milhone and Kay Scarpetta: Creating a Feminist Detective Hero', in Messent (ed.), *Criminal Proceedings*, p. 63.
34. Bethany Ogden, 'Hard-Boiled Ideology', *Critical Quarterly*, 34, 1, Spring, 1992, pp. 71–2.
35. Peter Messent, 'From Private Eye to Police Procedural: The Logic of the Contemporary American Crime Novel', in Messent (ed.), *Criminal Proceedings*, p. 7.
36. See Vanacker, in *Criminal Proceedings*; Kathleen G. Klein, *The Woman Detective: Gender and Genre* (Urbana and Chicago, IL: University of Illinois Press, 1988); Maureen Reddy, *Sisters in Crime: Feminism and the Crime Novel* (New York: Continuum, 1988).

37. Munt, *Murder by the Book*, p. 28.
38. Ibid., p. 30.
39. Ibid., p. 82.
40. Ibid., p. 58.
41. See Tom Hiney, *Raymond Chandler: A Biography* (London: Chatto and Windus, 1997), p. 101.
42. Munt, *Murder by the Book*, p. 33.
43. Vanacker, in *Criminal Proceedings*, p. 74.
44. Timothy Shuker-Haines and Martha M. Umphrey, 'Gender (De)Mystified: Resistance and Recuperation in Hard-Boiled Female Detective Fiction', in Jerome H. Delamater and Ruth Prigozy (eds), *The Detective in American Film, Fiction and Television* (Wesport, CT: Greenwood Press, 1998), p. 72.
45. Munt, *Murder by the Book*, p. 90.
46. Woody Haut, *Neon Noir: Contemporary American Crime Fiction* (London: Serpent's Tail, 1999), p. 98.
47. From the days of slavery onwards, Smith writes, 'the Creole People of color had their own well-developed society . . . The prettiest girls, meaning the ones with the most obvious Caucasian genes were sent to the Quadroon balls, where they met rich planters who bought them houses of their own', Julie Smith, New Orleans Mourning (New York: Avon, 1991), p. 59.
48. Julie Smith, *New Orleans Mourning*, p. 324.
49. See Vanacker, *Criminal Proceedings; Klein, The Woman Detective: Gender and Genre*.
50. Barbara Wilson, *Murder in Collective* (London: Virago, 1994), p. 95.
51. Vicky Hendricks, *Miami Purity* (London: Vintage, 1997), p. 7.
52. John Fiske, *Power Plays, Power Works* (London and New York: Routledge, 1995), p. 69.
53. The Neon Rain (1987), *Heaven's Prisoners* (first published 1988), *Black Cherry Blues* (1989), *A Morning for Flamingos* (first published 1990), *A Stained White Radiance* (1992), *In the Electric Mist with Confederate Dead* (first published 1993), *Dixie City Jam* (first published 1994), *Burning Angel* (first published 1995), *Cadillac Jukebox* (1996), Sunset Limited (1998).
54. See Fiske, *Power Plays, Power Works*, p. 10.
55. Burke, *A Morning for Flamingos* (New York: Avon, 1991), pp. 25–6.
56. Burke, *Dixie City Jam* (London: Orion, 1995), p. 205.
57. Burke, *A Stained White Radiance* (New York: Hyperion, 1992), p. 62.
58. Burke, *Burning Angel* (London: Phoenix, 1996), p. 172.
59. Pfiel, *White Guys*, p. 147.
60. Fiske, *Power Plays, Power Works*, pp. 10–11.

61. Burke, *Heaven's Prisoners* (London: Vintage, 1990), p. 45.
62. Burke, *A Stained White Radiance*, p. 65.
63. Burke, *In the Electric Mist with Confederate Dead* (London: Orion, 1994), p. 153.
64. Burke, *Sunset Limited* (London: Orion, 1998), p. 173.
65. Rutherford, *Identity: Community, Culture, Difference*, p. 26.
66. Burke, *A Stained White Radiance*, p. 55.
67. Cornel West, 'The New Cultural Politics of Difference', in Russell Ferguson (ed.), *Out There: Marginalisation and Contemporary Cultures* (Cambridge, MA: MIT Press, 1990), p. 19.
68. West, in *Out There*, p. 34.
69. Giroux, *Between Borders*, p. 30.
70. Stuart Hall, 'New Ethnicities', in *ICA Document 7* (London: ICA, 1988), p. 31.

CHAPTER 3

'Whose Genre is it Anyway?': Black Crime Fiction in the Contemporary US

If, up until the first half of the 1990s, some despairing critics were asking, 'What is it about race and genre fiction that doesn't mix?'[1] then a growing black[2] presence in the genre of American crime fiction in the second half of the 1990s perhaps, though not necessarily, makes such a question redundant. Questions raised about the ability of a generic form seen by many to be inherently conservative[3] to deal effectively with the complexity of black experiences in the United States cannot be easily dismissed, but the sheer variety and diversity of black crime fictions in circulation suggests, as has been the case in music and film, that the conflation of 'black' and the 'popular' continues to be highly productive.

A cursory glance at the evidence tells its own story. Walter Mosley, famously named as Bill Clinton's favourite writer, has seen two of his novels made into feature films, enjoys 'near' bestseller status, and now leads a vanguard of emerging and above all heterogeneous black voices within the genre. No longer is the setting for the black crime novel confined to east or west coast urban sprawls; though New York and particularly Los Angeles remain the favoured locations, black crime writers have also used settings as diverse as Chicago (Holton, Bland), the Deep South (Sherman), North Carolina and Maine (Neeley). Nor does the black crime writer or detective have to be male; the presence of Baker, Bland, Carter, Komo, Mickelberry, Neely and Wesley is ample proof of the growing visibility of female voices within the genre. Nor does 'he' have to be straight; George Baxt and Penny Mickelberry write about gay detectives. Nor does the black detective or writer need to be 'African-American'; Mike Phillips' investigator Sam Dean, in Paul Gilroy's terms, has a 'diasporic' identity, one that overlaps with but also elides mutually exclusive national definitions. Nor does the black protagonist have to be, in strict terms, a detective; Mosley's Easy Rawlins is at best a 'reluctant' investigator, while Mike Phillips' Sam Dean is a journalist. Nor, even, does the black crime writer necessarily have to be black; the fact that James Sallis is not but his novels, featuring African-

American private detective Lew Griffin, are among the 'best' examples of what we might call the black crime novel, calls into question the validity of essentialist arguments about cultural/racial authenticity and ownership.

Problems of definition associated with black crime fiction are significant because they draw attention to and feed out of wider debates ongoing in black cultural politics. Among others, Gilroy, Hall, Dyson and hooks, have called into question the ability of 'black' to operate as a trope of sameness, somehow connecting divergent experiences, identities and nationalities across space and time. Rather, fuelled by an interest in identity politics where points of identification are multiple and axes of race, ethnicity, gender, age, sexuality, nationality, religion and region continually merge and collide in the process of identity construction, these critics have sought to construct a more fluid, heterogeneous, even contradictory definition of blackness, one that resists the logic of racial essentialism and stresses the multiplicity of black tones, experiences and styles. The sheer diversity of the black crime novel outlined in the previous paragraph compliments and reinforces the trajectory of this project, opening up the category 'black' to multiple and sometimes conflicting interpretations, but it also throws up an important methodological challenge for the scholar; namely, whether one should focus on those elements which connect these various texts together, thus running the risk of re-inscribing an essentialist discourse of blackness, or whether one should focus on areas of difference between texts, thus ignoring the degree to which the nonetheless diverse experiences and histories of black-identified people in the United States overlap.

One approach has been that of Stephen Soitos whose timely study of the 'canon' of African-American detective fiction, *The Blues Detective* (1996), proposes that four 'uniquely African-American' tropes are present in black detective fiction in the United States – what he identifies as altered detective personas (i.e. rejection of the white myth of 'lone' hero), double-consciousness detection (i.e. positive appropriation of W.E.B. Du Bois' veil metaphor; 'trickster' detective using masks, mistaken identities for own purposes), black vernaculars (i.e. use of 'specific expressive arts of black Americans that form part of their culture and are derived from the folk tradition'),[4] and 'hoodoo' (i.e. a fusion of European and African forms to create something uniquely African-American).[5] Soitos' study draws heavily on the work of Henry Louis Gates (1984, 1988) and Houston A. Baker (1984) and their influential efforts to establish or rather delineate a transformative 'black' tradition or aesthetic based upon the premise of 'signifyin(g)' – the process by which Euro-American forms are appropriated and ironically reworked through the lens of African-American folk or oral culture. As Gates argues:

> Black texts employ many of the conventions of literary form that comprise the western tradition . . . but black formal repetition always repeats with a difference, a black difference that manifests itself in specific language use. And the repository that contains the language that is the source and the reflection of black difference is the black English vernacular tradition.[6]

My earlier reference to Soitos' timely study of the 'canon' of African-American detection is somewhat mischievous and perhaps a little unfair because, as Cobley notes, Soitos' approach has helped to excavate a rich vein of African-American culture 'buried by the white supremacist tendencies inherent in processes such as canonisation'.[7] Moreover to focus on the distinctiveness of African-American culture is useful because separation or segregation, enforced or otherwise, continues to produce a rich variety of cultural forms. And as Tara Mack points out, 'Without some space to maintain distinct cultural identities, white American culture could quickly take over, reaching into every nook and cranny of American life, stamping out all the cultural variety'.[8] Yet the danger remains that this kind of theoretical approach replaces one canon with another, a white European canon with one that privileges those texts whose formal and thematic properties dovetail best with the four tropes of black detection identified at the expense of texts whose formal and thematic properties do not. Cobley astutely observes that while Soitos' methodological approach is well suited to his analysis of particular authors, notably Pauline Hopkins and Rudolph Fisher (whose novel 1932 *The Conjure-Man Dies* is widely considered to be the earliest example of the form), it falters when assessing the work of writers like Chester Himes and Donald Goines:

> Undoubtedly it is unsatisfactory to say that Himes is effectively a 'white' writer because he operates in the hard-boiled frame . . . But suggesting that Himes's Harlem novels, composed to order in France, with a strong hard-boiled voice, are actually thoroughgoing African American narratives, contributing to a black vernacular tradition, clearly will not do.[9]

Himes, along with Walter Mosley, is considered at length in the following chapter and the relevance of this particular observation to his fiction will be discussed there, but the general argument is a significant one because it points to the inability of specific formal or structural models, however flexible they may be, to accommodate all voices and texts without inevitably organising them into hierarchies based on their appropriateness to the model.[10] Furthermore, though the resultant situation falls a long way short of re-inscribing racial essentialism, a sole focus on black difference as the key interpretative trope and a rejection of black works that are indistinguishable from other texts in the Western literary tradition, as Kenneth Warren argues, ignores the complex relationship between 'black' and 'white' that exists in the United States and risks becoming an 'obstacle to illuminating "fresh" interpretations'.[11] (One can perhaps better understand Gates' (et al.) omission of black 'experience' or 'street' writers like Iceberg Slim, Clarence Cooper Jr, Charles Perry, Herbert Simmons and Donald Goines from *The Norton Anthology of African-American Literature* (1997) in this context, because as Cobley observes, black characters in these novels are not joined by a vernacular tradition, nor do they allow for the exploration of a rich heritage of African-American culture. 'Instead, characters, rather than being unproblematically united by a common cultural heritage, are constantly in collision and are seen as part and parcel of conflicting social forces (for example, crime and law) and axes of identity beyond those of "race" or "ethnicity"'.)[12]

The approach taken in this chapter, and the next one, which treats the crime fictions of arguably the most significant African-American crime writers, Chester Himes and Walter Mosley, to a more rigorous analysis than would have been possible here, is perhaps more balanced, seeking to locate areas of common concern and experience, formal and thematic, between the range of texts considered, while at the same time, allowing for significant differences. In other words, to stress what some writers see as the 'positive' characteristics of communal identities, what Dyson refers to as an 'enabling solidarity', but without placing 'an ideological noose of loyalty around the necks of critical dissenters from received ideas about racial unity'.[13] This might sound like fence-sitting of the highest magnitude but there are sound critical reasons why such caution is necessary and why Soitos' approach requires some modification; reasons that relate to the function of popular texts in the context of the 'culture industry'.

The idea that a transformative African-American detective fiction, by employing the four tropes of black detection that Soitos identifies, manages to diffuse all of the reactionary elements inherent to the crime fiction genre, is less than honest. As we will see in the next chapter, Himes' detectives, Coffin Ed Johnson and Grave Digger Jones, despite their African-American identities, are nonetheless 'official' agents of law enforcement and thus deeply implicated in a system which is predicated on their own subordination. In other words the novels themselves are shot through with contradictions, with violently competing values and ideologies, perhaps an inevitable feature of 'unpopular-popular' texts that are formed within the shadows of the dominant culture but resist its colonising impulses. As Tony Bennett observes:

> It is no more possible in the past than in the present to locate a source of popular cultural activity or expression which is not, at the same time, shot through with elements of the dominant culture and, in some sense, located within it as well as against it.[14]

When one also considers that meanings are not simply locked up within texts but produced at the juncture of text, context and reader, and that the reader like the text, author and detective can simultaneously take up reactionary and progressive positions, we can begin to see the bewildering array of possible meanings available, meanings which are denied or closed-off by attempts to situate black crime fiction as a unified genre or sub-genre. Like all genres or sub-genres it is constantly being made and unmade. Or as Fiske points out, 'the popular' is determined by the forces of domination to the extent that is always formed in reaction to them; 'but the dominant cannot control totally the meanings that the people may construct'.[15]

'Sisters are Doing it for Themselves?': Valerie Wilson Wesley, Barbara Neely, Charlotte Carter

If the emergence of a significant number of black female crime novelists is a relatively recent phenomenon – the publication of Delores Komo's *Clio Brown, Private Investigator* (1988) marks the start of the contemporary cycle – then the traditions informing these works, inevitably, are somewhat older. There are the male-dominated traditions of American crime fiction and African-American detective fiction, as well as the predominantly white tradition of recent feminist crime fiction. On top of this, black female crime novels have also been informed by the kind of broader shifts in black cultural politics outlined in the introduction, as well as by the emergence of what Paula L. Woods refers to as the 'Third Renaissance of black thought and writing', a loosely affiliated 'movement' including voices as diverse as Toni Morrison and Ernest Gaines and presenting 'a more diverse range of black experience than ever before'.[16]

The danger in assessing black female crime fiction, then, is one of reductionism; a tendency to foreground race at the expense of gender or vice versa, or a tendency to foreground race and gender at the expense of a thorough investigation of how a shift in narrative perspective from that of white male, or even female, detective to black female detective affects the structural configurations and thematic concerns of the genre. Though it might seem self-evident that this mapping process will further destabilise the already fractured politics of the hard-boiled crime novel, this is not necessarily the case. In some, though by no means all, examples, subversive thematic critiques – of, say, white, patriarchal capitalism – are poured into all-too-familiar structural vessels, often without any acknowledgement of the problems or tensions that such a conflation can produce. The result, as Munt acknowledges, is that radical content can often be 'derailed by deep structures of conventionality undermining it'.[17] Or, as she goes on to argue in relation to Komo's *Clio Brown*, '[It] is a passing text . . . victim to the intransigence of the form'.[18]

Munt's influential study of feminism and the crime novel, *Murder by the Book*, was published before the arrival into the genre of a large number of the black female crime writers already noted, but her observations about the apparent generic incompatibility of a black female detective are significant because they call into question the ability of any crime writer, but especially a black or female or black female crime writer, to revise what she sees as a fixed set of codes and conventions that are inevitably resistant to subversive appropriation:

> The number of Black women writing formulaic crime is minimal. I see the intransigence of the form as a reason for this. There are aspects of the form which facilitate a self-conscious entry into the genre for Black authors, but ostensibly the crime novel does not meet the needs of Black women at the moment. A progressive race politics allows a limited restructuring in these texts, although it is mostly only foregrounded in theme. Orientalist discourse has conspired with the crime novel's structure of the threat as Other to contain a more radical break in the form.[19]

Compelling in the context of her argument, Munt's observations are nonetheless problematic for a number of reasons. Though the number of black women crime writers is still minimal, at least in terms of overall percentages, the figure is growing and this growth is perhaps testament to the fact that the crime novel does meet at least some of the needs of black women. Moreover, while Munt may well be correct in here belief that a progressive race politics *can* run up dead against the genre's structural conservatism and residual traces of an orientalist discourse whereby non-white 'others' are automatically constructed as a threat, this is by no means inevitable. Such an argument ignores shifts that have taken place in theories relating to Orientalist discourses (shifts discussed in the previous chapter which call into question the appropriateness of straightforward models on 'self' and 'other'). Perhaps more disturbingly, it also presupposes genre to be a kind of static, unyielding straitjacket, rather than a set of loosely defined codes and conventions that are constantly being made and remade by authors, publishers *and* readers. What Munt seems to be suggesting is that black female crime writers (or any crime writers) with a radical, transformative agenda will automatically fall victim to the genre's inherent conservatism; that failure to conflate thematic and structural radicalism – if it is a failure – is not down to the writers themselves but rather is a product of working within the genre. As we shall see, however, the fact that this 'failure' is not replicated across the board would suggest otherwise. Instead of filtering our assessments of particular texts through a static, theoretical grid, what requires far closer scrutiny are the range of conflicting forces at play within individual texts and the way in which these forces are arranged and interpreted by writers and readers in the process of constructing meaning. Or, to paraphrase that well-worn saying; generic structures don't matter, it's what you do with them that counts.

By far the most popular form for black female crime writers to work in is the private eye novel and the bulk of my analysis is directed towards these novels in particular; Barbara Neely's *Blanche on the Lam* (1992) and *Blanche Among the Talented Tenth* (1994), Valerie Wilson Wesley's series featuring Newark-based private detective Tamara Hayle, and Charlotte Carter's *Rhode Island Red* (1997) The popularity of the private eye novel with black writers in general is perhaps unsurprising, though it does require some kind of qualification.[20] Antagonisms between African-American communities and white-dominated police departments throughout the United States are well documented and present aspiring black police procedural with a myriad of potential difficulties and anxieties related to questions of agency and identity; whether it is possible, say, for the black public detective to work within the system without utterly compromising those qualities that might make him or her attractive, particularly to a mass audience. In many ways, this is a fascinating dynamic and one ripe for exploitation; in the next chapter, we shall see how gaps and ellipses produced in Himes' Coffin Ed and Grave Digger novels by their violently conflicted status as African-American *and* police officers constitute the key structuring tension for the entire cycle. Yet when one takes into account the demands of having to work within an explicitly popular genre, and remembers that by the end of Himes' Harlem cycle, his two 'ace' detectives are so disillusioned with and marginalised within the police department that they can no longer operate as agents, it is hardly surprising that it has been to the arguably less compromised and compromising private eye form that most African-American crime writers have turned.

Tamara Hayle, Valerie Wilson Wesley's private detective featured in a series of novels including *When Death Comes Stealing* (1994) and *No Hiding Place* (1997), used to be a police officer, the only black female officer in the Newark police department, but her position in the department is so compromised when her teenage son is subjected to the racist taunts of her white colleagues that she decides to take up as a private detective. Rather than being shorn of her power, this shift consolidates it, since freed from the pressures of departmental racism and sexism, Hayle is better able to exercise her agency as a detective. Freed from the shackles of departmental racism and sexism but exposed to the same forces in society as a whole, Hayle's power is undoubtedly 'weak', and like all private detectives, her relationship with the police, and by implication to mainstream ideologies and the 'dominant' culture, is necessarily unequal and adversarial. Nonetheless, in so far as her investigations, usually into crimes dismissed by a disinterested white-dominated police department as 'niggers killing niggers',[21] expose the conspiratorial configurations that underpin them, she is able to exercise some kind of control over the everyday, bringing individual incidents to albeit problematic, uneasy resolution.

Arguably the strongest novel of the series, *No Hiding Place*, describes Hayle's investigation into the murder of a young African-American man, Shawn Raymond, an investigation which appears to implicate a prominent black family from a prosperous Newark suburb and connects up to a range of racial, gendered and class-based conflicts at play within society as a whole. The family, headed by its patriarch, Gus Lennox, a retired police officer, is solidly middle class, unlike Raymond, who belongs to what could only be described as the city's racially determined underclass. Class-based antagonisms may lie at the root of their mutual antipathy but Raymond's brutal misogynism, when directed at one of Lennox's daughters who bears his child, perhaps best explains why Lennox decides to kill him, concocting an elaborate alibi to ensure that he escapes punishment. Interestingly, Raymond's misogyny is mirrored or replicated by Lennox in so far as they both possess 'the same aggressive, nothing-but-me-means-anything shit, the same foul mouth and ugly manner, the same rigidity' (p. 148) and is countered within the space of the narrative by the benign patriarchy of Hayle's neighbour Jake and her deceased brother, and revered police officer, Johnny, whose involvement in the department's 'Touch and Change' programme, 'set up to reach boys without fathers' (p. 16), brought him into contact with a younger Shawn Raymond and provided him with stability and hope.

The novel's class and gender politics – 'progressive' in so far as Hayle is a single mother trying to bring up her teenage son and an independent agent running her own business and 'reactionary' in so far as benign patriarchy is suggested as a solution to the problem of teenage delinquency – are subsumed by its racial politics. Race in the novel operates as a kind of structuring absence, determining the actions and motivations of the various characters in ways they themselves only partially understand. Played out against the backdrop of Newark, a post-industrial city in decline, still unable to come to terms with the 1960s riots, the violent tendencies of Lennox and Raymond could both be interpreted in terms of their anger at this legacy; Lennox, over the disintegration of community, having to watch 'property values slide into the toilet' as a result of the banks' post-riots 'redlining' policies, and Raymond, over the complete absence of opportunity for an emerging generation of working-class blacks. Yet Wesley subsumes and dissipates these tensions into a family drama whereby her plucky detective is able to make sense of a situation and landscape where, in macro-terms, the fractured politics of race, not to mention gender and class, would render her impotent. If this is a criticism that could be levelled at many crime novels, what disappoints about Wesley's novel is her failure to draw attention to this sleight of hand; offering individual resolutions that work to smooth over tensions which have been opened up by the various narrative configurations. What also disappoints is Wesley's failure to explore how the often conflicting axes of class, gender and race might work to undermine or dislocate the kind of secure, unproblematic identity that her detective seems to possess.

More successful in this respect is Barbara Neely's creation, Blanche White, a plump, middle-aged maid and amateur sleuth featured in *Blanche on the Lam* and *Blanche Among the Talented Tenth*. As a domestic servant well versed in the practice of role-playing, Blanche's identity is never fixed. The burden of double-consciousness, formally recognised by W.E.B. Du Bois when he wrote in 1903, 'It is a peculiar sensation, this sense of always looking at one's self through the eyes of others, of measuring one's soul by the tape of a world that looks on in amused contempt and pity',[22] is acknowledged but also transformed by this use of masks. The fact that Blanche's identity, in the eyes of her wealthy white employers, is reduced to that of cipher, a simpering Mammy figure whose function is to serve, may signify her lowly social status and foreground the power relations that underpin such hierarchies, but the practice of 'signifyin(g)', as Henry Louis Gates argues, also has a progressive meaning in so far as it functions as metaphor for the radical transformation of white norms and meanings once refracted through African-American eyes. 'By using the trickster qualities of masking', Sotios notes, 'they make their detection work and in the process outwit their enemies in trickster fashion'.[23]

As someone for whom 'reading people and signs, and sizing up situations, were as much a part of her work as scrubbing floors and making beds',[24] Blanche is well versed in the strategies of detection and her invisibility in the eyes of her white employers afford her the space and opportunity to turn her ratiocinative powers towards uncovering the complex web of murder and blackmail in which she is inevitably implicated. Neely's books celebrate a particular kind of black, female, working-class identity rarely seen in print. In so doing, Neely transforms the detective from isolated individualist (whether such a stance has been chosen or determined through external circumstances) into a figure whose agency is made possible by a mixture of personal guile and collective responsibility. As Munt argues, 'Blanche's opportunities are made possible precisely because she has a network of other women, family and friends, who support her ... Her survival depends on sharing a culture of resistance which Black women have necessarily made a community'.[25]

Yet the slippage between identities, part of what Soitos refers to as 'double-consciousness detection', is not altogether seamless and unproblematic. In *Blanche on the Lam*, Blanche is only too aware of the gap that exists between her role as 'Mammy' and that of 'trickster-detective' but finds herself moving uneasily between both identities, concerned about succumbing to what she calls the 'Darkies Disease' (of learning to love her employers or rather oppressors) but unable to deny the humanity of Mumsfield, a slow-witted white man with whom she forges some kind of, albeit problematic, friendship. The erosion of apparently fixed boundaries between black and white, and rich and poor, suggested by this relationship, however, is not a validation of the old liberal pluralist ethos that everyone is equal on the grounds of a common or essential humanity. Rather it is an acknowledgement that material inequalities and racial, class and gendered differences have not entirely destroyed a common humanity. The focus of Blanche's ratiocinative gaze is as much the complex terrain of identity politics as it is the social disorder generated by individual acts of criminal transgression, which her function as a detective requires her to address. In the former role, operating from a not-dispassionate perspective, she draws attention to the ways in which the interlocking and yet diverging forces of race and class operate to subjugate and dehumanise poor black subjects. This subjugation is most often practised by wealthy whites (such as Grace and Everett in *Blanche on the Lam*) but class and colour-based tensions within the black community, as Blanche finds out in *Blanche Among the Talented Tenth*, can be just as a pernicious:

> She hoped Ardell wasn't going to be proved right in her belief that well-off black folk were even more color prejudiced than the everyday folks

who'd tormented Blanche all of her life. Of course color wasn't the only
thing operating in a place like this. There was also the close relationship
between light skin and wealth. (p. 21)

The politics of her latter role, however, are not quite as clear-cut. Neely
has mapped the fragmented, divisive racial and class politics of
contemporary America on to a generic form that owes as much to
Agatha Christie as it does Dashiell Hammett. In *Blanche on the Lam*,
Blanche's movement from New York to rural North Carolina, both
affirms and undermines the logic of this shift. The association of the
rural South with the practices of the Klan and the brutal suppression of
the black population, and the narrative emphasis on this connection,
constitutes a radical departure from the codes and conventions of the
traditional country house form, where broader social concerns and
tensions tend to be noticeable only by their absence. Yet the very fact
that the crime and investigation take place in a self-contained world acts
as a kind of screen, distancing the narrative, detective and most
importantly the reader from such problems and associated anxieties.
The secure, ordered world promised or suggested by the kind of
unproblematic resolutions achieved in both novels is, of course, at odds
with their racial politics where the hierarchies which underpin this
orderliness are constantly being questioned and subverted. Perhaps all
one can say is that how these resolutions are interpreted, whether
Blanche's ratiocinative 'triumphs' unproblematically reinscribe the
status quo or whether they suggest that 'success' for poor blacks in
America will always be conditional and limited, is as much dependent
on the politics of the reader as it is on the politics of the author.
    This process, whereby the complex matrices of race relations and
identity politics are mapped on to the structures and conventions of the
crime fiction genre, is perhaps most effectively realised by Charlotte
Carter's *Rhode Island Red* (1997). Or rather Carter's appropriation and
reinvention of the structures and conventions of the hard-boiled
detective genre is sufficiently elastic to accommodate, and not diffuse,
radical or oppositional content. Carter does not fall victim, in Munt's
terms, to the genre's intransigence, because like the best crime writers,
she interprets its codes and conventions not as some kind of fixed,
inviolate blueprint but as a loose collection of signposts. Like jazz music,
which her protagonist Nanette adores, her conception of genre supposes
a vibrant, eclectic and above all open-ended form where variation rather
than repetition constitutes the dominant mode of playing.
    Nanette is emblematic of this free-wheeling elasticity. As someone
who is 'self-involved, mercurial, emotionally unstable . . . something of a
loner, apt to take off for ports unknown at a moment's notice'[26] it is

unsurprising that her identity is always shifting, Chameleon-like, in relation to her moods, her surroundings. What is surprising or at least refreshing is the extent to which her identity elides any kind of traditional constituency. The novel's first line – 'Ask any Negro. They'll tell you: a woman does not play a saxophone' (p. 1) – foreshadows the assault on essentialist racial and gendered tropes that is about to take place; Nanette, an African-American women in her late twenties, a 'Grace Jones lookalike in terms of coloring and body type' (p. 1) does play the saxophone, though by her own admission, not particularly well. In other ways, too, her identity is defined in terms of contradictions. She possesses a healthy heterosexual sex drive but has few maternal instincts; she plays the saxophone on the street for a living but nonetheless has a solidly lower middle-class background and a French degree from Wellesley. She dresses 'like a parody of a Civil Rights worker' replete with 'Stokely Carmichael shades' (p. 24) and defines herself in terms of a love of jazz but her affinity with France, with French poets like Rimbaud and Verlaine, is just as strong. 'France was hardly my home. Yet I kept fleeing there. It was where I felt safe, the most alive, the most understood, the most welcome' (p. 54).

This is not a rejection of her identity as African-American but rather a rejection of what Kobena Mercer has usefully characterised as 'the burden of representation',[27] that is, the demands placed on black artists and individuals to try and somehow 'represent' the whole of black experience. Nanette feels this burden only through the expectations of others, through white people who (mis)identify her 'either a half-wit, genetically determined criminal or an extraterrestrial with some kind of pipeline to the spirit' (p. 52), or black people who imagine that to enjoy French poetry is to somehow capitulate to hegemonic practices of white, Western culture. Nanette, for herself, is able to construct a space through which she is able to negotiate difference in non-hierarchical terms. Recognition that her love for Rimbaud and jazz is not mutually exclusive, that cultural products do not exclusively belong to the culture from which they originate, enables her to identify with Henry Valoukes, an eccentric Greek-born jazz aficionado with an obsession for Charlie Parker, and forges a bond between them which transcends racial-ethnic barriers.

Yet once this identity, one through which cultural, class and gendered differences can be negotiated, is re-mapped back on to the unsettled terrain of the crime novel, it threatens to unravel and break apart. Doubles proliferate; no one is as they appear to be. Sig, the musician who Nanette befriends at the start of the novel and who is murdered in her flat, turns out to be Charles Conlin, a corrupt detective with the New York police department. Henry Valoukes is also a gangster-turned-informer. Wild Bill, a homeless black man who wanders the streets of Manhattan, used to be Heywood Tuttle, a trumpeter and 'good musician' who had 'gigged once or twice with Bird' (p. 95). Nanette, too, is divided; free-wheeling jazz artist and prototype gumshoe, warts and all. Crucially, Carter represents her reluctant detective neither in Wesley's terms, as an old-fashioned fantasy or wish-fulfilment figure, able to expose social corruption while 'proving and maintaining [her] moral integrity',[28] nor in Neely's terms as a figure entirely grounded in a specific black working-class milieu and imbued with its 'values', but rather as a ambivalent, hedonistic, independent, cautious, moral, amoral black woman or in her own words, 'Bonnie and Clyde crossed with Wyatt Earp and a drug dealer from one of those death-in-the-ghetto movies' (p. 154).

The trajectory of the narrative brings Nanette into confrontation with Valoukes, who seems to hold the key to the mysteriously named Rhode Island Red, but like a jazz soloist, endlessly improvising on familiar themes or rhythms, Carter reconfigures the traditional ending of the crime novel in which events and situations are explained and ambiguity expunged. Rhode Island Red, Nanette discovers, is a saxophone filled with pure heroin and sealed with gold once given to Charlie Parker by a New England gangster in order to persuade him to play at his wedding. The cultural value of the saxophone, like that of the notorious statuette in Hammett's *The Maltese Falcon*, has been debased by its material value and significantly, like the statuette in Hammett's novel, the saxophone remains undiscovered, its significance, at least in terms of the narrative, ambiguous. Does the value of the saxophone signify the lasting impact of Charlie Parker's jazz and a continuing interest in his musical legacy or does it symbolise the tendency of white culture to exploit black cultural forms and icons for financial gain? The answer is left open to interpretation, as is the novel's concluding scene in which Nanette's confrontation with Valoukes comes to a head:

> I took the gun out, examined it one last time and headed over to Henry's chair./ I rested the barrel on his shoulder, perhaps an inch from his ear. / He slept on for a while, but then must have sensed me there. His eyes fluttered open. / 'This is for you,' I told him. 'I think it's time you learned a trade – my love.'/ The hotel lobby was no busier than when I'd arrived nearly five hours ago. / The clerk I'd bribed gave me what I guessed was his sexy look and hailed me winningly. / 'Well, hi there. Was he surprised?' / 'No,' I said, regretfully. 'He wasn't a bit surprised.' (p. 170)

Questions, rather than answers, proliferate. What has happened in this scene? Why does Nanette rest the barrel of the gun on his shoulder?

Why does she tell him that he needs to learn a trade? What kind of trade is she referring to? Does she still have feelings for him or is she being ironic when she calls him 'my love'? Has she actually shot and killed him, for betraying her? Or is her expression of regret in the final line not because she has killed him but more an admission of how much she still loves him? And what is it Henry is not 'surprised' about? That she left him? Loved him? Killed him? Perhaps most importantly, one could also ask, has justice been served? Or rather how can one tell whether justice has been served or indeed what the term actually means, whether it has any relevance to Nanette's situation. None of these questions are unambiguously answered and in so far as the burden of interpretation is shifted from writer to reader, Carter's *Rhode Island Red*, more than Wilson's Tamara Hayle series or Neely's Blanche White novels, successfully marries thematic and structural innovation, calling into question through its fluid, be-bop style and open-ended structure, the ability of detective, writer or reader to make conclusive judgements about who we are.

'Down These Ghetto Streets . . .' Gary Phillips and Gar Anthony Haywood

If the black female crime novel, with the notable exception of Pauline Hopkins's *Hagar's Daughter* (1901–2), is a relatively recent invention, perhaps unsurprisingly its male counterpart has a longer tradition, one that can be traced back from contemporary writers like Walter Mosley and Gary Phillips, through blaxploitation 'texts' like *Shaft*, and so-called 'street experience' novels by writers like Iceberg Slim, as far as Chester Himes' Harlem Cycle and Rudolph Fisher's *The Conjure-Man Dies*. To describe this disparate collection of writers and texts as a 'tradition' is perhaps misleading since it implies a uniformity of form and content, or at least some kind of continuity, that does not exist. What links them together, in so far as it reinforces the logic of this chapter, is their status as examples of black crime fiction, though the very diversity of styles and strategies of representation that characterises these works at once undercuts the basis for this kind of exercise. One could argue that these texts are joined, thematically, by their shared focus on the difficulties of living in a white-controlled world, or by their desire to revise the codes and conventions of what has been a predominantly white form. But how far can we take this idea? What does the 'black' in black crime fiction actually refer to? Is it the consumers, people who buy and read these novels, or just the producers? Is it the kind of structures used by writers or perhaps the content of their representations? And what is the relationship of these texts not just to the broader white public culture but also to hard-boiled crime fiction in general, a genre which is itself predicated on a distrust of public culture and anxiety about the repressive tendencies of the state?

My point is quite simply that the appropriation and revision of the crime fiction genre by various black writers is not the story of a conservative genre being transformed into a daringly subversive, or even an entirely different, genre by dissident authors. The challenge, then, for writers and readers of black crime fiction is to negotiate, rather than ignore these complexities, to understand how black writers and readers of crime fiction participate in the dominant culture through processes of accommodation and resistance without either transforming their means of participation (i.e. the crime fiction genre) into something altogether different or 'selling out', becoming commodities implicated in a voracious white capitalist culture. Mapped on to the fraught, divisive, fragmented landscape of the American inner cities, these complications are compounded; so that what becomes fascinating for the critic and reader alike is to see how the complexities of a genre, already shot through with contradictions, are heightened when the narrative focus switches from that of disaffected 'white' to disaffected 'black' subject and conflicting forces already at play within the genre collide head-on because the black detective, more so than his or her white counterpart, has to strive to restore an order whose essential nature is hierarchical and predicated on relations of domination and subordination.

Hammett's *Red Harvest* and his detective, the Continental Op are just as significant generic antecedents for Gary Phillips as African-American detectives like Fisher's N'Gana Frimbo (*The Conjure-Man Dies*) or Himes' Coffin Ed and Grave Digger (the Harlem Cycle). Indeed just as Hammett's novel responded angrily to the corrosive impact of industrial capitalism on the fabric of small-town life, Phillips' *Violent Spring* (1994) and *Perdition, U.S.A.* (1996) speak about the damaging impact of laissez-faire capitalism, what he describes as 'the rapaciousness of the big money boys who fed at the troughs Reagan and Bush slopped for them',[29] on the poorest residents of Los Angeles. Phillips persuasively argues that the effects of industrial 'downsizing' or 'outsourcing' on the city's African-American and Latino populations as the shipyards, car factories and chemical plants either closed down or 'moved to Mexico to cut costs'[30] were devastating and further compounded by Reagan-inspired cutbacks in social spending during the 1980s. Such policies effectively disenfranchised whole sections of the African-American working class and led to a not-unrelated rise in criminal activity; Robert 'Scatterboy' Williams is one such example, a shipyard welder turned petty thief in order to scrape together a living who is murdered at the start of *Perdition, U.S.A.*, apparently by a white serial killer randomly targeting members of the African-American criminal or underclass.

Described as a 'socialist private eye',[31] Monk is a more political or politicised figure than the Continental Op. The Op's actions are informed by a thinly veiled hostility towards the wealthy but as Christopher Bentley argues, he develops no political consciousness.[32] Monk, on the other hand, cannot help but develop a political consciousness because as an African-American with strong working-class affiliations, he has witnessed at first hand the catastrophic impact that a political shift to the right has had on his community. But this conflation of 'socialist' and 'private eye' is not unproblematic, because whereas Monk might recognise the importance of collective responsibility, and indeed be motivated by a desire to rectify 'wrongs done to African-Americans',[33] his distrust of political processes and preference for personal solutions is, in the end, just as significant. It is not that all politicians are necessarily corrupt; simply that progressive legislation, in Monk's view, stands little chance of successfully making its ways through a system which privileges the interests of white, patriarchal capitalism. Grainger Wu, a fictional senator in *Perdition, U.S.A.*, the first Asian to reach this level of political office, is well meaning and uses his office to try and push through Hate Crimes legislation aimed at curtailing the activities, and freedoms, of far right vigilante groups. Yet such legislation has little chance of becoming law, because of its implications for Constitutionally guaranteed rights like freedom of speech. Moreover since some of the police, at least at a local level, are sympathetic to the aims if not the practices of far right activists, responsibility falls on Monk to pursue and eradicate them.

If this description of Monk's function directly invokes that of Hammett's Continental Op in *Red Harvest*, it is intentional. The crucible of far right activity in *Perdition, U.S.A.* is a town in the Pacific Northwest whose name, Perdition, recalls the bastardised name given to Hammett's Personville – 'Poisonville'. Like Poisonville, Perdition is run by a corrupt alliance of police officers and a corporate patriarch whose name, Ira Elihu, borrows heavily from *Red Harvest*'s Elihu Wilsson. Elihu, meanwhile, might not be directly implicated in the activities of these far right groups but his purging of 'union sympathizers, uppity blacks, back-talking Mexicans, and women who wouldn't wear skirts in canning factories' (p. 160) in the 1950s institutionalised a perspective and social hierarchy privileging white over black, male over female, and upper and middle class over working class. His wife, too, is a key supporter of the War Reich, a group of skinheads responsible for firebombing a Puerto Rican family in Port Huron, while his son, Nolen Meyer, is the 'bone white' serial killer stalking the poor black communities of south Los Angeles.

Rather than misreading Hammett's detective as a 'hard-boiled hero [embodying] a vision of righteousness and justice',[34] or as 'tough, stoic, loyal to his own values, waging a lone battle against urban chaos',[35] Phillips embraces the full range of contradictions and ellipses that make the Continental Op in *Red Harvest* such a fascinating character. Tacit acknowledgement of these ellipses allow Phillips to explore the contradictory tendencies in Monk's character as he finds that his function as detective is not always, if ever, compatible with his personal desire for a vigilante-style justice. At once caring and moved to violent rage, Monk travels north from Los Angeles to Perdition to track down the white serial killer. Forging a path between well-meaning but ineffective politicians and ill-disciplined but impassioned anti-racist activists, Monk's preference for direct action leads him into immediate conflict with a group of far right activists known as the War Reich, but even as he savagely beats four of its members, he is not certain of his own motives, whether he should simply assassinate its leader and 'go down in the history books, at least the real ones, as a hero of the class and race struggle' (p. 172), or fulfil his obligation to his client, Clarice Moore, and focus his attention on finding the man who murdered her boyfriend.

Monk brings the narrative into resolution by tracking down the killer but his ambivalence over what to do and his passivity when faced by hoards of pro-fascist and anti-fascist demonstrators in Perdition threatens to paralyse him. Inability to steer an effective path between right and left positions splits Monk down the middle and disrupts the basic premise of the genre: that individual solutions to larger social problems can be achieved. In the end, though, Phillips draws back from Hammett's radical position. Unlike the Continental Op, who cannot help but succumb to the murderous forces redolent in Personville, Monk manages to pull himself back from the brink, the soothing balm of family and friends reigning in his aggression. Yet his rage and then ambivalence cannot be easily contained within a narrative form structured towards the idea or ideal of closure. The same could perhaps be said of Gar Anthony Haywood's private eye, Aaron Gunner, though Gunner's relative anonymity, and his detachment from his community, affords him a degree of protection from the violent excesses which often threaten to subsume Monk. On the other hand, Monk's anger is perhaps a sign that he believes that he can 'make a difference', whereas Gunner's circumspection is, in part, an extension of his acknowledgement that given the realities of power relations in corporate America, his 'failure' in some shape or form is inevitable. As Haywood admits:

> I wanted to create a black PI in LA who was not going to come off as John
> Shaft, who was not going to be a typical soul brother. And I knew that

somewhere along the line he was going to quit. That was one thing I was determined about. We've seen enough heroes who just deflect everything that comes their way.[36]

Part of Gunner's difficulty is that unlike Monk, who has easily identifiable targets upon which to vent his fury (white supremacists in *Perdition, U.S.A.* and multinational corporations in *Violent Springs*), his investigations, based almost exclusively within the poor black neighbourhoods of South-Central Los Angeles, usually expose the complicity of people from within these neighbourhoods and exonerate those who might appear to be obvious adversaries. *Not Long For This World* (1990) features an investigation into the murder of a young black gang member in which Gunner exposes the culpability of a black car mechanic who saw his pregnant girlfriend die in a botched 'drive-by' gang shooting, while Gunner's efforts in *You Can Die Trying* (1993) end up exonerating a racist white police officer who was dismissed from the LAPD, trying to rebuild its image in the aftermath of the 1992 riots. Which is not to suggest that Haywood wants to absolve white politicians and corporate bosses of responsibility for the continuing ghettoisation of poor blacks or disguise the extent of racial discrimination within American society. Rather novels like *You Can Die Trying* acknowledge that given the extent of poverty and divisions within the black community, and the extent of antipathy between poor blacks in South-Central and the mostly white police department, even Gunner can do nothing to break the cycle of violence and hopelessness that constitutes everyday life for most poor blacks:

> Someday, [Gunner] tried to reassure himself, the LAPD and the black community would find a way to break the vicious cycle that was pulling them further and further apart with every passing day . . . But in the meantime, there would only be a continuation of what Harry Kupchak had accurately described as a war, and everyone involved would lose . . . Almost no one would be spared. It was insane.[37]

Still, Gunner is efficient and thoughtful, someone able to tread a careful path through the minefield of contemporary racial and class politics, someone who understands the depth and extent of divisions between black and white America but refuses to frame them in essential terms, who dares 'to expand upon what some people insisted were the unalterable parameters of "blackness"' (p. 19) but is not bound by racial criteria when deciding who to see, where to live, and what to do. Phillips, too, explores the relationship between race, class and ethnicity and seen in this light, the conflicts played out in *Violent Springs* between

African-Americans, Chicanos and Korean-Americans are best understood in economic rather than racial or ethnic terms. As Stephen Steinberg astutely remarks, 'When ethnic groups are found in a hierarchy of wealth, power and status, then conflict is inevitable'.[38] Two scenarios present themselves. First, the Balkanisation of the city and its dissolution into a low-rent Blade Runner world with 'each ethnic group carving out its larger or smaller fiefdom' (p. 165). The other, emblematised by Monk's nicely drawn relationship with his Japanese-American girlfriend Jill Kodama, is a more hopeful one where the salvation of Los Angeles lies not with its corporate patriarchs but with its citizens drawn from a myriad of racial, ethnic and class backgrounds working together and 'trying to do their job because they believed it made a difference' (p. 166).

Racked by a sense of ambivalence that is the product of their peculiar mix of optimism and pessimism, Phillips' and Haywood's fictions resides somewhere between the 'cool motherfucker'[39] world of *Shaft* with its eminently capable tough guy hero and the bleak nihilism of Iceberg Slim's *Trick Baby* (1967) or *Black Mama's Widow* (1969). One could argue that their appropriation and reinvention of divergent traditions successfully negotiates attempts to categorise their fictions and audience in explicitly racial terms. One could also argue that their fiction falls between two stools, that for some readers, the excesses of *Shaft*, of a racially overdetermined 'super-stud' able to exercise his will in the face of opposition from the police and the Mafia, and the excessive, uncompromising violence, misogyny, racism and brutality that characterises Iceberg Slim's novels, constitute more 'popular' points of reference. Then again, maybe the very ambivalence of their work just makes them harder to market. Which, in the end, is the best compliment one could pay them.

'Would the Real Black Man Please Stand up?':[40] *George Baxt and Mike Phillips*

The flood of new arrivals from Latin America, the Caribbean and Asia has sharply transformed the social and ethnic composition of America's urban landscape, and in so doing has called into question traditional definitions of blackness. Manning Marable, for example, makes the point that although native-born African-Americans, Trinidadians, Haitians and Afro-Brazilians would all be termed 'black' on the streets of New York, they have 'remarkably little in common in terms of language, culture, ethnic traditions, rituals, and religious affiliations'.[41] In the same way, focus on the way in which gender and sexuality intersect with race to split the individual subject has gathered momentum. In this kind of environment questions of difference are increasingly being framed in terms of an examination of power and privilege. Black unity may be a desirable goal for those seeking a common reference point in the struggle against white racism but talk of unity presupposes that divisions based on class, gender and sexuality count for little. It would be wrong to conceive of blackness in terms of violent, irreconcilable difference but then again not all black cultural productions, as Isaac Julien argues, have been 'dialogic enough to think through the "hybridity of ethnicity" or liberated enough to include "queerness" in their blackness'.[42] Not all, perhaps, but what about the work of George Baxt and Gary Phillips? Julien is of course right in his assumption that black cultural productions, particularly in film and hip-hop, have been less than inclusionary in their representations of black masculinity but my focus on Baxt, who writes about a black gay New York police detective, and Phillips, whose detective moves comfortably between New York's various African-American, Caribbean and Latin American communities, suggests that things have started to change.

Related perhaps to what Michele Wallace once described as the damaging effects of 'Black Macho' – black men defining their masculinity by extending and reversing white stereotypes about black inferiority and using 'superficial masculine characteristics [like] demonstrable sexuality; physical prowess, the capacity for warlike behaviour'[43] – there has been relatively little attention paid to the diversity and complexity of African-American masculinities; how black male identities are constructed at the intersection of race, gender and sexuality. As Kendall Thomas argues, 'the jargon of racial authenticity insists, as the gangsta-rapper Ice-Cube has put it, that "true niggers aren't gay"'.[44]

Thomas argues that the politics of racial authenticity and its attendant homophobia are best understood as a displaced expression of internalised racism, and that corrective measures to challenge rigid adherence to outmoded notions of black identity are desperately required. That one such measure should emerge from the crime fiction genre in the form of George Baxt's Pharoah Love novels – *A Queer Kind of Death* (1966), *Swing Low, Sweet Harriet* (1967), *Topsy and Evil* (1968) and *A Queer Kind of Love* (1994) – is not an aberration or publishing fad intended to exploit a growing, lucrative market but rather demonstrates the elasticity and adaptability of the genre. Seeking to illuminate how the subordination of gays, lesbians and African-Americans manifests itself, Thomas identifies violence as a key issue.

Gay and lesbian Americans of all colors and African Americans of every sexual orientation live with and under the knowledge that at any time, anywhere, we might be attacked for being gay or lesbian or bisexual, for being black or being both.[45]

Yet such remarks risk positioning African-Americans and gays (and particularly gay African-Americans) as victims, something that Baxt appears to be concerned about; Pharoah Love's first act in *A Queer Kind of Love* is to 'tighten his grip' around his 9-millimeter Glock semi-automatic before shooting one of his oldest friends, Herbie Marks, in self-defence. Indeed rather than allowing himself to become a victim, or someone whose identity has been externally (mis)defined, Pharoah's aggressively confident and yet vaguely flirtatious manner affirms both his queerness and ability to 'kick ass' as a police officer. The two may appear to be contradictory but Pharoah expels this contradiction on to others and uses it as a weapon to disarm and disorientate his enemies inside and outside the department. As one such unfortunate remarks, more than a little bemused:

> A detective wearing a yellow-and-blue striped cowboy shirt? Wearing corduroy jeans torn at the knees? A detective wearing cowboy boots decorated with multicolored studs? A detective with a red AIDS pin fastened to his shirt and on his head a cap with a blue pom-pom?[46]

Having to operate within a racist, homophobic organisation and being discriminated against on the grounds of skin colour and sexual preference is not without cost. Earlier in his career, Pharoah suffered a psychological breakdown – 'Too much pressure on the brain from the sneers and jeers and snide remarks of my fellow officers. They didn't think black and gay was beautiful' (p. 201) – and throughout he has had to battle to earn the 'grudging respect' of his fellow officers. That said, Baxt is perhaps aware of the dangers of turning a black gay detective into a messianic paragon of liberal tolerance, a defender and protector of the oppressed and someone able to retain his or her principles working within a corrupt and corrupting system. Instead Pharoah has been cut from the cloth of a wildly overdetermined political incorrectness, an insensitive queer who wouldn't hesitate 'spitting in somebody's eye' or even killing them, if he had to. Rather than being paralysed by these contradictions, moreover, Pharoah opens up and exploits them, and in the process becomes someone for whom his gun is both a means of extermination and a fashion accessory, someone who is equally comfortable with using violence as he is honing his observational skills, someone who has taken flak from colleagues for being black *and* gay but who 'tore the hinges' of the closet door when he came out and who uses his sexuality and the discomfort it induces in others as a weapon. 'Christ', a suspect in a murder inquiry realises, 'I'm being intimidated by a fag cop' (pp. 160–1).

A connective tissue rather than an intricately woven puzzle, the plot itself is little more than a vehicle whose function is to bring Pharoah into contact with a wide cross-section of characters drawn from Manhattan's gay and straight communities, its ethnic and racial groups, its law breakers and law enforcers. A little disappointingly, perhaps, Baxt does not uncover the power structures and relations that criss-cross this terrain, nor does he fully explore the complexities of Pharoah's racial identity and the implications of his ability to 'pass' as white. Furthermore the successful conclusion of Pharoah's investigation (whereby he discovers who and what lies behind a series of Mafia 'hits') and the attendant restoration of a *status quo* which is, by its nature, racist and sexist, provokes little or no adverse reaction, no sense of the kind damage that upholding a law which discriminates against minorities might induce in non-white, non-straight police officers. At the same time, Pharoah's actions throughout the narrative undercut and overturn straightforward hierarchies of race, gender and sexuality, and his final *pièce de résistance*, the seduction of his homophobic partner, Albert, in the novel's closing passage is a clear affirmation of his agency, not just as a detective, but also as a gay black man.

The question of agency, of how to live or function in a world where the practices of white-dominated power elites and the inadequacies of essentialism as a vehicle for fostering racial and ethnic solidarity constantly threaten 'black' subjects, lies at the heart of Mike Phillips' *Point of Darkness*.[47] To claim that race has been and still is the primary axis of social organisation in Phillips' New York is tempting for his Jamaican-born, British-raised investigator, Sam Dean, in so far as the city's Caribbean population, like its African-American one, is externally defined or misdefined on the basis of skin colour alone. Inspired by a Pan-Africanist rhetoric, some of the city's black intellectuals, too, have appropriated this identity and turned it into a positive affirmation of blackness, of a transcendent black culture. When Dean's cousin, Bonnie, lecturer at a university in Queens, asks him to describe his dark-skinned Latino girlfriend Sophie, the choices she offers him reflect an apparently prevailing view built into many American racial/social attitudes. 'You've got two choices', she tells him, 'Black or white? Which one is it?'.[48]

Dean, however, rejects the kind of racial exclusivism that underwrites Bonnie's question. Though at the time he falls into her trap and blurts out, 'You'd definitely call her black', almost at once, he finds himself unsatisfied with his answer, not least because it fails to take into account significant cultural differences between his cousin and girlfriend. Indeed, when the two women finally meet and Bonnie disparagingly declares that Sophie is not 'one of us', Dean sets out his own position:

> I'm loyal to my friends and my memories and want progress for the race.
> That's how we were brought up, you know that. That don't change. But
> there's no reason, whether its psychological or sociological or mystical or
> whatever, that's gonna make me join that exclusion shit. (p. 149)

Dean, then, might be fiercely loyal to what he sees as his race but he uses
the term in its loosest possible sense. Just as Henry Louis Gates states in
his autobiographical account of his family's history *Colored People*, 'I want
to be black, to know black, to luxuriate in whatever I might be calling
blackness at any particular time – but to do so in order to come out of the
other side, to experience a humanity that is neither colorless nor reducible
to color',[49] Dean self-consciously foregrounds his pride in being black but
conceives of this blackness in multiple, diasporic terms. After all, belief in
a pure black identity is something of a misnomer, he suggests, because
most black people in the modern world have a mixed-race ancestry.
'Europeans, Indians and Chinese, all of them at one point or the other
stuck their fingers into the New World's black gene pool' (p. 196).

Diaspora discourses, James Clifford argues, articulate forms of
communal identities and consciousness 'that maintain identifications
outside the national time/ space' and acknowledge the overlapping and
diverging histories of black people – 'shared histories of enslavement,
racist subordination, cultural survival, hybridization, resistance and
political rebellion'.[50] As a detective, Dean's generic function is to locate
the daughter of an old friend who has gone missing in New York, but
the plot is something of a Trojan horse, a means of smuggling into the
novel a secondary and arguably more significant agenda, that of
identifying the areas where the experiences, interests and histories of
New York's black people differ and overlap. Furthermore, as someone
who moves chameleon-like between England, the Caribbean and the
transplanted Caribbean communities in New York, someone whose
identity – as Jamaican, English, black, Caribbean – shifts in relation to
where he is and who he is with, and someone who is only too aware of
the subtle nuances of cultural difference, it is a job that Dean is well able
to perform. When he visits a Spanish-Caribbean cafe in Queens with
Bonnie and Oscar, her African-American boyfriend, though many of the
faces are black, Dean senses their unease – 'as if they were in enemy
territory' (p. 212). In another restaurant, he is able to precisely identify
the ethnic identity of the waiters. To his trained eye, they are not simply
black or even Caribbean but specifically Haitian – 'That is to say, they
looked a lot like Jamaicans, but with a kind of prissy smoothness to their
style and movements' (p. 139).

Yet Phillips refuses to portray New York's ethnic and racial landscape in reductive terms, an assemblage of readily identifiable component parts or ethnicities, instead focusing on the teeming morass of sometimes conflicting, sometimes interlocking alliances that connect and also divide individuals and communities. Though Jamaicans and other Caribbean blacks share a nominal racial identity with the city's African-Americans, differences are clearly foregrounded. African-Americans, Dean claims, are fixed to one country while Jamaicans 'move between two countries' (p. 222) and from a cultural point of view, seem to have more in common with the various Latin Americans. Class and gender divisions, too, undercut racial and ethnic unity. Crucially, though, differences between particular individuals and communities, Dean realises, are best understood not in exclusively cultural, ethnic or racial terms, but rather as expressions of relations of social and economic power. Dean notices the transformation of a particular Brooklyn neighbourhood, how it fell into disrepair when the population was largely African-Americans and was revived once Caribbean immigrants from Jamaica, Trinidad and Haiti moved in, but refuses to yield to essentialist thinking. Interpreted via the interlocking relationships between racial discrimination, economics and historical experience, Dean understands that whereas African-Americans:

> had lost it in the grim struggles of the northern cities, and then TV had taught them human worth could be measured by possessions and happiness was an escape capsule, the Caribbeans still pulled together because that was part of their immigrant heritage. (p. 138)

It is here that Dean's function as sociologist and detective overlap. Not only must he bring to bear his considerable observational skills on the situation in order to track down Mary, his friend's daughter, whom he discovers has become embroiled in a complex conspiracy involving corrupt civic bureaucrats, the Mafia and a West African dictator. Dean must also use these same skills to identify and attack the 'epicentre' or source of the conspiracy. What he fails to realise until it is too late, however, is that this centre or source is everywhere and yet nowhere, that the 'villain' or 'evil' he must confront is not a deranged corporate megalomaniac or deviant politician but rather the system of cultural, economic and political power in operation throughout the world that privileges particular groups and individuals at the expense of others.

A scheme to discard toxic waste from the United States in an illegal chemical dump in West Africa not only results in the spread of disease and death throughout the indigenous population living close to the landfill, but also fractures, if not entirely shatters, the romantic notion of a Pan-African or 'black' identity capable of unproblematically joining diverse black individuals and communities across space and time. Involved in this scheme is Ben Schumann, a high-ranking African-American civil servant, George Barre, exiled minister of the West African country where the landfill is located, and Claude, an old friend of Dean's whose betrayal of this friendship for financial gain, underscores the logic of the system and forces Dean to re-evaluate his sense of selfhood and his relationship to the larger Caribbean diaspora:

> I had still been clinging to the illusion that we had crossed the ocean simply to be free of hunger and fear and that, after all, we could remain different, something like we had been at the beginning. But after this it would be impossible to think about my life or about the childhood that bound us together with the same belief. (p. 302)

Seen in this light, Dean's final act of killing both Barre, the West African minister, and Claude, his childhood friend, may be entirely recognisable as that of a private detective pursuing his or her 'alternative' sense of justice, but perhaps just as effectively, it demonstrates how 'black' communities and individuals, rather than being united by an invariant common racial or cultural heritage, are bound up in a dog-eat-dog capitalist system where identities are constantly being made and unmade. One does not have to yield to the logic of the system, of course, and strategies of resistance are an inevitable by-product of the hegemonic ambitions of a dominant culture. In the final analysis, this is perhaps what *Point of Darkness* illustrates most successfully; that Dean's action as a private detective may re-inscribe a kind of order that leaves existing power structures unchanged but his insistence that these structures can be challenged, if not overturned, and his acknowledgement that significant areas exist where the experiences, interests and histories of different black and Latin American communities overlap constitutes the beginnings of an oppositional politics.

Endings, Beginnings: James Sallis' Lew Griffin Novels

The trajectory of this chapter has been a linear one, introduction to conclusion, by way of showing how black crime writers utilise the codes and conventions of the genre, moulding them to their own purposes while retaining particular features or characteristics. How a subversive racial politics intent on uncovering hierarchies and relations of power, when mapped on to the ambivalent, contradictory politics of the crime novel, both atomises, diffuses and also resists dilution or commodification; and how the more original, innovative writers bring these forces – of dissent and assent – into complex configurations either by highlighting the rage or disillusionment these situations induce in the detective (Gary Phillips, Gar Anthony Haywood), or by muddying the process through which things are explained and made clear, forcing the reader into an interpretative role (Charlotte Carter) or by focusing on the 'crime' in crime fiction and its place within a white-controlled, capitalist society where definitions of 'right' and 'wrong' and 'crime' and 'punishment' are manipulated by those in positions of power and privilege (Mike Phillips).

At first glance, James Sallis may appear to be little more than a curious anomaly, a throwback to authors like Ed Lacy, John Ball and Ernest Tidyman, white novelists writing about African-American detectives. But on closer reflection Sallis' series, featuring his New Orleans-based private eye Lew Griffin, is remarkable in so far as it draws together all of these features, that is, all of the best features of what has been discussed so far, and blends them into a daringly original body of work where subversive content is married to formal innovation. In Sallis' deft hands, the component parts of the private eye novel are stripped down and reassembled in such a way as to question even its most basic assumption. Rather than treating the genre as a kind of unyielding monolith, a straitjacket that necessarily compels practitioners to operate within fixed, conservative and above all user-friendly parameters, Sallis understands that he can make what he wants of its codes and conventions, and does so to deliberately confound audience expectations and shatter the epistemological certainty that seems to underwrite a lot of crime fiction. As Sallis himself says of his first novel, *The Long Legged Fly*, 'A lot of [it] . . . is about setting up expectations of genre literature and just turning them over, standing them on their head'.[51]

Sallis' *The Long Legged Fly* (1992), *Moth* (1993), *Black Hornet* (1996), *Eye of the Cricket* (1997) and *Bluebottle* (1999), usually feature his detective, Lew Griffin, looking for people who have gone missing; friends, family, people he has been paid to find. Occasionally, he finds the people he is looking for and manages to pull them up out of the cracks into which they have fallen, or the people he is looking for in one novel turn up in another novel. But more often than not they disappear either for good or they turn up dead. *The Long Legged Fly* is illustrative. Divided into four sections, one part set in 1964, one in 1970, the next in 1984 and the final part in 1990, each section features Griffin's search for someone who has gone missing; Corena Davis, a black Civil Rights activist, who Griffin finds in a sanatorium and who manages to find her feet again; Cordelia Clayson, a young black girl who has run away from her strict Baptist parents and dies from a heroin overdose before Griffin can reunite her with her parents; Cherie Smith, the daughter of one of Griffin's friends, who reappears at the end of the third section, having narrowly escaped the violent recriminations of a pimp, only to learn that her father has been stabbed to death in an apparently random attack; and Griffin's own son David who disappears in the final section of the novel only to re-surface in a later novel, *Eye of the Cricket*.

Griffin's habitual bouts with alcoholism, his hard-bitten attitude, his flexible but still identifiable morality, and his preference for vigilante-justice, for avenging 'wrongs' done either to clients, friends or just innocents, are recognisable private eye traits. Yet almost at once, the familiar and reassuring dissolve and become something more problematic, less comforting. Throughout Sallis' work, Griffin's search for others is projected back on to himself, or rather his search for others also becomes a search for himself, an often futile, hopeless search for missing passages in his life, times that he has lost to alcoholism or near-fatal injury, the 'dots of period and ellipses, dashes, white space',[52] that stand in for his year long convalescence in *Bluebottle* after he has been shot. The search for knowledge, explanations and order that tends to characterise much crime fiction is always limited and provisional in Sallis' work. Challenging the conventional structures of the form, his novels have no real beginning and no real end, but rather narratives bleed into one another, within and between individual books. Stories, like a blues or jazz riff, are told and re-told, each variation similar but also different. Past, present and future merge and collide; the future is reflected in the past and played out in the present. The story of Griffin's son's disappearance in *The Long Legged Fly* is re-told in *Eye of the Cricket* but with a different conclusion. An incident at the start of *Black Hornet*, set in 1968, where a sniper shoots a female journalist, Esme Dupuy, as Griffin accompanies her out of a New Orleans bar is reconfigured, some thirty years later in the implied present of *Bluebottle*, but this time the sniper shoots Griffin and the female journalist escapes unscathed. As Griffin later observes, 'Stories never do end, of course. That's their special grace' (p. 44).

Interestingly, while recovering from concussion at the end of *The Long Legged Fly*, Griffin himself takes to writing detective stories, composing one called *Skull Meat* about a New Orleans-based Cajun detective by 'improvising wildly, throwing in whatever came to me' (p. 162). *Skull Meat* is followed by another, unnamed, then another, *The Severed Hand*, in which Sallis-as-Griffin, self-consciously referring to the codes and conventions of the form, remarks, 'My Cajun . . . was nosing closer and closer to the truth, improvising his way toward it the way an artist does, a jazz musician or bluesman, a poet' (p. 174). Potentially just a glib postmodern device, Sallis' fiction-within-fiction elides this criticism by drawing attention to the relationship between the 'real' and 'artificial', how we as readers are meant to be able to distinguish between them, between stories that never end and lives that do, how we should acknowledge the genre's status as artifice but also notice how the 'real' and 'artificial' constantly bleed into one another. Hence Griffin's fictional creation's apparent ability to nose 'closer and closer to the truth' is not replicated by Lew Griffin whose attempts to do likewise constantly meet with failure and frustration. To this end, the process of writing and detection are linked. Sallis, as writer, and Griffin as writer and detective, strive to illuminate 'why' – why someone has been killed, why someone has disappeared, why people act the way they do – though often without success. Having located Corena Davis in a sanatorium in *The Long Legged Fly*, Griffin is ultimately unable to determine what drove her there, and when he finally tracks down and kills Carl Joseph, the sniper in *Black Hornet*, he is unable to explain what motivated him to kill at random. 'Something in his head', a friend suggests, 'maybe, sunk in so deep there that we won't ever be able to find out. Or something in the air . . . We probably won't ever know' (p. 175).

Perhaps. Then again, even though nothing is ever clear-cut in Sallis' fiction, connections do exist between these conditions, between the dizzying rage that goes some way to explain what compels Carl Joseph – disaffected, half-black, abandoned by his white father – to assassinate people at will and the self-hate that drives Corena Davis to bleach her skin and eventually end up in an asylum. These are emotions that Griffin well understands, even more so after he has seen Corena inside the asylum and 'felt years of hatred, fear and anger draining out of me' (p. 44), and when he thinks about Carl Joseph's rage, he realises that 'at some level (at more than one level, truthfully), I identified with him' (p. 175). These contradictory feelings, of rage, of being unable to express this rage, of passivity and failure, of being conditioned by white society to react in certain ways and yet always rebelling against externally imposed identities, are not signifiers of 'criminality' or 'deviancy' but rather perverse expressions of what it is like to be African-American living in a racist society where power and privilege are exercised along interlocking axes of 'race' and class. As Chester Himes, the 'real' Chester Himes who gives a lecture at Dillard University that the 'fictional' Griffin attends in *Black Hornet*, declares:

> If our plumbing for truth, whether as a writer, like myself, or simply as individuals looking back over our experiences – if this plumbing for the truth reveals within the Negro personality homicidal mania, lust, a pathetic sense of inferiority, arrogance, hatred, fear and self-despite, we

must recognize this as the effect of oppression on the human personality. For these are the daily horrors, the daily realities, the daily experiences – the life – of black men and women in America. (p. 99)

If the homicidal mania that, implicitly, lies behind Carl Joseph's murder spree is a 'crime' that Griffin takes upon himself to punish, then within this context and explication, it is little more than a reaction to a far greater set of circumstances and pressures, the infinite and yet invisible strategies adopted by state institutions and, lower down the food chain, by the white man in the street in order to maintain their superior social, economic and political status. The casual beatings and random violence meted out by white police officers and vigilantes against blacks in New Orleans replicate, in an albeit infinitesimal way, the practices of institutions and even governments; covert wars, CIA-sponsored right-wing coups in South America, 'business as usual in [apartheid] South Africa'.[53] Seen in this light, the incidents that Griffin is called upon to investigate, the people who have gone missing or been killed, are not disruptions to the *status quo* but rather are the *status quo*. Griffin's function as a black private eye, therefore, is clear; as Willett observes, he can do little more than 'prevent individuals, including himself, from sinking into the abyss of drinks, drugs, self-loathing and despair that terminates in death or madness'.[54]

Capitulation to alcoholism, despair and self hate is not an inevitability, though. Survival tactics adopted by African-Americans throughout the history of the United States, practices of dissimulation, signifying, or mimicry, have exacted considerable damage, not least because having to wear masks or disguise one's feelings, to see oneself through the eyes of another and talk using someone else's language, is potentially alienating. As Sallis/Griffin acknowledges, 'That same masking remains in many of us, in their children's blood, a slow poison. So many of us no longer know who, or what, we are'.[55] Yet double-consciousness also has positive connotations, at least in so far as mimicry allows for parodic reinvention, the transformation of that which is being mimicked into something else, something specifically African-American, something that elides white control. 'We're all tricksters', Griffin declares more optimistically in *Bluebottle*, 'We have to be. Dissembling, signifying, masking – you only think you have a hold on us, tar babies all' (p. 92).

In such a racially divisive, disharmonious atmosphere, it is tempting to conclude, as Griffin does at the end of *Bluebottle*, simply that 'American society has set us against ourselves' (p. 154), as though racial divisions and conflicts are somehow inevitable and that nothing can be done to halt further disunity. Maybe so. But this is perhaps not the case.

Shorn of its colonising properties, whiteness *per se* is not necessarily a threat to blackness and the potential for cross-cultural or trans-racial friendships to blossom does exist. Griffin's best friend, Don Walsh, a cop with the New Orleans police department, is white, as is Vicky, a Scottish nurse whom Griffin briefly lives with in *The Long Legged Fly* and Hosie Straughter, a dissident writer who produces a weekly journal called *The Griot*, which speaks 'not only for blacks, but also for all of the city's eternal outsiders, all its dispossessed'.[56] This link is significant because it offers some kind of hope for the future; to use Manning Marable's language, some way of moving 'beyond "black" and "white"' to, new models, new relationships that more readily describe and represent the ongoing transformation of late capitalist society in the United States:

> By dismantling the narrow politics of racial identity and selective find new solutions self-interest, by going beyond 'black' and 'white,' we may construct new values, new institutions and new visions of an America, beyond traditional racial categories and racial oppression.[57]

In Sallis' fiction, such a vision remains an albeit distant hope but it is not without foundation. What follows explores how other crime writers have either anticipated, rejected or incorporated Marable's vision; and how the crime novel, in the hands of writers like Sallis, remains shot through with contradictions, with tensions that cannot be easily resolved. One of the products of this disjucture in Sallis' fiction at least is Lew Griffin's barely controllable rage, but even this is awash with ambivalence; either it is a signifier of failure and disillusionment or a subversive register of protest that cuts against the conservative tendencies of the genre.

Notes

1. Maxim Jakubowski, 'Crime Fiction', *Time Out*, 1287, 19–26 April 1995, p. 51.
2. In this chapter I use the term 'black' rather than 'African-American' because the latter term fails to acknowledge the diasporic nature of black identities and the extent to which black identities are being re-cast by the arrival of significant numbers of Caribbean immigrants since 1965. 'Black' moreover is not used to imply a static and homogeneous culture or identity but one defined in terms of multiple styles and experiences.
3. See Dennis Porter, *The Pursuit of Crime: Art and Ideology in*

Detective Fiction (New Haven, CT: Yale University Press, 1981); Stephen Knight, *Form and Ideology in Crime Fiction* (London: Macmillan, 1980).

4. Stephen Soitos, *The Blues Detective: A Study of African-American Detective Fiction* (Amherst, MA: University of Massachusetts Press, 1996), p. 37.

5. See Sotios, *The Blues Detective*, pp. 27–52.

6. See Soitos, *The Blues Detective*, p. 10.

7. Paul Cobley, *The American Thriller: Generic Innovation and Social Change in the 1970s* (London: Macmillan, 2000), p. 135.

8. Tara Mack, 'The US Isn't Great on Race. Are You Brits any Better?', *The Observer*, 20 February 2000, Review, p. 3.

9. Cobley, *The American Thriller* (see note 7), p. 137.

10. It is worth noting that *The Norton Anthology of African-American Literature* includes no reference to Harlem Cycle, despite its considerable reputation, and no mention is made of so-called 'street experience' writers like Iceberg Slim, perhaps because their work falls outside the kind of tradition that Soitos, Gates and Baker describe.

11. Kenneth Warren, *Black and White Strangers: Race and American Literature* (Chicago, IL and London: University of Chicago Press, 1993), pp. 135–6.

12. Cobley, *The American Thriller*, pp. 139–40.

13. Michael Eric Dyson, 'Essentialism and the Complexities of Racial Identity', in David Theo Goldberg (ed.), *Multiculturalism: A Reader* (Oxford and Cambridge: Blackwell, 1992), p. 221.

14. See Sally Munt, *Murder by the Book: Feminism and the Crime Novel* (London and New York: Routledge, 1994), p. 31.

15. John Fiske, *Understanding Popular Culture* (London and New York: Routledge, 1989), pp. 45–6.

16. Paula L. Woods, *Spooks, Spies and Private Eyes: An Anthology of Black Mystery, Crime and Suspense Fiction of the 20th Century* (Edinburgh: Payback Press, 1996), p. xvi.

17. Munt, *Murder by the Book*, p. 58.

18. Ibid., p. 112.

19. Ibid., p. 118.

20. Only Hugh Holton, Elizabeth Taylor Bland and Penny Mickelberry write police procedurals.

21. Valerie Wilson Wesley, *No Hiding Place* (first published 1997) (London: Headline, 1998), p. 16.

22. Du Bois, W.E.B., *The Souls of Black Folk* (New York: Dover, 1994), p. 2.

23. Soitos, *The Blues Detective*, pp. 35–6.

24. Barbara Neely, *Blanche on the Lam* (first published 1992) (New York: Penguin, 1994), p. 3.
25. Munt, *Murder by the Book*, p. 117.
26. Charlotte Carter, *Rhode Island Red* (London: Serpent's Tail, 1997), p. 121.
27. See Kobena Mercer, *Welcome to the Jungle: New Positions in Black Cultural Studies* (London and New York: Routledge, 1994).
28. John G. Cawelti, *Adventure, Mystery, Romance: Formula Stories as Art and Popular Fiction* (Chicago, IL: University of Chicago Press, 1976), pp. 156–7.
29. Gary Phillips, *Violent Springs* (Portland, WA: West Coast Crime, 1994), p. 166.
30. Gary Phillips, *Perdition, U.S.A.* (first published 1996) (Harpenden: No Exit Press, 1998), p. 4.
31. Phillips, *Violent Springs*, p. 67.
32. Christopher Bentley, 'Radical Anger: Dashiell Hammett's Red Harvest', in Brian Docherty (ed.), *American Crime Fiction* (London: Macmillan, 1988), p. 68.
33. Phillips, *Perdition, U.S.A.*, p. 93.
34. Timothy Shuker-Haines and Martha M. Umphrey, 'Gender (De) Mystified: Resistance and Recuperation in Hard-Boiled Female Detective Fiction', in Jerome H. Delamater and Ruth Prigozy (eds), *The Detective in American Film, Fiction and Television* (Westport, CT: Greenwood Press, 1998), p. 71.
35. Munt, *Murder by the Book*, p. 71.
36. See John Williams, *Into the Badlands* (London: Paladin, 1991), p. 99.
37. Gar Anthony Haywood, *You Can Die Trying* (New York: St Martin's, 1993), p. 211.
38. Stephen Steinberg, *The Ethnic Myth: Race, Ethnicity and Class in America* (Boston, MA: Beacon, 1989), p. 170.
39. See Cobley, *The American Thriller*, p. 129.
40. Title from essay by Kendell Thomas, 'Would the Real Black Man Please Stand Up', in Marcellus Blount and George P. Cunningham (ed.), *Representing Black Men* (London and New York: Routledge, 1996).
41. Manning Marable, *Beyond Black and White: Transforming African-American Politics* (London and New York: Verso, 1995), p. 186.
42. Isaac Julien, 'Black is, Black Ain't: Notes on De-Essentializing Black Identities', in Gina Dent (ed.), *Black Popular Culture: A Project by Michelle Wallace* (New York: Dia Center for Arts, 1992), p. 258.
43. Michele Wallace, *Black Macho and the Myth of Superwoman*, 2nd edn (London and New York: Verso, 1990), pp. xix–xx.

44. Kendell Thomas, *Representing Black Men*, p. 59.
45. Ibid., p. 63
46. George Baxt, *A Queer Kind of Love* (first published 1994) (New York: St Martin's Press, 1995), p. 31.
47. A version of this section on Phillips' *Point of Darkness* appears as 'Bridges and Boundaries: Race, Ethnicity and the Contemporary American Crime Novel', in Kathleen G. Klein's (ed.), *Diversity and Detective Fiction* (Bowling Green: Popular Press, 1999), pp. 252–9.
48. Mike Phillips, *Point of Darkness* (London: Michael Joseph, 1994), p. 39.
49. Henry Louis Gates, *Colored People* (Harmondsworth: Penguin, 1995), p. xv.
50. James Clifford, 'Diasporas', in Montserrat Guibernau and John Rex (eds), *The Ethnicity Reader* (Oxford: Polity, 1997), p. 287.
51. See Wally Hammond, 'Into the Black', Time Out, 1359, 4–11 September, 1996, p. 50.
52. James Sallis, *Bluebottle* (Harpenden: No Exit, 1999), p. 61.
53. James Sallis, *The Long Legged Fly* (first published 1992) (Harpenden: No Exit, 1996), p. 114.
54. Ralph Willett, *The Naked City: Urban Crime Fiction in the USA* (Manchester and New York: Manchester University Press, 1996), p. 126.
55. Sallis, *Bluebottle*, p. 24.
56. James Sallis, *Black Hornet* (New York: Avon, 1996), p. 36.
57. Marable, *Beyond Black and White*, p. 202.

CHAPTER 4

'The Fire this Time': Social Protest and Racial Politics – From Himes to Mosley

Music notwithstanding, in popular cultural forms where African-American players have struggled long and hard to achieve parity with their white counterparts and where their efforts have only started to bear fruit, there has been a marked tendency, particularly on the part of white critics and commentators, to shoehorn the most high-profile African-American figures together simply on the grounds of a shared racial-ethnic identity. Thus, the film-maker John Singleton is spoken of in the same breath as Spike Lee; Denzel Washington is compared to Samuel L. Jackson, and Morgan Freeman to Danny Glover. It should perhaps come as no surprise, then, that the two writers who have loomed largest over the field of black crime fiction in America, Chester Himes and Walter Mosley, have suffered inevitable comparison. One rarely reads a review of Mosley's crime fiction without some kind of reference to Himes, even if it is to emphasise their differences. Mosley himself is keen to put some ground between himself and Himes, asserting, 'even though Chester Himes wrote crime, I'm entering the genre in a different way'.[1] Their differences, too, do seem to be pronounced. Himes, after all, grew up in America in the 1930s and prior to his foray into crime fiction, wrote bleak, coruscating 'social protest' novels like *If He Hollers Let Him Go* (1946) and *The Primitive* (1949) which featured doomed but rage-fuelled black protagonists battling in vain to find voice and visibility in a hostile white-controlled world. His crime novels, too, were uncompromising, despairing and full of grotesquely violent incident. Mosley, on the other hand, grew up in the era of Civil Rights and perhaps as a reflection, his fiction is noticeably gentler than Himes', less polemical, the product of a kinder, more conciliatory era. Certainly his writing has gained the kind of mainstream recognition that Himes never achieved, or perhaps hoped to, a situation emblematised by Mosley's near bestseller status and most famously by the politically astute approval given to his work by America's newly elected President, Bill Clinton, in 1992.[2]

Still, to overlook similarities in their outlook and their body of work merely on the grounds that they wrote at different times, and arguably for different audiences, would seem to be an equally suspect critical practice. Times have changed, of course, but the question of how much they have changed, particularly for African-Americans, remains a point of much debate. African-Americans are entering the middle classes in rapidly increasing numbers and yet the black underclass is also growing. 'New' immigrants from Latin America, the Caribbean and Asia have transformed the social landscape of urban America almost beyond recognition and yet racial-ethnic divisions based on 'old' cleavages remain endemic. Rioting in South-Central Los Angeles in 1992 evoked bitter memories of Watts in 1965 and yet the presence of Koreans, Mexicans and poor whites as aggressors and victims caused commentators to describe the disturbances as America's 'first multicultural riot'.[3] Himes' and Mosley's crime fictions reveal much about the 1960s and 1990s and much about the extent to which black cultural politics and racial-ethnic relations have both changed and remained the same. What follows, then, is an attempt to provide a close critical reading of their writing which both acknowledges this situation and anticipates the final chapter in which the changing relationship between race and ethnicity, and between African-Americans and Jewish, Cuban, Mexican and Korean-Americans, is more fully explored.

Black Rage and Racial Transgressions: Himes and Harlem on the Edge

It is perhaps unsurprisingly that Himes' so-called Harlem Cycle, a series of loosely worked police procedurals featuring his two 'ace' black detectives Coffin Ed Johnson and Grave Digger Jones written between the late 1950s and the late 1960s, should have coincided with the proliferation of black social protest and its culmination in the most serious race riots that the United States had ever witnessed, first in Watts, then in Newark, Detroit, Chicago and New York. Of course, one must be careful about conflating the unfolding situation in Watts too closely with that described in Himes' fiction, not least because Watts and Himes' albeit fictionalised Harlem are different communities with their own distinctive social, economic and political histories. However since Himes himself is adamant that his Harlem is not an unproblematic rendering of the 'real' – 'the Harlem of my books was never meant to be real'[4] – his fictionalised city is, to some extent, emblematic of a black 'every-ghetto' and as a result, one can identify significant areas of overlap between the two situations. It is hard not to notice the parallels between the incident described below, from *Cotton Comes to Harlem*, and the unfolding situation in the initial stages of the Watts riots:

> Colored people poured into the vicinity from far and wide, overflowed the sidewalks and spilled into the street. Traffic was stopped. The atmosphere grew tense, pregnant with premonition. A black youth ran forward with a brick to hurl through the plate-glass window ... Suddenly the air was filled with the distant wailing of the sirens, sounding at first like the faint wailing of banshees, growing ever louder as the police cruisers roared nearer, like souls escaped from hell. The first cruiser ploughed through the mob and shrieked to a stop on the wrong side of the pavement with pistols drawn, shouting, 'Get back! Get off the street! Clear the street!' Then another cruiser ploughed through the mob and shrieked to a stop ... Then a third ... Then a fourth ... Then a fifth. Out came the white cops, brandishing their pistols like trained performers in a macabre ballet entitled, 'If You're Black Get Back'. The mood of the mob became dangerous. A cop pushed a black man. The black man got set to hit the cop.[5]

The above situation is diffused peacefully when a police chief orders his men to back off and the crowd disperses, but later in the novel, as another crowd congregates outside the headquarters of the Back-to-Africa movement to listen to a speaker from the Harlem branch of the Black Muslims and is confronted by a group of white supremacists, full-scale anarchy beckons. Enter Coffin Ed and Grave Digger. Anticipating trouble, Himes' 'ace' detectives manage to cut-off the white supremacists before they have the chance to confront the black crowd, and proceed to humiliate their leader, Colonel Calhoun, by drawing their nickel-plated pistols and shooting a hole in his hat. Calhoun goes to retrieve the hat and they shoot it again, turning a potentially violent situation into a comic one. Comic, perhaps, but rather than being a cause for optimism, there is a curiously ambiguous quality about the incident and the way in which it is described. On the one hand it serves to confirm Coffin Ed and Grave Digger's already fearsome reputation and underline their agency as police officers. On the other hand, it serves to remind readers of the depth of racial divisions, and foreground Coffin Ed and Grave Digger's conflicted status within the department; revered trouble-shooters whose interventions help to secure and police existing social and racial boundaries and subversive outcasts whose subordinate hierarchical status is guaranteed by their skin colour and whose 'lived experiences' have forever tarnished their faith in the promise of justice-for-all.

Of course, one of the distinctive features of the emerging hard-boiled school of detective fiction has always been the problematic nature of the 'law' and 'justice'. Unlike the classical detective fiction of Christie and Sayers where the moral interventions of respectable, middle-class investigators ensured a seamless restoration not just of law and order but also of the entire social structure, American novelists like Hammett presented a world so corrupted, so endemically violent, that his detectives could only ever hope to achieve partial understanding and a flawed, provisional justice. Himes' detective novels are riven with some of the same complications but the extremity of this disjuncture once it has been mapped on to the canvas of a racially segregated Harlem is so intense that it threatens to shatter the awkward equilibrium negotiated even by Sam Spade and the Continental Op. This disjuncture also renders Himes' black detectives Coffin Ed Johnson and Grave Digger Jones virtually impotent and incapable of exercising their will except through acts of uncontrolled, undirected rage.

The two situations are not unrelated because this kind of rage is a product of Coffin Ed and Grave Digger's conflicted status as African-Americans, nonetheless compelled to preserve, through whatever means necessary, an exploitative and racially oppressive system that subjects or rather subjugates them. Peter Rabinowitz and H. Bruce Franklin describe Coffin Ed and Grave Digger as 'Black-killer detectives' and argue that in so far as they impose the laws of white capitalist America upon the people of Harlem and do so with brutal and often blinding violence, they embody 'the ultimate stage of social disorder masquerading as order'.[6] Such a reading, though, is only partially accurate because the process of dissolution which Rabinowitz and Franklin allude to is exactly that – a process – one that gradually grinds Coffin Ed and Grave Digger down, transforming them in the course of the cycle into modern-day grim reapers who inhabit a Hobbesian world in which 'monsters prey on weaker monsters'.[7] One is struck in *The Real Cool Killers* by just how conventional Grave Digger seems, responding to a situation in which a white man has been murdered by jettisoning his desire to exercise vigilante justice and embracing 'official' procedures, 'I'm not going to shoot you', he tells an informer, 'I'm going to try and find out who killed [the white man] because that's what I'm paid for and that was my oath when I took the job'.[8] This is not to suggest that either Grave Digger or Coffin Ed, who is suspended from the department after shooting a black youth for throwing what he believes to be acid at him, are without flaws, but rather in the context of other similarly compromised hard-boiled detectives, their deeply problematic and often contradictory impulses constitute recognisable hard-boiled characteristics. Even their final act of turning the killer loose is symptomatic of their generic status. Since Galen, a white man and the victim, is also the villain, at least in so far as it is his (deviant) obsession for young black girls that caused one of them to shoot him, and since the law is unable to recognise the complexity of the situation, it is the responsibility of Coffin Ed and Grave Digger to assume what John Cawelti calls the basic generic functions of 'exposure, protection and judgement',[9] and allow the so-called 'crime' to go unpunished.

Their conflicted status as defenders of a law that does not represent black interests invariably takes its toll, though, manifesting itself in a series of increasingly grotesque and often misogynistic violence. *The Heat's On* sees Coffin Ed, driven to such rage during his hunt for the assassins who shot and wounded his partner that he does not hesitate to cut a six-inch line across the throat of an unwilling female informer and proceed to show her the wound in a mirror. At once, he realises that what he had done was 'unforgivable' but it does not lead him to modify his behaviour. Martha Diawara argues that the Harlem cycle is littered with similar expressions of misogyny, from Grave Digger's threat to pistol-whip Immabelle, a 'hot-bodied, banana-skin chic with . . . the ball-bearing hips of a natural born amante'[10] who offends his sense of masculine propriety, so badly that no man will ever 'look at her again',[11] to Coffin Ed's impulsive desire to crush the windpipe of a female suspect during an interrogation scene in *Cotton Comes to Harlem*. One could argue, not as a justification, that this kind of misogynism is business as usual for the hard-boiled genre, but Diawara makes the point that Himes' representation of male-on-female violence does not secure or legitimise the detective's masculinity (as it arguably does in Chandler's fiction), and is better understood as part of a wider expression of black rage which is itself the product of the dehumanising conditions that Himes' detectives and the rest of black Harlem have to endure:

> Rage often takes the form of eroticized violence by men against women and homosexuals, a savage explosion on the part of some characters against others whom they seek to control, and a perverse mimicry of the status quo through recourse to disfigurement, mutilation, and a grotesque positioning of weaker characters by stronger ones.[12]

The trajectory of the Harlem Cycle is towards apocalyptic disintegration. If an early novel like *The Real Cool Killers* successfully papers over the tensions and contradictions writ large in the actions and ambitions of Himes' 'ace' detectives, the final (completed) novel of the Cycle, *Blind Man With a Pistol* (1969), lays them bare to reveal a city and world so riven by racially determined conflict that nothing that Coffin Ed or Grave Digger can do comes even close to prevent New York from sliding into a nihilistic anarchy. If there is some debate about the status of Himes' detective fiction as a whole – Gary Storhoff, for example, makes no distinction between Himes' early and later novels arguing that the entire Harlem cycle radicalised the social and political ideologies of the detective fiction form, while Woody Haut is more circumspect, arguing that Himes' detective novels, tended 'to be more conservative than they appear'[13] – it might be more helpful to argue that as the cycle progressed, Himes found it increasingly difficult to reconcile the various formal and thematic tensions which had characterised his work from *A Rage in Harlem* onwards.

The brooding opening of *Blind Man with a Pistol*, in which a multiple stabbing takes place in the rancid, delapidated home of a black religious trickster, replete with his eleven wives and fifty children, reflects the dark, generically unsettling terrain into which Himes was increasingly steering his crime writing. Coffin Ed and Grave Digger are virtually unrecognisable as the 'tough-guy' anti-heroes who so effectively diffused racial tensions in the earlier *Cotton Comes to Harlem*. By way of an introduction, their car passes 'practically unseen, like a ghostly vehicle in the dark, its occupants invisible' (p. 33), a description which prefigures their increasing anonymity within the police department and the wider black community. Marginalisation has bred cynicism which, in turn, has bred desensitisation to violence. Violence is a necessary weapon in the hard-boiled detective's arsenal, of course, but the extent of Coffin Ed and Grave Digger's rage in this final novel far outstrips anything seen previously, and while Grave Digger in earlier novels had been a moderating influence on his partner, there is little to tell them apart. Their interventions, too, are that much more problematic because what actually constitutes a 'crime' or rather the difference between a 'crime' and social turmoil or even revolution is not clear. The multiple stabbing and the murder of an unidentified white man are the most obvious manifestations of criminal transgressions, but not only do they remain unsolved, they also become component parts in a much broader picture of malaise and corruption involving a nefarious alliance of white gangsters, politicians and police chiefs, over which Coffin Ed and Grave Digger have no authority or control.

Their overbearing attempts to impose even a semblance of order upon a volatile, angry black population are exposed as hollow and redundant. Faced with social unrest on an unprecedented scale, their familiar, aggressive tactics result in stalemate. Confused and angered by their inability to channel their rage into generically 'useful' activities, Coffin Ed and Grave Digger can only watch the rapidly disintegrating situation with detached bemusement. Flanked on either side by an increasingly militant group of black protesters and a racist police captain who refers to them merely as 'black sons of bitches' (p. 61), Coffin Ed and Grave Digger contemplate their future with cynicism and bitterness. The detectives may pay lip service to their generic function, hollowly declaring 'We're the law' (p. 150) but the curtailment of their powers and their marginalisation within the department is enough to convince them that the 'law' is better understood as a mechanism responsible for perpetuating racially conceived relations of domination and subordination.

The novel races towards a conclusion but the various murders that Coffin Ed and Grave Digger have been called upon to investigate remain unresolved. As the unrest spreads beyond the carefully demarcated borders of Harlem, the novel ends not with the conventional generic denouement in which the contradictions and tensions generated within the narrative are smoothed over, but rather with a blind African-American man who has played no part in the narrative until this point producing a pistol and firing it, wildly and indiscriminately at passengers, black and white, on a crowded subway car. The blind man is a symbolic register for the latent and unresolved frustrations of all the African-American characters, as well as an emblematisation of the fragmented, undirected nature of black protest in the novel. As the survivors of the attack swarm up from the subway platform to the Harlem streets, meanwhile, Coffin Ed and Grave Digger have been reduced to firing their legendary nickel-plated Colts at rats on a derelict building site.

Right at the end of his writing career, Himes seemed to be drawing our attention to a quite fundamental paradox – namely, that the crime novel was flexible enough to accommodate black writers with radical political and aesthetic ambitions but was also limiting, at least in so far as black protagonists working within official hierarchies simply could not provide the kind of albeit problematic solutions that the mostly white audience for crime fiction tended to demand. Hence Gary Storhoff suggests that Himes' rage manifests itself not just in the actions of his detectives, and other black characters, but also in his own deliberate and sustained assault on the conventions of the genre and its mainly white readership. The chaos and bloodshed which tend to characterise the start of Himes' novels are symbolic registers of the mayhem which inevitably follow; violence begetting more violence. As Storhoff argues, it is impossible for the reader 'to reassemble the logical sequacious order of clues and evidence leading inexorably to a resolution [since] the author continually intervenes with increasingly bizarre acts of violence'.[14] Coffin Ed's search for his partner's assassins in *The Heat's On*, for example, has to vie for our attention with Himes' gleeful description of what happens when a religious trickster, Sister Heavenly, disembowels a pet dog in order to recover heroin believed to be hidden in its intestines. 'We return to Digger and Ed as they disentangle clues',

Storhoff remarks, then wryly adds, 'but with what interest?'.[15]

Storhoff's conception of the crime fiction audience as predominantly white may be hard to refute, yet his assumption that this audience, to a person, expected 'vicarious thrills' but not 'the kind of shock Himes prepares'[16] is misguided because it ignores the extent to which readers, then and now, have enjoyed Himes' writing precisely because of such 'excesses'. In fact, Himes' current popularity and the re-issuing of the entire Harlem cycle in the UK (including the unfinished *Plan B*) in three brand-new volumes is perhaps linked to a growing interest in the kind of explicitly violent, generically innovative and savagely distopian crime novel produced not just by Himes but also by practitioners as diverse as Jim Thompson and James Ellroy (and arguably at the expense of a declining interest in the more mannered and generically conventional hard-boiled fiction of writers like Chandler and Robert B. Parker). To be fair, though, it is not hard to see how such 'excesses' may have contributed to Himes' neglect by earlier audiences and in a fine study of Himes' career, James Sallis describes how, in the United States at least, the Harlem novels were 'brought out indifferently by various publishers' and remained out of print for thirty years or more. Sallis also describes how critics 'typically considered the Harlem books potboilers that pandered to excessive violence and grotesque characterisations, and not a few bemoaned the loss of a serious writer'.[17] What Sallis only hints at, though, is that a good deal of hostile criticism was levelled at the Harlem cycle from within the black community by those who felt that too much of his violence remained *within* the black ghetto and that his 'excessive' focus on intra-racial, black-on-black violence somehow let the dominant white culture off the hook, or simply that the cycle seemed to advocate little more than a dead-end politics of nihilism and despair.

What links these criticisms of Himes is an unwillingness to see beyond what Michelle Wallace calls 'the binary opposition of "negative" versus "positive" images', a formula which for Wallace at least has too often 'set the limits for Afro-American cultural criticism'.[18] Hence, while white critics have tended to assume that the function of African-American artists is to 'uplift the race', there has been a related pressure coming from within the black community on artists to focus their collective imaginations to salvaging the denigrated images of African-Americans in white public culture. Wallace argues that both are inherently limiting because the act of swapping 'negative' images for 'positive' ones ends up tying African-American cultural production 'to a racist ideology in a way that makes the failure to alter it inevitable'.[19] Significantly, her suggestion that this kind of formula tended to set the limits for black popular cultural production throughout the 1960s and 1970s, marks out Himes' Harlem cycle as distinctive because he never pandered to such reductive stereotypes and instinctively understood the need the represent his black characters as 'more' than victims of white racism:

> Maybe it was an unconscious protest against soul brothers always being considered victims of racism, a protest against racism itself excusing all their sins and faults. Black victims of crime and criminals might be foolish and harebrained, but the soul brother criminals were as vicious, cruel and dangerous as any other criminals.[20]

Himes' belief that African-Americans were 'more' than victims of racism, and that black culture, by implication, was not formed simply in response to forces of white oppression, did more than challenge the complacent simplicity of this 'positive/negative' images formula. Just as significantly, it alluded to the heterogeneous nature of African-American culture and experiences and in doing so unsettled the kind of essentialist view of 'race' that might have been in vogue at the time Himes was writing. Michael Eric Dyson argues that racial unity or 'black' essentialism in the United States was conceived in the mid nineteenth century 'as a socially useful way of speaking about the need to offset slavery's divisive effects on black culture'.[21] Stuart Hall, meanwhile, suggest that 'black' essentialism emerged in the 1950s and 1960s as 'a way of referencing common experiences of racism and marginalisation . . . among groups and communities with different traditions and ethnic identities'.[22] To some extent, both definitions are relevant to Himes' crime fiction, for while it is hard not to notice the extent of racial segregation in the Harlem of his novels, it is equally hard not to notice the significant faultlines running through his black community; how class and gender divisions in particular constantly threaten to shatter the black unity that Himes' political activists crave so much.

To some extent divisions between black and white appear to predominate throughout Himes' fiction. Hence Harlem is described as a battleground where black residents are locked into inexorable struggle with their white slumlords:

> [Harlem] is the Mecca of the black people just the same. The air and the heat and the voices and the laughter, the atmosphere and the drama and the melodrama, are theirs ... They are the managers, the clerks, the cleaners, they drive the taxis and the buses, they are the clients, the customers, the audience; they work in it, but the white man owns it. So it is natural that the   white man is concerned with their behaviour; it's his property. But is the black people's to enjoy.[23]

Though Himes is also quick to celebrate the cultural achievements of black writers and artists, in practice, he is all too aware of the material and economic forces that prevent what Dyson refers to as an 'enabling solidarity'[24] from becoming a lived reality. The harshness of ghetto life means that poor blacks are pitted against one another in a desperate struggle for survival and while the idea that they should, in the words of The Rolling Stones, 'come together' to protest against the conditions in which they are forced to live is admirable, more often than not they are exploiting each other in order to stay alive. The finite point of this disintegration is reached, unsurprisingly, in *Blind Man with a Pistol*, when four separate protests – organised by the Brotherhood, Black Power, the Black Jesus movement and the Black Muslims – converge in Harlem and instead of joining forces to attack the police and other emblems of white authority, turn on each other and ignite further disturbances. In this context, tensions within Himes' community are destructive rather than creative; hence one should be careful about holding his novels up as symbols of progressive black cultural diversity. Still, in so far as Himes' Harlem cycle in general resists attempts to impose an artificial order on what Dyson calls 'the perplexing and chaotic politics of racial identity',[25] one could argue that it anticipates shifts in black cultural politics towards a discourse of diversity and difference, where the multiple tones and styles of black cultures are emphasised.

Himes' preoccupation with hue and skin colour is in itself an implicit assault on racial essences. Though racial boundaries are strictly policed, transgressions through miscegenation and attempts to 'pass' as either black or white are commonplace. Figures like Pinkie and Sister Heavenly from *The Heat's On* are visual reminders of America's mixed-race ancestry; Pinkie, an albino giant with milk-white skin, pink eyes, battered lips, cauliflower ears and thick, black, kinky hair and Sister Heavenly, whose daily applications of bleach creams have 'lightened her complexion to the color of pigskin'.[26] The fact that Pinkie proceeds to dye his skin black – black as 'wet, bituminous coal' (p. 69) – in order to disguise himself, merely heightens the confusion and foregrounds the absurdity of a situation where arbitrary classifications, which do not even come close to reflecting the complexity of racial mixtures, become powerful devices by which one group exercises power over another. Most absurd of all is the tragic tale of Pinkie, who fits into neither black nor white worlds, who finds himself excluded from a trip to Africa on the grounds that he looks 'white' but who enjoys none of the privileges of whiteness because his 'black' ancestry is writ large in his lips, nose and hair.

Furthermore, just as Gerald Horne's probing analysis of the Watts riots of 1965 points towards the existence of very significant class

divisions within the local black community,[27] close analysis of Himes'
Harlem cycle unearths similar patterns. The problem, as Martha
Diawara astutely observes, is that these divisions are concealed or
flattened out by the tendency of white figures and white culture in
general to reduce black characters to stereotypes. Jackson, a mild-
mannered, God-fearing man from *A Rage in Harlem* is one such victim
of this process. Though he might wish to establish his superior class and
upwardly mobile economic ambitions in terms of his work ethic and
moral fortitude, viewed through a white lens, he is just another black
man. As Diawara argues, Jackson's intention to locate 'his Blackness in
an ethics of responsibility that is class-derived', collide with the
ambitions of white public culture – a culture that only permits 'the
reproduction of such Black subjects as whores, lawbreakers, and
falsifiers who have to be policed'.[28] Perhaps Himes had grasped,
instinctively or otherwise, what is only now becoming theoretically
fashionable, namely that differences between individuals and
communities are most significant when they are underscored by unequal
relations of power (whether this inequality is expressed in terms of race,
class, gender etc.), and that race cannot be understood in simple
biological terms as a poisoned chalice pitting an essential black against
an essential white subject, but rather as a convergence of physiological
and cultural factors within a network of micro and macro power
relations where the position of the latter is 'always-already' privileged
over that of the former.

'Taking the "Black" out of Noir': Walter Mosley's New Black Cultural Politics[29]

When Los Angeles went up in plumes of black smoke following the
acquittal of four white LAPD officers accused of beating an African-
American motorist in May 1992, commentators were divided in their
assessment of the situation, whether it represented a new set of
problems or ones swept under the carpet after the fallout from the Watts
some thirty years earlier. While some felt that the similarities between
the two incidents were impossible to ignore, pointing to the similar
locations and to the harsh treatment of LA's black population at the
hands of the mostly white police department, others sought to explain
the fire this time in terms of a different, more complex set of conditions.
Some called it a class riot, others described it as the nation's first
multicultural riot, while others characterised it as 'several different,
overlapping, riots'.[30] Howard Omi and Michael Wincant read the
situation similarly, noting that the riot 'took unprecedented form' in so

far as the disturbance revealed class and ethnic cleavages to be as significant as racial ones and manifested itself in the potentially confusing scenario whereby the rioters were black, Latino and white and the victims were Latinos, whites and Koreans. 'The riot', they concluded, 'demonstrated the unity – partial and real – which links the urban poor regardless of race',[31] while at the same time uncovering and exacerbating a myriad of tensions between competing communities of whites, Chicanos, Koreans, Vietnamese and African-Americans.

The riots exposed divisions, then, not just between the black population of South-Central Los Angeles and mainly white police department but also between blacks and Latinos, blacks and Koreans, Latinos and Koreans, between the middle classes or entrepreneurial capitalists and the working poor, between Chicanos and recently arrived immigrants from Central America, between documented and un-documented people, and between 'solidly middle class Japanese-Americans, largely working class Filipinos, generally low-income south-east Asians and Chinese- and Korean-Americans whose class position varied significantly'.[32] At the same time, the disturbances or rather the response to the disturbances particularly from within the worst affected neighbourhoods suggested that a kind of 'enabling solidarity' involving not only African-Americans but also a broad spectrum of non-whites and the working poor could potentially bear fruit. Soon after the riots, Lynell George noted:

> People have become more optimistic about the possibilities because of the brief sparks of unity emanating from within: the scuttlebutt of a black gang truce; an east-side Latino gang that worked to keep their home turf market guarded and safe from harm; and the presence of a new police chief, who unlike the old chief, will pause and bend to listen.[33]

The question of whether it was possible to negotiate 'difference' without either fanning the flames of ethnic conflict or collapsing distinctive experiences and identities on top of one another predominated. Himes' Harlem cycle had grappled with these issues, drawing attention to the diverse nature of black experiences, styles and identities but without suggesting that it was anything but chaotic and ultimately self-destructive. Twenty years later, Mosley would do likewise, but perhaps informed by significant shifts that had taken place in black cultural politics, would come much closer to reconciling the attendant tension or dilemma; namely, whether or rather how it was possible to cherish black cultural norms, values and ideas and promote what Michael Eric Dyson calls 'love, friendship and mutual co-operation among black folk' without 'placing an ideological noose of loyalty around the necks of critical dissenters from received ideas about racial unity . . . ones that stress that black Americans have one overriding vision, purpose and destiny'.[34]

Mosley is the author of a series of crime novels set in Los Angeles in the years between the end of the World War Two and the mid 1960s, featuring African-American detective, Ezekiel 'Easy' Rawlins. He has also written *RL's Dream* (1995), a novel which tells the story of an elderly blues musician who is dying of cancer, and *Always Outnumbered, Always Outgunned* (1997), which tells the story of Socrates Fortlow, a ex-convict attempting to renounce his violent ways and find a usable morality amid the poverty and deprivation of contemporary Los Angeles. There are important differences between the mood and tone of the Easy Rawlins novels and *RL's Dream* and *Always Outnumbered, Always Outgunned*, differences which are touched upon later in the chapter and which relate, in part, to the function of genre fiction, but what is instructive about all of Mosley's work, at least in relation to the question posed earlier, is the extent to which they appear to have been written in response to the kind of shift in black cultural politics alluded to in the last paragraph. In other words, not only does he tacitly acknowledge problems associated with definition (what it means to be 'black' or 'African-American') and try to mark off what is distinctive about African-American culture and history, but at the same time he also explores areas where the experiences and interests of other communities and individuals overlap. What ultimately emerges from his various novels is a complex, contradictory portrait of African-American identity, one with its roots in the idea or ideal of a collective black experience but which represents that experience in fluid, fragmented terms.

It would be wrong to suggest that Mosley is writing against rather than out of a rich tradition of African-American letters. Unlike Himes who operates in a much tighter hard-boiled frame and through his focus on economic and racial disharmony challenges the idea that his characters are unproblematically united by a common cultural heritage, Mosley is perhaps more circumspect. In fact it is tempting to consider his novels, first and foremost, as contributions to the ongoing project of re-writing the history of black America using the words and stories of black Americans themselves; as documents of what it was like to be black and living in Los Angeles either in the post-war years or at the time of the 1992 riots, or in the case of *RL's Dream*, growing up along the Mississippi delta in the 1940s; as testaments to the vitality of black culture and particularly black musical forms like the blues; and as novels which set out to debunk official (white European) power structures and overturn official discourses. Some commentators have even sought to locate Mosley's work exclusively within this particular tradition. Time argued that his writing 'hums with the particular rhythms and blues of the black American experience'; Richard Liston remarked in *The Weekly Journal* that Mosley was 'skillfully unfolding the untold history of the African-American people'; while Stephen Moore, in *The Guardian*, described Mosley as 'perhaps the most important black literary figures to appear on the scene since James Baldwin's death' and argued that he had joined 'the ranks of some of our best black writers, particularly Ralph Ellison'.[35]

Certainly Mosley's use of a 'blues' idiom throughout his work is a reminder that African-American culture is not merely a reaction to white racism but rather a complex and sophisticated blending of European and African-American discourses, whereby the hegemonic aspects of the former are re-constituted as 'positive' affirmations of an enabling black culture. Using a distinctive black Southern dialect, for example, connects Easy Rawlins and other black characters to their collective past, encourages them to reject externally imposed identities and helps them to forge a sense of selfhood from the multiple strands of black culture and community. As Easy himself acknowledges, 'I always tried to speak proper English in my life but I found over the years that I could only truly express myself in the natural, uneducated dialect of my upbringing'.[36] The inversion, here, of terms like 'natural' and 'proper' supposes that dialect has subversive potential in so far as it reflects an entire worldview that exists outside of the domains of the majority white culture. As Tommy L. Lott concludes, 'Spirituals, sermons and literature written in dialect are held to be forms of cultural expression that are distinctly African-American because they contain elements of African-American culture ... that are readily distinguishable from the Euro-American mainstream'.[37]

The link between the blues as a kind of authentic, vernacular-based form of African-American cultural expression and existing, or rather having to exist, on the margins of American society is one of the key themes of Molsey's *RL's Dream*. The novel's central character, Atwater 'Soupspoon' Wise, is an elderly blues musician who once played with the legendary R. L. Johnson while he was growing up along the Mississippi delta but who in the present of the narrative is dying of cancer in New York. Soupspoon wants to tell his story to Kiki Waters, a young woman from a poor white home in Arkansas who takes him into her flat after he has been evicted and left to die on the street. The physical act of speaking his story is significant because, as one character remarks, 'black people's history is stories and words and music'.[38] Blues music connects up to this project because the words spoken and sung by its performers were 'like the talk people talked every day' (p. 74), but for Soupspoon at least, blues is not simply a form of cultural expression, it is

an entire way of life, a way of temporarily getting outside of his own life
and forgetting about the tribulations of having to live in a world where
people died all the time – 'from hard blows, disease, from taking their
own lives' (p. 91). The association of the blues with hardship and
suffering is foregrounded in the opening chapter when Soupspoon is left
lying on the pavement outside his apartment. 'Music thrummed in his
body; the rattles of death in the tortured song of his breathing' (p. 13).
But the blues is not a funereal dirge; it is a vibrant form of expression
that might extend out of a culture of suffering – a milieu of 'harsh talk,
hard liquor, hot smells and hot tempers' (p. 104) – but which ultimately
turns into a positive affirmation or celebration of a cultural tradition
emanating from the American South. 'We [may have been] the bottom
of the barrel', Soupspoon says, about himself and other black
Southerners, but the blues, whenever he hears or plays it, 'made him
want to dance, so he knew it had to be good' (p. 140).

The blues, Leon F. Litwack argues, has its roots in gospels music and
in the field hollers, shouts, chants and work songs of black Southern
field hands:

> 'The blues is a low down aching old heart disease / And like consumption,
> killing me by degrees.' It was more violent, subversive and
> threatening . . . and it had a language of its own, touching on aspects of
> black life seldom addressed . . . More directly than any other form of
> expression, it captured the consciousness, the day-to-day experiences,
> anxieties and despair of a new black generation.[39]

Litwack's description of the blues, as a violent, subversive, authentically
African-American form of expression which captured the day-to-day
experiences and anxieties of a new generation of black Americans, nicely
summarises why Mosley has sought, both in *RL's Dream* and the Easy
Rawlins series, to use it as a kind of organising metaphor for his work as
a whole. Mosley's fiction gives voice to Leroi Jones' 'blues people', poor
working-class blacks who struggle in different ways to navigate a path
through a hostile, white capitalist world without losing a sense of who
they are and where they came from. When Soupspoon Wise recalls the
plaintive, tormented cries of Robert Johnson or Easy Rawlins wanders
along Bones Street, listening to sounds drifting out from the various bars
or walks into the Black Chantilly and hears Lip McGee blowing in his
horn, Mosley is reminding us of the rich tradition of music that
continues to give meaning to black lives. As Rawlins himself says, 'That
horn spoke the language of my history; traveled me back to times that I
could no longer remember clearly – maybe even times that were older
than I; travelling in my blood, back to some forgotten home'.[40]

Yet at the same time Mosley also suggests that this tradition, rather than being locked up in history, can and indeed has adapted as black lives change and relations between blacks and whites are brought into new, complex configurations. The fact that the past continues to invade and inflect the present of Mosley's world is only part of the point. One could also argue that the present, in albeit subtle and perhaps more interesting ways, invades and inflects the past. What I mean is perfectly illustrated in *RL's Dream*. The blues, as a form of expression, reminds the reader of the suffering and hardship borne by African-Americans throughout the history of the United States and reminds us of the suffering and hardship endured by Soupspoon. Present-day New York may not be exactly the same as the Mississippi Delta of Soupspoon's youth but reminders of the depth and extent of racial oppression nevertheless abound. Randy, who is not quite light enough to pass as white, insists that he is an exotic Caucasian but no one who knows him is convinced and the extent of his self-delusion or denial is best understood as a register of the way in which blackness is demonised by the wider white public culture.

In the main part, blacks and whites continue to co-exist in a state of uneasy disharmony. However at the start of the novel Soupspoon meets with Kiki Waters, a transplanted white Southern women, who has suffered terribly at the hands of her abusive father and who, like Soupspoon, is seeking, if not redemption, then a way of putting to rest the demons that have stalked her throughout her life. As their friendship develops, the possibility of a different type of relationship between 'black' and 'white' is suggested and the blues assumes a slightly altered significance. This is not to suggest that the blues remains anything but an authentically African-American form of expression and as I suggested previously, Mosley weaves the music into his stories in order to give voice to the trials and tribulations endured by his black characters in the past and present. However in *RL's Dream* the dynamics of Soupspoon's friendship with Kiki upsets this logic in so far as the blues comes to reflect the anxieties and aspirations not just of Soupspoon but also of Kiki and Randy too. Alone with the two of them in Kiki's apartment, Soupspoon picks up his guitar and begins to play. Randy joins him, keeping the beat with a spoon and mayonnaise jar and Kiki starts to sing. A while later Soupspoon realises that although Kiki is white and neither she nor Randy were 'even born when he came around', they were nevertheless 'playing his music' (p. 182). With Kiki facing an uncertain future, made even more uncertain by unemployment and alcoholism, and scarred by the memories of an unhappy past, Soupspoon is forced to concede that 'they were living it, too' (p. 182), something which attests to a shared sense of suffering, a common humanity and the falsity of racial essences.

Like *RL's Dream*, Mosley's crime fiction demonstrates how the ugly imperfections of the past – the legacy of slavery and institutional racism – continue to invade and shape the present, but they also focus upon the various strategies of negotiation and resistance employed by figures like Easy Rawlins in order to achieve even a modicum of control over their lives. This tension – between Rawlins' desire for agency and his inability to transcend the limits imposed on him by white-controlled institutions and their representatives – is played out on both a thematic and formal level throughout the series. Though he may want to operate as Phillip Marlowe does, going where he wants to, seeing whom he wants to, choosing how he spends his time, his ability to do so is severely eroded by externally imposed restrictions relating to his racial identity. Marlowe is far from a rich man but his decision to reject or accept an assignment is not taken on the basis of financial remuneration alone, and thus affords him a degree of agency.[41] For Rawlins, though, the need to survive, to pay his mortgage, and to feed and clothe his children, are what motivate him rather than a vaguely defined desire to do what is 'right'. Which is not to say that he is morally bankrupt; just that as a black man subject to the injustices of having to live in a hostile, white-controlled world, he is forced to compromise any kind of moral or personal 'code' simply in order to remain afloat.

Rawlins may prefer the comforting anonymity of the margins, prefer to attain agency through the reassuring minutia of everyday life – the sanctity of home, the joys of family, the satisfaction of work – but his ability to do so, to live on his own terms, even if these terms are not at all extravagant, is constantly under threat. The very fact that Rawlins owns his own home, has a job, cares about his family, means that people (usually white people) are able to threaten him, threaten the things and people he cherishes, force him into complying with their demands. In *Devil in a Blue Dress*, his job is taken away from him and his home threatened; in *A Red Death* his business is undermined and in *White Butterfly* he must help the police in order to secure his family's freedom. Always a reluctant investigator, Rawlins' hopes for a quiet life are always shattered by those who are a position to make demands of him and expect these demands to be met. Furthermore these demands, and his inevitable acquiescence to them, are not without cost. Freedom and the ability to live as he wants to, for Rawlins, can only be achieved through significant sacrifice, because as others before him have discovered, self-advancement or even just survival can only usually be achieved by exploiting those things, those friendships that are dearest to him. Involvement in 'crime' is always damaging; damaging in a physical sense, of course, but damaging in an emotional sense too, because the consequences of his involvement are often tragic and far-reaching. The death of Mouse in *A Little Yellow Dog* is particularly affecting because Rawlins is only too aware of his own complicity in his best friend's demise.

Like Himes, Mosley understands that the hard-boiled crime novel is most effective as a vehicle for black social commentary when its inherent tensions are stretched to breaking point. The kind of difficult, strained resolutions that tend to characterise their work is a feature of much hard-boiled crime fiction, of course, but what is particularly noticeable about Himes and Mosley is their willingness to push at this particular generic boundary until it dissolves in their hands. With Himes this willingness manifests itself in his representation of crime in such grotesque terms that the partial resolutions achieved by his detectives cannot help but fail to conceal those tensions which produced the disruptions in the first place. With Mosley, this willingness manifests itself in his repeated assertion that for a poor black man, mere survival is a political act. As Haut suggests, Mosley's fiction may lack some of Himes' 'psychological complexity and bitterness' but its subtle investigations into the impact of oppression – in which characters are presented not as passive victims but as people for whom violence and death are the inevitable consequences of having to live in a dog-eat-dog world – constitutes an equally powerful indictment of the American system.[42]

In Rawlins' case, having to do the dirty work for his white taskmasters or blackmailers and yet struggling to free himself from their tentacle-like grasps, creates a dramatic tension which is arguably missing from Mosley's forays outside the crime fiction genre. Still, *Always Outnumbered, Always Outgunned* (1997), featuring Socrates Fortlow, an ex-convict living in the wastelands of contemporary South-Central Los Angeles, brings into sharp focus many of the preoccupations which loom largest over the Easy Rawlins series. The novel is anecdotal, featuring a series of superficially unrelated incidents that nonetheless all draw attention to the difficulties of living a 'good' life in conditions where it is tempting and indeed more financially lucrative to hurt and steal from others. Neither a proponent of vigilante justice ('I'm sayin' that killin' ain't no answer for civilized men')[43] nor a believer in the desire or ability of the police to represent the interests of African-Americans ('Going to the cops ovah a brother is like askin' for chains'),[44] Fortlow advocates a complex and uneasy mixture of aggression and 'turning the other cheek' in order to get by in an unequal world in which a black man will 'always be outnumbered, always be outgunned' (p. 131).

In narrative terms, the time that has lapsed between *A Little Yellow Dog*, the most recent instalment in the Easy Rawlins series, and *Always Outnumbered, Always Outgunned* (1963 to 1992) constitutes one of the most important periods in African-American history, one that saw both the passing of Civil Rights legislation and the noticeable failure or inability or unwillingness of the system and its representatives to punish racially motivated attacks on African-Americans. One of the more recent manifestations of this situation was the attack propagated on a black motorist, Rodney King, by four police officers in Los Angeles and their subsequent acquittal. The subsequent unrest, which spread rapidly throughout the city, provides the backdrop for part of *Always Outnumbered, Always Outgunned*, and although the smoke from the fires comes 'through the cracks in his apartment walls' (p. 153), Fortlow's decision not to join the protesters but sit in his apartment and watch 'aerial shots of the blocks burning around him' is a triumph of pragmatism over sentiment. Though 'every scar on his body and curse in his ear . . . wanted out in that street' (p. 153), his refusal to get involved constitutes an acknowledgement that such actions would ultimately be detrimental to the interests of African-Americans living in South-Central Los Angeles:

> 'Buy you know, you burn down your own home in the face 'a enemy an' it's just followin' his rule; doin' what he wants you to . . . I wanted to loot and burn. I wanted to firebomb a police car an' then take their guns an' shoot down helicopters. But them helicopters woulda crashed in my own people's homes.' (p. 167)

Easy Rawlins and Socrates Fortlow pass through life in an environment where 'race' shapes and moulds the contours of one's identity, where their every thought and action is measured against a yardstick drawn up by a hostile white world. Just as Fortlow endures a series of ritual humiliations at the hands of white bureaucrats simply to 'win' the right to be considered for a menial supermarket packing job, Rawlins cannot move outside the carefully demarcated boundaries of the black ghetto without external agencies asking questions about where he is going and what he is doing. As Liam Kennedy remarks, in so far as Rawlins' movements through the city are constrained by the various agencies of white power, race 'moulds the boundaries of social identity'.[45] Marlowe might not have much respect for the law and those who enforce it but he is, nevertheless, treated with a certain degree of respect by most of the police officers he encounters. In Mosley's Los Angeles, however, police officers not only fail to show any interest in investigating crimes that remain within the carefully demarcated borders of black neighbourhoods, they also treat African-Americans like Rawlins with an ill-disguised contempt. In every novel, he is assaulted by racially motivated physical and verbal abuse while in police custody, and throughout the series has to deal with the consequences of racial discrimination and oppression at the hands of employers, government officials, businessmen, local politicians and civil servants. One could even argue that Rawlins' ability to operate as an individualist detective is undermined by the consequences of racism. Unlike Marlowe, who works alone and prefers it that way, Rawlins cannot effectively function as a detective without the support and protection that friends like Mouse offer. Mouse, meanwhile, pours scorn on the frontier-inspired myth of 'success' through individual action, telling Rawlins that such a myth is a white construction:

'Nigger cain't pull his way out of the swamp wit'out no help, Easy. You wanna hole on t'this house and git some money . . . ? Alright. That's alright. But Easy, you gotta have somebody at yo' back, man. That's just a lie them white men give 'bout makin' it on they own. They always got they backs covered.'[46]

Nonetheless, Rawlins and other black characters in Mosley's fiction are not depicted simply as powerless victims of racial oppression, just as the different black neighbourhoods, though poor and at times dangerous, are not represented as unremittingly bleak ghettoes. Mosley's setting is neither romanticised nor demonised. Despite the dangers that confront Rawlins when he moves outside the various black neighbourhoods in Los Angeles, he remains captivated by the city's physical landscape – the desert sun, fluffy white clouds slowly making their way across the pool blue skies towards the snow-capped San Bernadino mountains – and for everywhere like Ricardo's bar, 'the kind of place you could get killed in',[47] there are other places like John's, where black working men and women come together to drink, gossip, laugh, fight and listen to music, particularly the blues:

People were shouting and talking, kissing and laughing. John's place felt good after a hard day's work . . . Big names in Negro music came there because they knew John in the old days when he gave them work and didn't skimp on the paycheck. There must've been over two hundred regulars that frequented John's place and we all knew each other.[48]

Part of the African-American post-World War Two migration from Texas and Louisiana to Los Angeles, Rawlins is both connected to and disconnected from this transplanted African-American community. Unlike Marlowe, who remains entirely separate from the wider community, Rawlins cannot and does not want to do likewise. It is not merely that his function as a 'fixer' or a reluctant detective and his position within this transplanted Southern black community are linked – in *A Red Death*, for example, Rawlins declares that his was 'a real country way of doing business' (p. 15), a way of doing business based upon a system of favours rather than the wage-earning principles of mercantile capitalism. Nor is it simply that Rawlins' link to his own community are strengthened after he adopts Jesus and Feather and has to assume the responsibility of fatherhood, although this is a significant generic departure. As Mosley admits, 'The difference between Easy and other old-time detectives is that he is part of the world. He has a house, a family'.[49] Much of the complexity of the Easy Rawlins series stems from the fact that his desire to be part of his community is born out of necessity – as a black man living in a hostile white world, he needs his family and the wider African-American community and culture to sustain him – and yet in order to survive he is forced into alliances which compromise those values which he holds most dear; friendship, community, loyalty.

Furthermore, though Easy Rawlins may be proud to be African-American, to be part of a long and rich African-American culture and ancestry, to view him simply as black, or rather to conceive of and understand 'black' in secure, homogeneous terms, is to misread the way in which Mosley draws attention to the multiple, syncretic nature of all identities. In other words, Mosley seems to be suggesting that African-American culture and identity has evolved not simply as a result of interaction between and among African-Americans but syncretically, in relation to other influences, other cultures, other communities. In *A Little Yellow Dog*, Rawlins visits a white gangster who is reading a book called *Meditations* by the Roman Emperor Marcus Aurelius. Stetz, the gangster, does not expect Rawlins to have read the book, but he has taken a course in European history and knows that it was written during a military campaign against the Germans. They talk about the book and as Rawlins is about to leave, Stetz asks him how he knows about it. To which Rawlins replies, 'Rome is a lot closer to Africa than it is to here, Mr Stetz' (p. 245). Referring to this particular scene, Mosley says:

> It's just a little statement. I'm not didactic in the novels. Easy just wants to reclaim what is his. Very often in Black America people say that we should be back in Africa. But Easy says no, we've evolved everywhere, so that everything belongs to us as it belongs to everyone else.[50]

Crucially, Mosley depicts the teeming morass of sometimes interlocking, sometimes conflicting alliances that characterise relations in his city without allowing himself to become carried away by its optimistic possibilities. From *Devil in a Blue Dress* onwards, one is made acutely aware of the separation or rather segregation of the white and black population. In fact, given the extent of the social and economic divisions

– reflected in *Black Betty* by the gulf separating the fabulous wealth of the Cains, a white family living in Beverly Hills, and the sheer desolation of black children living in Watts for whom the 'future's so bleak that it could make you cry' (p. 216) – it is difficult not to think of the title of Andrew Hacker's book, *Two Nations: Black and White, Separate, Unequal, Hostile*. Yet Mosley does not allow himself to fall into the essentialist trap of representing black America in one-dimensional terms. The sheer variety of different skin colours worn by his various black characters is testament to the falsity of biological definitions of 'race' and racial difference. In *Devil in a Blue Dress*, for example, Coretta James has 'cherry brown' skin, Odell Jones is coloured like a 'red pecan' and Jackson Blue is 'so black that his skin glinted blue in the full sun'.[51] Meanwhile in *A Red Death*, whereas EttaMae is a 'sepia-colored' brown, Mofass is 'dark brown but bright', Mouse is 'dusky pecan', Jackie Orr is more of an 'olive brown' and Andre Lavender has distinctive 'orange-colored' skin.[52] Such a racial melange, if nothing else, draws attention to the degree to which black and white communities are already implicated in one another, and have been so for as long as they have lived in close proximity. As Henry Louis Gates once said about his own multicoloured family: 'no need to point out that those with lighter skin were either part Irish or part English or part European because they were the complexity of their bloodline on their faces'.[53]

Emblematic of this racial mixing is Holland Gasteau, a middle-aged man of apparently indeterminate ancestry who turns up dead at the start of *A Little Yellow Dog*:

> 'I didn't think he was a white man; his skin was dark olive and his nose was wider than most Caucasian's. I wasn't claiming him for a Negro either. His racial roots could have been from at least four continents, or a thousand islands around the world.' (p. 23)

Holland Gasteau, like his twin brother Roman, has come to Los Angeles having emigrated from French Guiana and settled in Philadelphia and if any doubt remains as to the extent to which cultural and ethnic differences shatter neat, clear-cut racial configurations, these are expunged when another Guianese émigré, Bonnie Shay, whose skin is darker than Holland's and might otherwise be categorised as 'black', turns up. Bonnie, like the Gasteau twins, is implicated in a scheme to smuggle heroin into Los Angeles from Paris, France, but reveals her non-American background when she tells Rawlins that if he was innocent then he had nothing to worry about. As Rawlins himself remarks, 'I knew right then that she wasn't a fully American Negro. A black man or woman in America, with American parents, knew that innocence was a term for white people' (p. 172). Class differences also abound. The dialect spoken by most of the characters from Watts and Compton resonates with a distinctively African-American rhythm and operates as a signifier of their working-class status. Middle-class African-Americans like Quentin Naylor, a police detective who comes not from Texas and Louisiana like most of the black population in Los Angeles but from Philadelphia, have an 'educated way of talking' and live on particular streets that are somehow supposed to establish their class superiority. One such community, who live on Bell Street in Watts, 'thought that their people and their block were too good for the rest of the Watts community'. Indeed, 'They frowned on a certain class of people buying houses on their street and they had a tendency to exclude such people from barbecues and whatnot'.[54]

In the main part, race and class tend to be interlocking systems, so that the overlap between the African-American and working-class population in Los Angeles is considerable. Yet the working-class population is by no means exclusively African-American and throughout Mosley's work there is a persuasive reference to white, Mexican and Jewish working-class suffering as understood by African-Americans and vice versa. Archie Muldoon, a white janitor in *A Little Yellow Dog*, is described by Rawlins as 'a kindred spirit; a man trod on by history, his poverty' (p. 205). Primo, a poor immigrant, is similarly oppressed on account of his Mexican ancestry and Rawlins draws attention to the link between ancestry and poverty when he remarks, 'Back then . . . a Mexican and a Negro considered themselves the same. That is to say, just another couple of unlucky stiffs left holding the short end of the stick'.[55] Meanwhile the Jewish characters who populate Mosley's novels, like Chaim Wenzler in *A Red Death* and Abe and Johnny in *Devil in a Blue Dress*, are either Holocaust survivors themselves or understand the suffering endured not just by Jews in the Polish concentration camps but also those who live with the painful consequences of violent discrimination. Wenzler uses this knowledge to draw attention to the comparisons between the situation facing African-Americans and Jews in Poland, something that Rawlins has already reflected upon in *Devil in a Blue Dress*:

> I'll never forget thinking how those Germans had hurt that poor boy so terribly that he couldn't even take in anything good. That was why so many Jews back then understood the American Negro; in Europe the Jew had been a Negro for more than a thousand years. (p. 144)

The term 'Negro' is used here as a euphemism for those groups like Polish Jews and African-Americans who have been oppressed but such a definition, failing as it does to take into account differences based on skin colour, runs up dead against a comment made by Jackson Blue in *A Red Death*. The novel takes place in a country and city in the grip of McCarthyism but within this particular context Mosley is careful not to exactly equate the experiences of all those marginalised by the repressive legislation. Jackson informs Rawlins that he has heard about a list circulating in the business community which names not just black Americans but also Jews who are to be excluded from the workplace because of apparently un-American political affiliations. Yet as Jackson glumly acknowledges, significant differences do exist between the discrimination suffered by African-Americans and Jews:

> 'One day they gonna th'ow that list out, man. They gonna need some movie star or some new bomb an' they gonna th'ow that list away. Mosta these guys gonna have work again,' he said, then winked at me. 'But you still gonna be a black niggah, Easy. An' niggah ain't got no politician gonna work fo' him. All he got is a do'step t'shit in and a black hand t'wipe his black ass.' (p. 230)

The way in which Jackson Blue frames black oppression in exclusively male terms draws attention, if only through its absence, to a common complaint of African-American women; namely, that male historians and novelists have tended to ignore the double marginalisation faced by black women, at the hands of white culture and black and white men. Certainly Mosley is partly complicit in this context. If he successfully exposes the fraudulent nature of essential racial identities, he is perhaps less successful at contesting essential gendered identities. Recalling the noir model, women tend to be either hard-working family types or femme fatales. Daphne Monet (*Devil in a Blue Dress*), Black Betty (*Black Betty*) and Idabell Turner (*A Little Yellow Dog*) are all drawn as the latter – duplicitous, aggressive women who use their powerful sexuality to ensnare men who happen to stumble across their paths and cannot resist their wily 'feminine' lures. As Rawlins says of *Black Betty*, '[she] wasn't your warm sort of home-making girl. Betty was a great shark of a woman. Men died in her wake' (p. 5). Similarly Mosley's portrait of masculinity is perhaps less inclusionary and heterogeneous than his portrait of blackness. Rawlins, like most of the male characters in the series, defines himself, and is defined by others, in traditionally 'masculine' terms, particularly in terms of his voracious appetite for heterosexual relations. 'I was used to being in charge with women', he admits in *A Little Yellow Dog*, 'at least I was used to playing that role in love' (pp. 107–8).

Of all his novels, *White Butterfly*, the third instalment in the Easy

Rawlins series, stands out in this respect because Mosley explicitly uses the novel as a vehicle to explore gender relations and manages to contextualise, if not overturn, these essential or stereotypical identities. Unlike the other novels of the series, Rawlins is married in *White Butterfly*, though strains in the marriage are quickly exposed. Rawlins' claim that his wife Regina 'was perfect in every way'[56] – he places her on a pedestal, one way in which men have traditionally objectified women – is almost immediately followed by a scene in which Rawlins forces himself on her, an alternative method of achieving the same goal:

> She tried weakly to pull away but I held her and stroked her in the ways she liked it. She gave into my caresses but she wouldn't kiss me. I rolled on top of her and held her head between my hands. She let my leg slip between hers but when I put my lips to hers, she wouldn't open her mouth or eyes . . . 'Stop, Easy,' she cried, but I knew she meant, 'Go on, do it.' (p. 36)

This scene is a particularly disturbing and effective one because the reader's identification with Rawlins, which has been secured by thirty-odd pages of first-person narration (and two previous novels), is broken. The suffering experienced by Regina at the hands of her husband (later, she describes this act as rape) goes a long way to redressing previous gender stereotypes and rectifying a situation in which the voices of black women have been deliberately suppressed or silenced. When Regina says to him, 'Sometimes you look at me the same way a dog be lookin' after raw meat' (p. 130), Mosley is drawing attention not just to the sexual exploitation of black women even within marriage but also to the ways in which this particular practice connects up to other, more overt male strategies of domination, notably a serial attacker who is responsible for the brutal murders of a number of women, black and white, during the course of the narrative.

The fact that Regina eventually leaves Rawlins for another man at the end of *White Butterfly* is a sign of the shift in power relations that takes place during the course of the novel, though her reasons for doing so are only partially connected to this particular incident. Of more concern to her is the way in which Rawlins has shut her out of his life, telling him, 'You don't understand. I want to be part of something. I ain't just some girl to suck your dick and have your babies' (p. 131). Such an assertion is a powerful affirmation of female subjectivity but it also compels Rawlins to examine his own motives and in doing so he realises that the kind of unyielding, inscrutable, apparently essential male identity he has adopted, particularly in his relations with women, is not one modelled on a traditional white patriarchal 'norm' but rather is the product of white oppression. As a black man for whom survival will always be the greatest achievement, Rawlins has made it his rule never to reveal anything about himself. 'Nobody knew me. They didn't know about my property . . . I felt safe in my secrets' (p. 35).

Trapped by his needs and by his second-class status, Rawlins moves cautiously and reluctantly within his own community and beyond, through the treacherous environs of a racially segregated LA. Yet in so far as his narrative function is as much observational as investigative, he must also read and decipher the fragmented social landscape of the city he loves and loathes. Chameleon-like, his identity is never fixed but rather shifts in relation to where he is, who he is with, what he is doing. Among his 'own' people, he prides himself in the achievements of black musicians and writers and celebrates the energy and vitality of black culture, takes care to talk in the 'uneducated' dialect of his upbringing, and seeks out friendships in order to sustain himself and his family during difficult times. Yet to conceive of his identity as provisional and fluid is liberating for Rawlins because it allows him to move an interest solely in black literature and history, beyond a reliance only on black friends and community, allows him to move beyond the limiting position where he is only identified and identifies himself as black.

This assessment of Rawlins' character perhaps does Mosley a disservice, though. For as much as Rawlins may comes across a manifestation of late twentieth-century liberal humanism replete with a politically correct agenda stressing the importance of cross-cultural dialogue, there is a harder, tougher edge of his character, an acknowledgement in his words and actions of the violence and suffering, funk and dynamism, that have informed and shaped his identity. Mosley's writing may have evolved out of, and in turn anticipated, a new black cultural politics predicated on an assumption of the inadequacy of the binary language of race relations and essentialist definitions of racial identities, but he is by no means blind to the frustrations experienced by those with dark, as opposed to light, skin and the different ways in which these frustrations can manifest themselves – in acts of violence, rape, murder and self-mutilation. Because lurking beneath Rawlins' apparent liberalism is a damning vision of the United States in which different cultures and individuals do not co-exist in a state of blissful harmony but rather in a grim, deterministic world where relations of domination and subordination inevitably assume a racial complexion.

It is here, perhaps, that the interests and concerns of this chapter finally come together, or rather that the project of comparing Himes and Mosley – reading Himes in relation to Mosley and vice versa – is fully realised. Because whereas Himes, in the past, has been criticised for the grotesquely violent, reactionary politics of his novels and Mosley, for his apparent liberalism, a strain or tenet in his fiction which makes it politically acceptable for a 'poll-monger'[57] like Bill Clinton to nominate him as his favourite author, such a reading ignores the underlying bleakness of Mosley's vision and the subtle, thoughtful dissection of racial politics to be found in Himes' writing. For Himes and Mosley, like Ellroy, Sallis, Carter and all the 'best' crime writers, cannot be neatly situated somewhere on the political spectrum. Their writing and characters are manifestations of an at times bewildering mixture of attitudes, ideologies, politics and ambitions; moving between hegemonic and counter-hegemonic positions, their detectives consciously subvert the values of an established or dominant culture while simultaneously policing its not so fluid boundaries. Cleavages of race, but also ethnicity, class and gender, further complicate an already complicated landscape and in so far as the detective, particularly where his or her marginality is foregrounded, does not or cannot bring attendant tensions even into problematic resolution, these writers, collectively and individually, portray an America on the verge of violent disintegration.

Notes

1. Walter Mosley, in Paul Duncan (ed.), *The Third Degree: Crime Writers in Conversation* (Harpenden: No Exit Press, 1997), p. 150.
2. Following his election to the Presidency in 1992, Bill Clinton was asked to name his favourite writer and nominated Walter Mosley.
3. Raphael Sonenshein, *Politics in Black and White: Race and Power in Los Angeles* (Princeton, NJ: Princeton University Press, 1993), p. 222.
4. Chester Himes, *My Life of Absurdity: The Autobiography of Chester Himes Volume II* (New York: Doubleday, 1976), p. 126.
5. Chester Himes, *Cotton Comes to Harlem* (London: Allison and Busby, 1988), p. 66.
6. See Gary Storhoff, 'Aggravating the Reader: The Harlem Detective Novels of Chester Himes', in Jerome H. Delamater and Ruth Prigozy (eds), *The Detective in American Film, Fiction and Television* (Westport, CT: Greenwood Press, 1998), p. 46.
7. Storhoff, *The Detective in American Film, Fiction and Television*, p. 49.
8. Chester Himes, *The Real Cool Killers* (New York: Berkeley Medallion Books, 1966), p. 60.
9. John G. Cawelti, *Adventure, Mystery, Romance: Formula Stories as Art and Popular Fiction* (Chicago, IL: University of Chicago Press, 1976), p. 152.

10. Martha Diawara, 'Noirs by Noirs: Towards a New Realism in Black Cinema', in Joan Copjec (ed.), *Shades of Noir: A Reader* (London and New York: Verso, 1993), p. 264.
11. Ibid., p. 266.
12. Ibid., p. 266.
13. Scott McCracken, *Pulp: Reading Popular Fiction* (Manchester and New York: Manchester University Press, 1998), p. 46.
14. Storhoff, *The Detective in American Film, Fiction and Television*, p. 50.
15. Ibid., p. 51.
16. Ibid., p. 47.
17. James Sallis, *Difficult Lives: Jim Thompson, David Goodis, Chester Himes* (New York: Gryphon Books, 1993), p. 74.
18. Michelle Wallace, *Invisibility Blues: From Pop to Theory* (London and New York: Verso, 1990), p. 1.
19. Ibid., p. 1.
20. Himes, *My Life of Absurdity*, p. 111.
21. Michael Eric Dyson, 'Essentialism and the Complexities of Racial Identity', in David Theo Goldberg (ed.), *Multiculturalism: A Reader* (Oxford and Cambridge, MA: Blackwell, 1992), p. 219.
22. Stuart Hall, 'New Ethnicities', in Bill Ashcroft, Gareth Griffiths and Helen Tiffin (eds), *The Post-Colonial Reader* (London and New York: Routledge, 1995), p. 225.
23. Chester Himes, *Blind Man with a Pistol* (London: Allison and Busby, 1986), p. 24.
24. Dyson, *Multiculturalism*, p. 221.
25. Ibid., p. 219.
26. Himes, *The Heat's On* (London: Allison and Busby, 1992), p. 39.
27. See Gerald Horne, *Fire This Time: The Watts Uprising and the 1960s* (University of Virginia Press, 1995).
28. Diawara, Shades of Noir, p. 270.
29. Extracts from this section have appeared elsewhere as '"Taking the Black Out of Noir": Deconstructing "Blackness" in Walter Mosley's Fiction', *Borderlines: Studies in American Culture*, 27, 3, Summer 1997, pp. 251–66 and 'Bridges and Boundaries: Race, Ethnicity and the American Crime Novel', in Kathleen G. Klein (ed.), *Diversity and Detective Fiction* (Bowling Green: Popular Press, 1999), pp. 187–208.
30. Sonenshein, *Politics in Black and White*, p. 222.
31. Michael Omi and Howard Wincant, 'The Los Angeles "Race Riot" and Contemporary U.S. Politics', in Robert Gooding-Williams (ed.), *Reading Rodney King, Reading Urban Uprising* (London and New York: Routledge, 1993), p. 105.

32. Ibid., p. 106.
33. Lynell George, *No Crystal Stair: African-Americans in the City of Angels* (London and New York: Verso, 1992), p. 5.
34. Dyson, *Multiculturalism*, p. 221.
35. See 'Presidential Private Eye', *Time*, 28 November 1992, p. 57; Richard Liston, 'The Gentle Literary Giant', *The Weekly Journal*, 9 September 1993, p. 8; and Stephen Moore, 'Black and Blue', *The Guardian*, 13 October 1993, p. 4.
36. Walter Mosley, *Devil in a Blue Dress* (London: Serpent's Tail, 1991), p. 17.
37. Tommy L. Lott, 'Black Vernacular Representation', in David Theo Goldberg (ed.), *Multiculturalism*, p. 243.
38. Walter Mosley, *RL's Dream* (first published 1995) (London: Picador, 1996), p. 220.
39. Leon F. Litwack, 'Trouble in Mind: The Bicentennial and the Afro-American Experience', *Journal of History*, 74, September, 1987, pp. 315–37, reprinted in Leonard Dinnerstein and Kenneth T. Jackson (ed.), *American Vistas 1877 to the Present* (Oxford and New York: Oxford University Press, 1995), pp. 19–20.
40. Walter Mosley, *A Little Yellow Dog* (London: Picador, 1997), p. 152.
41. At the start of *Farewell My Lovely*, Marlowe chooses to follow Moose and elects to try and find Velma once Moose has killed someone and disappeared.
42. Woody Haut, *Neon Noir: Contemporary American Crime Fiction* (London: Serpent's Tail, 1999), p. 107.
43. Walter Mosley, *Always Outnumbered, Always Outgunned* (first published 1997) (London: Serpent's Tail, 1998), p. 30.
44. Ibid., p. 32.
45. Liam Kennedy, 'Black Noir: Race and Urban Space in Walter Mosley's Detective Fiction', in Peter Messent (ed.), *Criminal Proceedings: The Contemporary American Crime Novel* (London: Pluto, 1997), p. 50.
46. Mosley, *Devil in a Blue Dress*, p. 158.
47. Ibid., p. 129.
48. Ibid., p. 36.
49. See Joanne Glaseby, 'Profile: Walter Mosley', *Esquire*, December, 1995, p. 20.
50. Mosley, *The Third Degree*, pp. 147–8.
51. Mosley, *Devil in a Blue Dress*, p. 44, p. 42, and p. 120.
52. Walter Mosley, *A Red Death* (London: Serpent's Tail, 1992), p. 26, p. 13, p. 72, p. 86 and p. 120.
53. Henry Louis Gates, *Colored People* (London: Penguin, 1995), p. 73.

54. Mosley, *A Red Death*, p. 197.
55. Mosley, *Devil in a Blue Dress*, p. 182.
56. Walter Mosley, *White Butterfly* (London: Serpent's Tail, 1993), p. 31.
57. Haut, *Neon Noir*, p. 7.

CHAPTER 5

America's Changing Colour: Towards a Multicultural Crime Fiction

Like a magician who produces a rabbit from a top hat only to make it disappear, the logic of the book so far has been to affirm the significance of the black/white racial binary in American life, if only by focusing on examples of 'black' and 'white' crime fiction, while simultaneously questioning its validity and existence. The idea that this kind of model reflects the full range of lived experiences in a nation whose city streets vibrate to the rhythms of diverse ethnic cultures and whose population can be traced back to every corner of the world from Laos and Cuba to El Salvador, Colombia, Korea, Armenia and China, is clearly misguided. Nonetheless, while the idea that 'blackness' and 'whiteness' ever described fixed, natural essences has been well and truly dismissed, the persistence of race and racism as a continuing blight on the American landscape has been noted. After all, who could have failed to notice the racial fault-lines exposed and opened up by the melee to condemn and explicate Mark Fuhrman or Louis Farrakhan in recent years? And who could assert, with any degree of conviction, that race in America is of no consequence, when much of the evidence points to the contrary. However unreal or problematic 'race' as a biological or scientific category might be, belief in the existence of race, like belief in the existence of witches, as Kwame Anthony Appiah notes, continues 'to have profound consequences for human life'.[1] Or as Howard Wincant puts it:

> As we watch the videotape of Rodney King being beaten up by Los Angeles police officers; compare real estate prices in different metropolitan neighbourhoods; select a radio channel to enjoy while we drive to work; size up a potential client, customer, neighbour, or teacher . . . we are compelled to think racially, to use the racial categories and meaning systems into which we have been socialised.[2]

Indeed, the continuing and pervasive influence of race in American life and concurrently, the problematisation of race as a viable method of classification is the structuring tension that will inform much of this final chapter. What follows, then, is an attempt to address and, if not to resolve then at least unpack, this contradiction, by opening up the generic frame of reference to include not just examples of 'black' and 'white' crime fiction, but also crime novels featuring and written by protagonists of Jewish, Cuban, Mexican, Ojibwa and Korean extraction.

Certainly this list speaks about the growing ethnic diversity in American life but what to make of this diversity is by no means self-evident. To those on the conservative right like Arthur Schlesinger Jr diversity begets fragmentation and fragmentation, of course, threatens the grand American project invoked by the Founding Fathers' maxim, *E Pluribus Unum*. 'The U.S. escaped the divisiveness of a multiethnic society by a brilliant solution: the creation of a brand new national identity', Schlesinger argues, with more than a passing reference to the 'melting pot' theory. 'The point of America was not to preserve old cultures but to forge a new, American culture'.³ Other critics, however, like Lawrence Fuchs, have celebrated the diverse nature and origins of American society and conceived the United States as a 'kaleidoscope' or 'mosaic' of different-but-equal cultures and individuals whose interactions necessarily change but do not exactly transform one another.⁴ This view, as we shall see, perhaps comes closer to informing my own treatment of the novels and novelists to be discussed in this chapter, but missing from both versions, nonetheless, is any idea of the way in which racial and ethnic identities have, and continue to be, constructed through, and in relation to, a hierarchical system of domination and subordination in which the role of the 'State' (or at least the institutional and legal apparatus established to regulate and order social relations) cannot be overlooked. Smith and Feagin helpfully illustrate how this process has functioned in the United States:

> State power has often been the object of the politics of racial representation; and state policies, the means to enforce relations of domination-subordination. In the American case, the archetypal foundations for centuries of subsequent racial-ethnic incorporation, negotiation and conflict began with the early colonial struggles between European settlers and Native Americans and between early colonial settlers and their imported African slaves. The latter involved a multi-layered construction of dominance and oppression that cut across all major institutions.⁵

To conceive of the 'State' as monolith and its power as all-pervasive, to the point where individual agency – the ability of individuals to define themselves – is extinguished, would be overstating the case. But who could deny that from its inception the United States has been founded upon principles, and legislation, which have explicitly excluded peoples of non-white, non-European descent from enjoying privileges and benefits extended to their white, Euro-American counterparts? Though the Declaration of Independence was rhetorically a 'colour-blind' document, the US Constitution amended the latter's claim that all men should be allowed to enjoy 'certain unalienable rights' to effectively define African-American slaves out of existence.[6] Subsequent legislation further reinforced the subordinate status of non-whites in the early Republic and gave institutional legitimacy to racist practices that would be replicated elsewhere, in the economy, education, housing and politics. The Naturalisation Act of 1790 extended citizenship only to 'free, white people'; Chief Justice John Marshall's ruling, in the case of *Cherokee Nation* vs *Georgia* (1831), that Indian tribes were to be seen as 'domestic, dependent nations' effectively placed Native Americans outside America's political and constitutional borders; and two Supreme Court rulings in the 1920s, *Ozawa* vs *United States* and *Thind* vs *United States*, underlined both the artificial, arbitrary nature of racial classification as well as the power of such classifications to determine (unequal) social, economic and political relations across all spectrums of American life.[7]

Takao Ozawa, a middle-class, University of California-educated immigrant from Japan, appealed to the Supreme Court that he should be considered for naturalisation on the ground not simply that he was a 'model' citizen who had severed all cultural and religious links with his 'home' country but more pertinently because his skin colour was 'white' or at least whiter than the average Spaniard or Italian. The Supreme Court rejected Ozawa's appeal, arguing that 'skin color does not correlate well with racial identity',[8] and that 'the words "white person" are synonymous with the words "a person of the Caucasian race"',[9] which Ozawa was deemed not to be. However in arriving at this decision, the Court ignored the basic implications of Ozawa's argument – that scientific racial classifications were actually untenable – and thus opened the door to further citizenship applications from other non-white European immigrants. One such applicant, Bhagat Singh Thind, an Indian immigrant from the Punjab, argued that since anthropologists had classified certain Indians as 'Caucasian' rather than 'Mongolian', under the terms laid down by the earlier Supreme Court ruling, he was eligible for citizenship. In its 1923 ruling, however, the Court threw out his appeal arguing that a 'white person' and a 'Caucasian' were not, in fact, synonymous, and that the distinction between, say, an Indian and someone from north-west Europe was, quite simply, a matter of 'common sense':

It is a matter of familiar observation and knowledge that the physical group characteristics of the Hindus render them readily distinguishable from the various groups of persons in this country commonly recognized as white. The children of English, French, German, Italian, Scandinavian and other European parentage quickly merge into the mass of our population and lose the distinctive hallmarks of their European origin. On the other hand, it cannot be doubted that the children born in this country of Hindu parents would retain indefinitely the clear evidence of their ancestry.[10]

Intentionally or otherwise, the Court's decisions exposed a gaping contradiction at the heart of the American system. On the one hand, racial classifications, at least in a specifically biological sense, were rejected for being too nebulous and inadequate for the purpose of distinguishing between persons with different physiological characteristics. On the other hand, differences between persons of white, European and non-white, non-European extraction were enshrined and legitimised with reference not just to their cultural background and in the case of Thind, his Hindu religion, but also to their visible, physical characteristics. 'Race', as Haney-Lopez points out, was shown *not* to be a matter of physical difference but rather 'what people believed about physical difference',[11] something which inevitably entailed not just physiological but also cultural factors – not just how a person looked but also what language he or she spoke or what religion he or she practised. In so doing the Court bowed to popular, or rather nativist, concerns about the cultural and physiological impact of wholesale mixing between persons of European and non-European descent. Mr Justice Sutherland's haughty summary that people 'intuitively recognize' racial difference and 'reject the thought of assimilation'[12] legitimised a hierarchical model of social relations, whose origins lay in the 'black/white' binary established in the popular imagination with the arrival of African slaves on American shores as early as the 1630s, and whose impact continues to be felt, despite the passage of civil rights legislation in the 1960s.

The conflation of 'race' and 'ethnicity' here, and implicitly in the Supreme Court's ruling in the case of *United States* vs *Thind*, raises important questions about the relationship between both terms. Indeed, given their intertwined historical associations, it is tempting to simply collapse 'race' and 'ethnicity' on top of one another. William Peterson observes that the terms 'ethnic' and 'racial' have at different times been used to describe similar properties or attributes (i.e. the Irish 'race' and Irish as an 'ethnic' category) and argues that since the Greek term ethnos (from which our word 'ethnicity' is derived) originally pertained to a biological grouping, it was perhaps closer to our definition of 'race' (a word most likely derived from the medieval Latin term ratio which was used to designate species). Peterson also states that separation between the two terms has been further undermined by the confusion in real life between cultural and physiological criteria; he points out, for example, that African-Americans have been defined in ethnic and racial terms – as belonging to a specific 'ethnic' group with its own distinct culture and history and possessing certain physiological features.[13]

Nomenclature may indicate a close historical interrelationship between race and ethnicity but cultural critics have fiercely debated the relative significance of both terms, whether race or ethnicity should be the dominant paradigm through which the contemporary United States is read and understood; in other words, whether race, as Harold Abramson and latterly Werner Sollors argue, is merely 'one of the dimensions of the larger cultural and historical phenomenon of ethnicity',[14] or, as M. G. Smith and more recently Howard Wincant and E. San Juan Jr contend, whether race needs to be treated as a special 'objective' category on the grounds that racial, and not ethnic, categorisation 'became the principle of exclusion and inclusion that continues to inform and reinforce all other social antagonisms [in the United States]'.[15] Certainly it would be hard to deny that the historical experiences of immigrants from Europe and, say, Asia and Africa were not quantitatively and qualitatively different, but does this kind of acknowledgement necessarily involve the rearticulation of race as the only usable trope of difference (and the corresponding obliteration of ethnicity)? And what of all classifications in this brave new, post-structualist world, where 'essences' (racial and ethnic) have been exposed as subjective fictions?

My answer is admittedly circumspect. Rather than succumb to the temptation either to collapse race and ethnicity on top of one another, or to excessively privilege one at the expense of the other, what follows is underpinned by a discourse that is flexible enough to view race and ethnicity as overlapping and yet diverging categories, sophisticated enough to acknowledge that commonalities between and among individuals and communities do not necessarily override equally significant cultural, historical and physiological differences, and clear-headed enough to accept that the social, political and economic consequences not just for those with, say, dark as opposed to light coloured skin have been very profound. At its heart, this model embraces a definition of race and ethnicity which focuses on the mechanics of social power, or rather foregrounds the way in which differences are constructed to reinforce relations of domination-subordination. Significantly such a model does not preclude, but rather depends upon, the ambitions and efforts of individuals and communities to contest and even overturn such relations, so that race and ethnicity, ultimately, need to be theorised in suitably complex terms, as an unstable, 'decentred' set of historically diverse experiences situated within fluctuating but nonetheless hierarchical relations of social, political and economic power.

Those who conceive race as merely one of the dimensions of the larger cultural and historical phenomenon of ethnicity, who want to entirely subsume 'race' into the wider category of 'ethnicity', by implication, are either blind to, or do not properly account for the kind of historical and material forces of racial inequality responsible for the passage of the Naturalization Act of 1790. Disturbingly such a position informs and shapes a liberal but bland multiculturalism where similarly minded groups, communities and individuals exist as 'equal' component parts of a falsely utopian, pluralistic America. I say, disturbingly, because who could argue with any conviction that the historical experiences of African-Americans or Native-Americans differed from that of, say, Irish or Italian-Americans only in degree (of suffering, marginalisation)? Yet those who consider race as a special objective category that cannot be discussed under the heading ethnicity, who resist all attempts to subsume race into the category of ethnicity run a different kind of risk; that of essentialising racial difference and compartmentalising those who have been ascribed racial identities in the United States into hermetically pure enclaves. This position informs and shapes an equally disturbing multiculturalism built upon the rhetoric of essentialism, whereby the different racial and ethnic properties of Europeans and non-Europeans are naturalised and presented as being somehow fixed, unchanging.

To view race and ethnicity as overlapping and yet diverging categories, conceived and situated in relations of unequal power, however, frees us from the tyranny of both of these positions. Informing and shaping what Manning Marable has called a 'radical democratic multiculturalism' this model emphasises the distinctive properties of particular groups and communities, foregrounds differences within and among these same groups and communities, and forges links between different groups and communities. Crucially, though as Marable notes, such interactions are conceived of and understood in relation to the functioning of power – 'and the ways in which ideology and aesthetics are used to dominate or control oppressed people'.[16]

Significantly, a model that acknowledges the logic and history of patterns of racial and ethnic domination while simultaneously conceiving of race and ethnicity as fluid, dynamic, unfixed categories, corresponds with the prevailing view of the United States contained in and expressed by the crime novel; that of a nation in which the existence of a central power source and a dominant culture neither guarantees the loyalty nor ensures the oppositionality of the detective or his or her surrogate, but rather replicates, within his or her persona, the kind of dynamic struggle which characterises the process of identity formation at large. The logic and trajectory of this final chapter, therefore, extends out of what has come before; namely, an acknowledgement that whereas 'top-down' power seeks to bind, control and condition the fabric of people's lives, individual agency invariably challenges, transgresses and elides its ability to do so. In terms of the American crime novel, this contradiction manifests itself most visibly in the persona of the detective (or his or her surrogate) who is both an agent of the state and an '*agent provocateur*'; someone operating according to his or her own code or values, or values constructed within a broader community whose opposition to the 'dominant' culture has been forged along axes of, say, race, ethnicity, gender, or sexuality.

As the scope and framework of the book opens up not just to 'black' and 'white' voices and perspectives, but also to a whole spectrum of hyphenated American identities (Jewish, Cuban, Mexican, Korean), the question of what unites and divides groups and individuals in an age when the ideas or ideals 'of coherent communities and consistent subjectivities, of dominant centers and distant margins . . . no longer seem adequate'[17] is brought into sharper focus. The emerging portrait of a multi-ethnic, multiracial American society is a complex one – a society where changes are being fuelled by a cultural politics that recognises the fragmented, provisional nature of identities and the intersecting modalities of race, ethnicity, class, gender and sexuality that criss-cross and atomise individual subjectivities. Of course, shared properties inevitably connect crime novels, whatever the racial or gendered identity of the author or protagonist, but differences, as we shall see, are often more revealing. It would be far too trite to suggest that differences between, say, Burke's Dave Robicheaux novels and Mosley's Easy Rawlins series can be explicitly attributed to the ethnic or racial identity of the author or protagonist. After all, both writers, as we have already seen, skilfully open up tensions between competing values and ideologies at play in American society in order to challenge the 'preferred' view of the United States as harmonious and progressive. That said, as Feagin and Smith argue, internal differences within racial and ethnic groupings 'constitute an important form of resistance to the homogenization by dominant centers of power'.[18] In other words, differences – between ethnic and racial groupings and by implication their cultural artifacts (i.e. crime novels) – are not entirely arbitrary and require further investigation. If this is one starting point for the chapter, another is the recognition that 'internal differences within ethnic and racial groupings' manifest themselves not just along ethnic or racial lines, but also in terms of gender, class and sexuality. To this extent, the kind of 'radical democratic multiculturalism' to which Manning Marable refers, acknowledges the link between ideology, power and culture, in its broadest sense, and envisages a radical restructuring of the 'system of cultural and political power itself'.[19] The crime novel may not share such explicitly utopian goals, but as we have already seen, the maverick, dissenting detective is better placed than most to reveal links between existing political and cultural systems and the marginalisation and oppression of oppositional voices.

'Ties That Fray But Won't Snap': Ritual, Tradition and Memory in Jewish-American Crime Fiction

When Walter Mosley alluded, in *A Red Death*, to the discrimination and suffering experienced by Jews in Europe at the hands of the Nazis and African-Americans in the New World, he was making an implicit reference to the close, though often antagonistic, relationship that African-Americans have traditionally forged with their Jewish counterparts in the United States. Both Jews and Blacks, as Cornel West observes, have been, and to some extent, continue to be a 'pariah' people – 'a people who had to make and remake themselves as outsiders on the margins of American society and culture'.[20] The brutal extremities of slavery in America and the Holocaust in Europe have given each group at least partial insight into the suffering and hardships experienced by the other, and opened up significant areas of common ground. Rather than succumbing to the cult of victimhood, moreover, both groups have responded with verve and imagination to the challenges of living in the United States; in a very real sense, their achievements have helped to define and characterise America in the twentieth century. 'A century that begins only a generation after the emancipation of penniless, illiterate enslaved Africans and the massive influx of poor Eastern European Jewish immigrants', West asserts, 'is unimaginable without the creative breakthroughs and monumental contributions of Blacks and Jews'.[21] And who could disagree, when the list of creative influence from both groups includes, among many others, Louis Armstrong and George Gershwin, Miles Davis and Irving Berlin, Bessie Smith and Leonard Bernstein, Charlie Parker and Jackson Pollack, August Wilson and Arthur Miller, Richard Wright and Saul Bellow, Zora Neale Hurston and Phillip Roth, Amiri Baraka and Allan

Ginsberg, James Baldwin and Harold Brodsky, Ralph Ellison and Joseph Heller?

Certainly, within the realm of culture at least, the achievements of blacks and Jews have made a mockery of attempts to define 'America' and American culture in anything but multi-ethnic terms. Yet this unanimity of success has not been replicated across the board. While Jewish-Americans, particularly in the post-World War Two era, have by and large moved en masse from working to middle and upper-class status, the disparity of wealth and opportunity for middle and working-class African-Americans has never been greater. Though the ranks of the black middle classes continues to grow, as David Theo Goldberg points out, 'nearly half of black American children now live in poverty ... [and] in the public mind of America, "black" and "underclass" have tended to become synonymous'.[22] Such disparities have provoked many African-Americans to question the wisdom of comparing the experiences of blacks and Jews. Increasingly relations between the two groups have been defined by mutual distrust and hostility. Crown Heights and Williamsburg in Brooklyn have played host to violent confrontations between poor blacks and Hassidic Jews, while Louis Farrakhan's ill-concealed anti-Semitism has merely poured petrol on to the flames of discontent. While some Jewish-Americans have looked to their own experiences and set out to explain continuing African-American poverty in terms of the latter group's inability to make the most of opportunities, growing numbers of African-Americans have sought to explain so-called Jewish economic 'success' and their own so-called 'failure' in explicitly racial terms. In other words, Jewish-Americans, by their own volition and with the tacit approval of the dominant culture, have enjoyed and been allowed to enjoy 'white-skin privilege' – despite virulent claims by certain right-wing extremist thinkers that Jews constitute a distinctive race. This privilege, furthermore, has come at the expense of, or at least has been predicated upon, the presence of a 'polluting' blackness. Consequently, as Goldberg notes, in much black anti-Semitic rhetoric, the 'Jew' has come 'to stand metaphorically for the figure of the capitalist, of capitalism, of prevailing social power ... of whiteness itself'. He concludes, 'Jews are perceived and now mainly perceive themselves as white'.[23]

Whether or not such claims stand up to closer scrutiny, however, is a debatable point. Certainly, precisely because of their 'light' skin colour, most Jews in the United States, have choices that most African-Americans, quite simply, do not have. The choice, that is, to blend or assimilate into the dominant American culture, to renunciate their Jewish heritage and learn to enjoy the fruits of being white in America. In these terms, or at least in terms of how individuals and groups identify themselves and are recognised or more pertinently *mis-*recognised by others, race and ethnicity need to be understood as diverging categories. Mary C. Waters makes the telling point that the choices available to someone defined in ethnic terms are often far greater than those defined in racial terms:

> The reality is that white ethnics have a lot more choice . . . than they themselves think they do. [But] the situation is different for members of racial minorities, whose lives are strongly influenced by their race or national origin, regardless of how much they may choose not to identify themselves in either ethnic or racial terms.[24]

That said, the apparently seamless conflation of 'whiteness' and 'Jewishness' has also been called into question. To be 'white' in America, Michael Lerner argues, is to fit into the social construct of the beneficiaries of European imperialism. Yet, Lerner continues, far from benefiting from this situation, Jews 'have been socially and legally discriminated against, have been the subject of racism and genocide, and in those terms . . . are not white'.[25] In this case, race and ethnicity need to be understood as overlapping categories, because discrimination against Jews in America and elsewhere, has assumed different forms; attacks based on both physiological properties (i.e. looks) and cultural and religious factors (i.e. different attire, religious rituals and beliefs, eating habits etc.). Consequently, many have argued that it has not been easy or straightforward for Jews to blend into the American mainstream, or rather that such a process comes at a heavy cost. As Lerner concludes, 'By and large, the way to get into this system is to take off your kippah, cut off your beard, hide your fringes; in other words, to reject your entire cultural and religious humanity'.[26]

The vexed question of what it means to be an American Jew or rather 'Jewish-American'[27] has occupied writers throughout the twentieth century. Leslie Fiedler once wrote that 'the very notion of a Jewish-American literature represents a dream of assimilation, and the process it envisages is bound to move towards a triumph (in terms of personal success) which is also a defeat (in terms of survival)'.[28] This tension is picked up upon and developed, as we shall see, by Faye Kellerman, Kinky Friedman and Jerome Charyn, three contemporary Jewish-American crime writers whose respective detective-protagonists (Peter Decker, Kinky Friedman and Isaac Sidel) reflect upon the difficulty of knowing what it means to be Jewish-American, or rather reflect upon the slipperiness and fluidity of Jewish-American identity in an uncertain age when the ties that bind them to their ancestors and co-religionists overseas have frayed but not snapped. This process of reflection, whereby each figure finds himself caught, figuratively, between America and Judaism, between an awareness of their ancestry and an acknowledgement of their 'Americanness', is mapped on to the generic framework of the crime novel, whereby the ambiguous cultural politics of the hard-boiled detective perfectly expresses or at least mirrors this atmosphere of anxiety and uncertainty. The tensions opened up as a result of the maverick detective's implication in the hegemonic practices of the state and the 'ethnic' detective's anxiety about being 'ethnic' *and* 'American' may not be as pronounced or violent as those characterising, say, Himes or Mosley's work but in so far as such tensions are never entirely closed off, Kellerman, Friedman and Charyn skilfully marshal the various component parts of the genre into fresh, illuminating patterns that speak about the ambiguities of contemporary life and the fractured nature of modern identities.

This question – in essence, 'how do you know who you are?' – constitutes an ongoing line of enquiry that runs through most, if not all, of Faye Kellerman's eleven (to date) crime novels, featuring LAPD detective, Peter Decker.[29] Decker, in many ways, is cut from a familiar generic mould. Embodying what Dennis Porter has called 'an ideal American-ness'[30] Kellerman's detective not only possesses many of the qualities the genre conventionally demands of its practitioners – toughness, determination, clarity of purpose and vision, humanity and a sense of self-reliance that is the product of the detective's awareness of the failings of the institution he or she serves. The ranch and horses Decker owns are also not-too-subtle signifiers of a mythic past where the kind of 'American' values Decker appears to possess were forged on the frontier. Yet Kellerman transforms Decker from cliched totem to complex, contemporaneous figure by giving him a Jewish ancestry which is brought into sharper focus as his relationship with Rina Lazarus, an attractive widow, develops throughout the series. Adopted and raised by Baptist parents, Decker has always known of his Jewish ancestry but has made little effort to investigate it, or come to terms with what it means, until he meets Rina, herself an orthodox Jew, in the first novel of the series, *The Ritual Bath*. There after, his curiosity and desire piqued, Decker's quest for self-knowledge, and Rina, compels him to embrace Judasim and as the series unfolds, Kellerman skilfully charts his attempts to come to terms with his fractured identity and bring its various constituent parts into albeit uneasy equilibrium.

Rina's anxiety about the conflicted nature of her own identity once precipitated a shift in her own religious beliefs and practices from the modern orthodox Judasim of her parents, where 'we were indistinguishable from the rest of the neighbourhood kids except that we kept kosher and observed Shabbos',[31] to the traditional orthodox

Judaism of her first husband, Yitzchak, where the differences were more pronounced. In a clever mirroring device, it also anticipates and reflects Decker's own quest for self-knowledge, at least in so far as it leads him in a similar direction; into an apparently secure, familial environment of ritual and tradition, to some extent shielded from the corrosive influences of a capitalist-fuelled modernity. Yet in both cases, this shift is not nearly as conclusive as it might appear. In Rina's case, the trajectory of the series leads her in precisely the opposite direction; from Kellerman's first novel, *The Ritual Bath*, where she is part of an enclosed, isolated, orthodox Jewish community built around a religious teaching institution and strictly adheres to its codes and values, Rina's relationship and eventual marriage to Decker compels her to open up to the modern world of which Decker, by the very nature of his job and his Christian/American upbringing, is inexorably a part.

In Decker's case, meanwhile, one if left to ponder upon the difficulty or even impossibility of transforming himself in line with the strictures of orthodox Judaism and, perhaps more pertinently, in Rina's image. In a later novel, *Serpent's Tooth*, Decker realises that he had become 'the type of Jew she wanted'[32] and acknowledges the value of prayer – if only because the ritual forces him to contemplate the nature of God and his own spiritual quest for 'twinkle of time' (p. 255). Still, his reasons for doing so are grounded just as much in the practical and romantic as the spiritual – failure to embrace orthodox Judaism on his part would have ended his relationship with Rina – and as a committed, long-serving police detective who has no intention of giving up his job, it is impossible to shield himself, or his family, from the brutal realities of life in contemporary Los Angeles.

Decker's quest for spirituality is both a signifier of his orthodox Judaic beliefs and a reaction against the grotesque excesses of degenerate late capitalist culture. Yet as a police detective who, to a great extent, defines himself through his work, Decker depends, and in a perverse way, thrives upon the presence of such excesses. This contradiction is played out through the structure of the novels. Decker's criminal or public investigations – into LA's pornographic industry in *Sacred and Profane* or a mass shooting in *Serpent's Tooth* – parallel but also clash with his private search for spiritual meaning. Diana Arbin Ben-Merre argues that Kellerman's double plots suggest both the 'difficulties of integrating Decker's public life as a detective with his private life as a . . . returning Jew' and the 'difficulties of trying to integrate the world of secular endeavors with the world of spiritual belief'.[33] That said, both worlds are marked, surprisingly perhaps, by a similar sense of indeterminacy. Throughout the series, the apparently rigid, unchanging properties of orthodox Judaism splinter to reveal a more ambiguous constitution; in

Sacred and Profane, for example, Decker is told by Rabbi Schulman that 'uncertainty is a condition of belief'.[34] This ambiguity both mirrors and informs the trajectory of Decker's investigations and the character of the 'justice' he dispenses. Tensions that are the product of the detective's contradictory function as state-sponsored enforcer and subversive dissenter, to a lesser or greater degree, shape the structure of the American crime novel. Here, they perform a similar function, but also speak about the difficulties of 'knowing' – knowing in a ratiocinative and metaphysical sense. Decker's actions in *Day of Atonement* when he kills an adolescent delinquent in the line of fire, and then proceeds to fire 'a chamber and a clip' into the dead man's head, oversteps his function even as dispenser of 'alternative-sense' justice, and prefigures his anxiety about setting free the dead man's accomplice, Noam Levine, who may or may not have killed someone in a botched robbery, simply because he is repentant and is the teenage son of a close family friend. This anxiety, too, assumes an overtly religious character, both when Decker cannot quite reconcile his actions with the strictures and demands of orthodox Judaism, and when Noam seeks in vain for a forgiveness he knows is beyond his reach. As Ben-Merre concludes:

> [The novel] shows how one person becomes a victim, another a victimizer, and how both these categories begin to overlap. Even after the criminals are found and guilt is aportioned out, the final image is that of a victim who is also a victimizer praying to a God who does not answer.[35]

Jewish-American identities are multiple and forged through a myriad of political, economic, social and religious affiliations. Indeed, if one is struck in Kellerman's *The Ritual Bath* by the introspective, insular nature of the novel's orthodox Jewish community or in *Day of Atonement* by the similarly distinctive character of Brooklyn's Boro Park, with its Hebrew-emblazoned storefronts displaying black hats, wigs and kosher foods, then one only has to look at other Jewish figures in Kellerman's novels whose assimilation has been more pronounced or at the visible presence of liquor stores, pizza parlours and doughnut luncheonettes at the fringes of Boro Park, to realise that cultural or religious homogeneity is no longer a possibility. Which is not to pretend that the ability and will of the State, as refracted through the desires and ambitions of a 'dominant' culture, to determine and arrange social relations is negligible. Rather it is to suggest that the tangible changes and concessions that Decker and Rina make in respect to the other, ultimately, represents a perhaps albeit utopian hope that we can all speak from a particular position, voice or culture without being imprisoned inside an ethnic enclave whose imagined boundaries are policed from outside and within to maintain a purity that does not actually exist, at least in terms of the experiences of many Americans.

The dynamic configuration of perspectives, cultures, religions and voices is nicely expressed, too, in Kinky Friedman's many crime novellas, featuring the author's private detective alter-ego, also named Kinky Friedman. Friedman – the detective and by implication the author, too – is an eccentric, protean figure; he plays in a country and western band called the Texas Jewboys, who were Jewish 'by inspiration'[36] if not ancestry, and best known for deliciously named tracks like 'They Ain't Making Jews Like Jesus Anymore'. Friedman is a cigar-chomping New Yorker, a Greenwich village bohemian with a collection of oddball friends, a collection of cats and a penchant for the unconventional, someone whose sense of identity has been forged in the image of the vibrant, multi-ethnic, dangerous, intoxicating culture the city has spawned. Just as significantly he is also a private detective; an eclectic figure constructed with more than a passing reference to both Sherlock Holmes, the doyen of ratiocinative investigators, and action-orientated, hard-drinking 'gumshoes' like Raymond Chander's Phillip Marlowe. Friedman's eye for detail and razor-sharp intellect often leaves his close friends, and by implication the reader, astounded but he is not afraid to 'mix it up', physically speaking, with adversaries who cross his path. In 'Frequent Flyer', he is beaten, spat at, gassed, shot at and left for dead but still manages to triumph over his neo-Nazi antagonists.

In some respects, the satirical elements of Friedman's crime fiction manoeuvre and locate it outside of the kind of hard-edged, uncompromising vision of a racially divisive urban America in terminal, unremitting decline which increasingly characterise the genre. Perhaps for this reason, Friedman's detective is not affected to the same extent as, say, Himes' Coffin Ed and Grave Digger, by rage which is the product of their implication in a system predicated upon their own subordination. Perhaps, too, this is because Friedman, the detective, is able to pass as white or enjoy the benefits of white-skin privilege; as Mary Waters suggests, he is to some extent able to choose which constituent parts of his ancestry, his culture and his religion to make a part of his life, whether this means eating bagels or attending classes run by the Jewish Defence League. However, this situation by no means guarantees the eradication or non-existence of anti-Semitic prejudice, nor does the satirical tone of Friedman's writing necessarily blunt its political or oppositional ambitions. Friedman's quip about the rise of Germany in the post-World War Two world – 'I understand they've come up with a new microwave oven; seats forty'[37] – may well be humorous but it masks a deep-seated concern about the terrible plight suffered by European Jews and Gypsies at the hands of Hitler's Nazis. In fact, the humour somehow makes the actions and ambitions of the Nazis that much more shocking, perhaps because one is disarmed by it and hence unprepared for revelations that follow.[38]

Being 'Jewish' in America is not entirely symbolic or without cost because the past cannot simply be sealed-off in a capsule and forgotten. As Friedman, the detective, acknowledges, about the Holocaust, 'I was too young to have been there at the time but I was a Jew. There would always be a piece of yesterday in my eye'.[39] Intrusions of the past into the present, moreover, do not only take the form of 'remembering'. A violent conspiracy hatched by neo-Nazis in 'Frequent Flyer' to conceal the contemporary whereabouts of Josef Mengele, a Nazi doctor responsible for the death and torture of thousands of Jews in the Polish concentration camps, alludes to the continuing persistence of anti-Semitic sentiment and the marking of Jewish-Americans, in the eyes of extremists at least, as different. The sheer scale of the Nazis' crimes against people of Jewish extraction makes the detective's traditional task of restoring even a fragile, temporary 'order' that much more problematic. Of course, one of the features of hard-boiled American crime fiction has always been the provisional, incomplete nature of 'justice' and the problemisation of detection as a vehicle for social control. That said, the sheer enormity of the Holocaust renders even this paradigm unworkable and while Friedman, the detective, successfully thwarts the neo-Nazi conspiracy, at least on American soil, he can do nothing to prevent horrific images of Jewish suffering in World War Two from punctuating his fevered dreams.

Perhaps reflecting Jewish-American 'success' at being able to infiltrate or blend into the white mainstream, Jerome Charyn's detective fiction charts the meteoric rise of Isaac Sidel, during the course of six (to date) novels,[40] through the ranks of the New York Police Department to the eventual and dizzy heights of Commissioner, the city's premier policeman. Yet rather than signalling his implication in the hegemonic ambitions of a 'dominant' culture (which itself is something of a fiction because it is the Irish who hold the purse-strings of power) Sidel's lofty but precarious position in the hierarchy of the department is little more than a gift that others have bestowed upon him. Of particular concern to the Irish king-makers, who have seen their preferred candidates move on to the FBI and pastures outside New York, is relinquishing power to the growing African-American presence in the department. Indeed, though boundaries which are conceived of in racial terms (between the city's various white ethnic groups and, say, African-Americans or newly arrived Cuban immigrants) tend to be drawn as unyielding and fixed, those denoting differences between the city's white ethnic population are constantly on the verge of collapse. Patrick Silver, an ex-cop of Irish extraction who gives his name to the third instalment of the series, *The Education of Patrick Silver*, may affirm his 'Irishness' by drinking Guinness in the King of Munster saloon but he also runs an unofficial synagogue for Jews and gentiles by pulling people off the streets, sticking a prayer shawl over their heads and including them in the 'minyan'.[41] Meanwhile Isadore Wasser, a Jewish 'melamed' or spiritual teacher in *The Good Policeman*, may speak perfect Yiddish but he is also 'an anarchist who didn't care about kosher things'[42] and acts as chief advisor or 'consigliori' to his Italian-American son-in-law, Jerry DiAngelis, a fearsome mafioso who nonetheless has a strong affinity for Judaism.

Like Friedman's novellas, Charyn's crime fiction flirts with satire and certainly the playfulness implicit in the idea of an Irish ex-cop running a synagogue or a Jewish 'melamed' advising an Italian gangster also manifests itself in Charyn's construction of Isaac Sidel himself. Sidel is a wildly unorthodox, improbable creation: a cultural hybrid, born of a Jewish father and Irish mother; a bohemian imbued with the spirit of artistic genius; a detective with a razor-sharp intellect and memory bank 'that could give you the size of a criminal's smelly sock';[43] a politician juggling allegiances and favours in order to remain afloat; and a reckless, renegade vigilante, cursed with a tapeworm and obsessed with bringing down the Guzmanns, a family of Peruvian immigrants from Marrano Jewish stock who operate a prostitution racket out of the Bronx. Still, the satirical elements of Sidel's character, and Charyn's novels, sit uncomfortably alongside the explicit and often disturbing violence exercised by Sidel and the Guzmanns in their ongoing struggle. The tension produced by this unease, moreover, opens up a space for Charyn to investigate the origins of Sidel's rage – rage that eventually drives him to deliberately maim one of Papa Guzmann's sons by running him down in his car. On the surface, the nature of Sidel's dispute with the Guzmann's is purely material. As pimps and murderers, it is perhaps understandable that they should be so firmly fixed in his sights, not least because they were responsible for killing his beloved son-in-law, Manfred Coen, in the second novel of the series, *Blue Eyes*.

Yet there is also an ethno-religious or spiritual element to their conflict. Though Sidel's identification with Judaism, in any shape or form, is severely strained, he cannot divorce himself entirely from its spiritual dimension. A self-confessed atheist and 'skeptical Jew',[44] Sidel's desire for forgiveness and spiritual salvation, nonetheless, is brought into sharper focus as the series develops. Concerned about the possible consequences of his violent ways, he starts to experience overdetermined ethno-religious hankerings – '[he] wished he could enter some little shul, cover his balding skull with a prayer shawl, and sing his way to God'.[45] Sidel's conflict with the Guzmanns assumes religious significance because Papa Guzmann's ancestry is founded upon a rejection of Judaism, at least in so far as Marrano Jews, during the time of the Spanish Inquisition, were forced to covert to Christianity, leave Spain or face execution. Sidel himself is convinced that Papa Guzmann's ability to cast spells in order to further his criminal ambitions is the product of this 'deviant' heritage. 'Only men who drank the boiling piss of Christian Jewish saints could be such strong magicians', he says, scathingly, about his arch-enemy. Guzmann, meanwhile, is equally convinced that Sidel is not merely a 'whore cop' but rather his own 'personal devil' who 'had been born into this world to plague [him]'.[46]

Charyn himself has suggested that the contemporary writer, like a destitute craftsman, 'has been left with little else than a sense of dislocation, a splintered reality, and the shards and bones of language'[47] to work with. The contemporary crime writer, too, has struggled to come to terms with a world in which answer, and meanings, are only ever subjective, provisional and incomplete. Sidel's anger, and the violence it spawns, could well relate to what he sees as a policeman or be the product of a more personal grievance against the Guzmanns and what they stand for, but conclusive answers are not forthcoming. Instead one is left to speculate on the perhaps more interesting thought that Sidel's antipathy towards his nemesis could also be antipathy towards himself; his ambition to destroy Papa Guzmann, a veiled attempt to destroy that side of his character founded upon the same principles of violence and intimidation that Papa Guzmann has used to establish his criminal empire. Guzmann's confused ethno-religious ancestry also mirrors Sidel's, as does his spiritual yearnings and quest for salvation. In a revealing essay on Charyn's fiction, Mike Woolf suggests that a key structuring tension of the Isaac Sidel series is the 'persistence of a notion of redemption in an ostensibly doomed and damned world'.[48] Such a notion remains only a possibility, but when Sidel visits a Rabbi in *The Good Policeman* and acknowledges his failings, the fact that he has often broken departmental rules, killed people when it wasn't his job or place to do so, the dynamic between crime, religion and the mechanics of city life is brought into albeit uneasy resolution. One could also say that Woolf's claim for Charyn, that he is 'reflective of contemporary fragmentation and responsive to the persistence of spiritual potential within the contemporary environment'[49] goes equally for Kellerman and Friedman too. Charyn himself playfully suggests that the legacy bestowed on New York, and by implication on America, by Jewish culture cannot be found in the concrete physicality of bricks and mortar but in the imaginative projections of its subjects. 'And the deepest, darkest thinkers are always criminals of one kind', he concludes, maybe a little too knowingly, 'There's an odd relationship between Jews, cities and the metaphysics of crime'.[50]

'Through Barrios and Across Borderlines . . .': 'Latinos' in the City of Angels

If African-Americans, throughout the long and often bloody passage of American history, have been singled out and subjected to the most violent, inhumane punishments by the white-dominated majority in the United States, and Jewish-Americans, for an admittedly much shorter, less sustained period and to a less vitriolic extent, encountered prejudicial discrimination on the basis of an uneasy cocktail of ethno-religious and racial[51] factors, then white fears of Latino 'difference' has been brought into sharper focus by the mass influx of Mexican immigrants into the United States, and large number of so-called political exiles escaping from Castro's Cuba to the El Dorado of south Florida. Spurred on, in California at least, by fears of a Latino or Hispanic takeover, a fractured alliance of native-born voters, politicians and businessmen drawn from right across the racial and ethnic spectrum, came together to ensure the passage of Proposition 187, denying illegal immigrants access to emergency health-care and other public services. In doing so, they mobilised anti-immigration sentiment throughout the United States; sentiment whose origins in part relate to the large numbers of Asians and particularly Latinos arriving in America since changes to the immigration laws in 1965.

To a certain extent, the influx of large numbers of immigrants from countries throughout Latin America – not just Mexico but also Puerto Rico, Cuba, Guatemala, El Salvador, Honduras and Colombia – has further questioned the viability of binary racial caste in which a dominant white population is situated in opposition to a minority black one. Ethnic, class, gender and regional diversity makes this kind of model untenable in both a practical and theoretical sense. In part, too, Latinos themselves bridle at attempts to corral them on to either side of the binary divide, particularly the black side. Linda Chavez, president of the Center for Equal Opportunity and author of *Out of the Barrio* (1991) is quick to underline the differences between Latino- and African-Americans, arguing haughtily that, 'Most native-born Hispanics have leapt over blacks in achievement . . . [and] within one or two generations living in the United States, the great majority of Hispanics are integrated into the social and economic mainstream'.[52]

In fact Chavez's efforts to distance Hispanics from African-

Americans, to position Hispanics within the social and economic mainstream, ends up reifying this binary mode of thought or at least implicitly suggesting that what happens when Hispanics arrive and settle in the United States is that they somehow cross this divide and march triumphantly into the promised land of whiteness. Smith and Feagin make a similar but also diametrically opposed point; namely that while Hispanics and other newcomers to the United States have often been 'able to negotiate a higher status for themselves entailing less discrimination than that faced by African-Americans', higher has not meant equal – 'for equal political and economic citizenship . . . has not yet been effectively won by any groups of color'.[53] Furthermore the post-1960s' tendency to marshal previously disparate ethnic or national groups (Cuban, Puerto Rican, Mexican etc.) into the homogeneous categories of 'Latino' or 'Hispanic' suggests both the indeterminate and also impervious nature of racial divisions in America. As David Theo Goldberg argues, the category 'Latino' or 'Hispanic' problematises certain prevailing assumptions about racial formation in so far as it becomes 'not so much a third race . . . black and white melding into brown, as an evidencing that race is politically fabricated and contested'.[54] To this end, 'the 'Hispanic' is recognised by the ethno-racial technology of the census as white, but the nervous insecurity of this recognition is reflected in the qualifications about when to count 'Mexicans' or 'Hispanics' as 'black'.[55]

Anxieties over how to identify oneself, and the dynamic tensions between being able to define oneself and being defined by others, are played out in Alex Abella's *The Killing of the Saints* (1992), featuring Cuban-American court-appointed investigator Charlie Morell, and Michael Nava's *Goldenboy* (1989), *How Town* (1991) and *The Hidden Law* (1992), featuring Mexican-American lawyer and surrogate detective, Henry Rios. Moving freely but also awkwardly between 'centre' and 'margins', both in a physical sense, as their investigations transport them between the *barrios* of east Los Angeles and cocktail parties of west Los Angeles, and in a cultural sense, as their ancestry and physiology marks them as 'different' from whites who occupy most of the positions of power and privilege and blacks who do not, Morell and Rios cut across but also run up against traditional hierarchical designations.

In doing so, of course, they recall Raymond Chandler's prototype detective, Phillip Marlowe, who also trod an uneasy path between the 'centre' he unwillingly belonged to and the anonymity of the 'margins' he preferred, but their ability to do likewise, to choose, in a sense, is limited by a schizophrenic tendency on the part of the majority white culture to identify them as insiders and outsiders, often simultaneously.

Moreover, while the latent anxieties in Chandler's fiction as a result of Marlowe's conflicted status and ambitions were usually reconciled, albeit problematically, at the end of each narrative, Abella's *The Killing of the Saints* in particular opens up and exploit the tensions produced by Morrell's fractured identity as insider and outsider, in order to undermine if not explode one of the basic cornerstones of the genre; the retrieval of knowledge or the ability of the detective, and reader, to piece together the fragments he or she come across in order to arrive at a rationally deduced 'answer' which might not punish the 'guilty' and exculpate the 'innocent' but which at least explains what has happened.

The generic ruptures are prefigured in the first pages of the novel when two Cuban immigrants walk into a jewellers in downtown Los Angeles, armed with a .357 Magnum, .45 Colt automatic, sawn-off Browning shotgun with retractable butt, black Sten machine pistol, gray Uzi sub-machine gun, six sticks of dynamite and two grenades, and apparently possessed by Oggun, 'the mighty warrior of the [Afro-Cuban] *santeria* religion',[56] proceed to murder six people, store employees and customers, during the course of a botched robbery attempt which is eventually foiled by battalions of armed police. The sheer scale of the carnage is unprecedented, even by Los Angeles' own violent standards, but even more disruptive, at least in generic terms, is the presence of *santeria* as a complicating factor in the subsequent investigation and trial. Hired by one of the defendants, Ramon Valdez, to be his legal representative, because of his own Cuban ancestry, Charlie Morell's official function is to gather information that could help to exonerate his client. Unofficially, as a detective defined in terms of his own private sense of justice, his job is to determine for himself, and by implication the reader, exactly what has happened and more significantly, who or what is to blame – and in the spirit of his generic antecedents, take action to rectify any perceived 'injustices'.

Yet throughout Morell's investigation, the politics of race and ethnicity, and his own ambivalence about his Cuban heritage and how this heritage manifests itself in lived experience, pollutes his judgement and renders him unable to perform this function. On the surface the case against his client, Ramon Valdez, is convincing. Valdez has been apprehended at the scene of the crime and there are witnesses to confirm his culpability in the jewellery store massacre. As a 'Marielito'[57] Cuban with a lengthy prison record, moreover, Valdez's fearsome reputation and penchant for violence, is confirmed by Morell's subsequent investigations when he is told that Valdez slit another man's throat in an argument. Still, this alone fails to guarantee his guilt and as Morell's investigation continues, another portrait of Valdez begins to emerge; that of an intelligent, cultured, well-educated man whose violent tendencies have been fuelled by a long history of racially motivated rejection and discrimination. His story is a distopic inversion of Horatio Alger's heroic tales of immigrant success. As a dark-skinned Cuban, Valdez is frustrated even by his plans to find menial work. His position as a salesman peddling kitchen appliances to South American housewives is terminated because his boss decides that his 'black' skin could scare off potential buyers. He is rejected by a number of Cuban entrepreneurs because of his status as a 'Marielito' and by an African-American businessman because he is 'too Hispanic', and in the end has to support himself by selling marijuana, a situation which sends him into a downward cycle of drug-taking and dependency which culminates in his discovery of *santeria* and his alleged transformation into violent sadist.

Emerging from Morell's fraught investigations into his client's past is a sophisticated picture of racial–ethnic relations in which the cheerful optimism of those like Ollin, a light-skinned Cuban-American television presenter, who declares, 'people of all colors and origins get to rise and prosper here' (p. 128) collides head-on with the bleak pessimism of those like Valdez whose apocalyptic musings have been shaped and informed by lived experience of race and class-based discrimination. In fact Valdez's response to Ollin's patriotic rhetoric is persuasive:

> You're white, educated, from the middle class. You have no idea what it's like to be brown or black and be treated like an idiot just because you are not fluent in the language . . . You don't know how it feels to be afraid of Immigration all the time, to be lost in a place where all you can hope is forty dollars a day if you can find the work. You don't know how it feels to know that you're not even second class, you're third class, that even American blacks are better than you. (p. 128)

On the one hand, Valdez's appears to conceive of 'race' and 'ethnicity' as diverging categories, at least in so far as he distinguishes himself, as a dark-skinned Cuban, from 'American blacks' and elsewhere in the novel differences between immigrants from Cuba and Mexico – 'Castro's children and the sons of Montezuma' (p. 13) – are emphasised. On the other hand, 'race' and 'ethnicity' are conceived of as overlapping categories, at least in so far as Valdez's views confirm the presence of a racial-ethnic cleavage where an albeit fluid, diverse white population (or those permitted to enjoy the privileges of whiteness) is set against an albeit fluid, diverse non-white population whose physiology marks them as 'different' (or different from a white European 'norm').

Morell's experiences in the United States both confirm and undermine the existence of such a cleavage. In many ways he is a model

American citizen, someone who has chosen to shed his Cuban ancestry (and been allowed to do so) on his way to becoming a Porsche-driving lawyer with a degree from an Ivy League college. As a light-skinned Cuban who is able to 'pass' as white, discrimination has not prevented him from achieving wealth and status, but he is not blind to the prejudices that shape and inform social relations in his adopted home. In fact his awareness of the scope and extent of racial-ethnic divisions and his concerns that Los Angeles might 'by some twist of fate [have] slipped into a big Johannesburg' (p. 149) mean that he is less quick to condemn Valdez's actions than figures from the white establishment. His ambivalence towards Valdez's culpability is underscored by an inability to dismiss, as his colleagues do, a key tenet of his client's defence; diminished responsibility on the grounds that he was acting under the influence of *santeria*. To blue-blooded Anglos like Clay Smith III, *santeria* is merely 'voodoo shit' but Morell is more circumspect, describing it as a 'mystery cult that claims millions of followers and powers beyond description' (p. 32). But circumspection dissolves into confusion and doubt and while Morell attempts to explode his client's posturing as hollow and without foundation, incidents which appear to have no rational explanation compel him to think otherwise. Morell can expose some of these, like the supposed 're-appearance' his late father, as cynical tricks played on him by his client in order to elicit his sympathy and support, but others elide and problematise notions of rational logic. So when a thunderbolt strikes the courtroom just as the trial is reaching its climax and sweeps Valdez's co-conspirator, Ramon Pimienta, out of the room in a dancing ball of fire 'never to be seen again' (p. 290), it is perhaps not surprising that Valdez himself is eventually found not guilty.

Abella skilfully maps the familiar tropes of hard-boiled crime fiction on to a perhaps more unfamiliar racial-ethnic landscape where the order and rationality upon which the former depends are fatally undercut by eruptions of spiritual excess. Santeria, here, is emblematic of a 'Cubanness' that Morell can neither fully embrace nor reject and caught between the Cuban world of his father and ancestry and the WASP-dominated American culture he has aspired to join, he finds himself drifting, unsure of who he is. As I have argued throughout the book, the identity of the (white) hard-boiled detective, despite assertions to the contrary, has never been fixed or secure but as we have seen, this liminality is compounded by the competing claims placed on the detective not just by his or her allegiance to state-sponsored and alternative notions of 'justice' but also by the inevitable 'colouring' of both terms along particular racial-ethic lines. Following Valdez's acquittal, Morell stumbles across evidence pointing towards his guilt and enraged by the cynical manner in which his clients has manipulated not just him but the entire legal system, he confronts him and when Valdez tries to escape, Morell attacks him and Valdez falls to his death. Justice is therefore served. Or is it? For however much Valdez's words and action expose him as a charlatan, one cannot dismiss his justifications out of hand, neither the ones relating to the effects of racial-ethnic discrimination nor the influence of *santeria*. Moreover while it may be tempting to conceive of Morell's final intervention in palliative or even heroic terms – a victory for justice – one could equally argue that his vigilante assault on Valdez is as much the product of rage, resentment and bitterness at his own inadequacies and failings as a detective.

In deliciously radical fashion, the trajectory or movement of Abella's narrative is not, to use Porter's reductive terms, one of 'perceptual de-familiarization' to 're-familiarization'[58] but rather one where an overall core of doubt remains. In the end, we do not know whether Valdez was possessed or not, nor what caused the disturbance in the courtroom and the earthquake which also disrupted the trial, nor even what happened to Valdez's partner Jose Pimienta after his 'disappearance' during the trial. Significantly 'not- knowing' in a generic context (i.e. not knowing why Valdez and Pimienta did what they did) becomes 'not-knowing' in a personal context (i.e. not knowing who you are). From apparently secure moorings at the start of the novel as a middle-class lawyer able to pass as white, Morell is soon forced to reassess the legitimacy of the identity he has chosen for himself. Identifications based on race-ethnicity, class, gender and sexuality project him like a pinball from 'centre' to 'margins' and in doing so undermine the fixity of this relationship and shatter the wholeness of his projected identity. At once an insider and outsider, Morell both rejects his Cuban ancestry, at least in so far as it connects him with poor dark-skinned 'Marielitos' like Valdez and embraces it because only by knowing where he has come from can he hope to know who he is – as he later acknowledges, while watching immigrant families from Central America picnicking in a local park, 'I wanted to know about these people and by doing so to come to know myself as well, the pieces of myself that were scattered among these Caribbean exiles like arms of a starfish' (p. 74).

Furthermore, while he might initially want to identify himself as white, and though he might drive a fancy car and move freely around the city cocooned by the privileges of class and skin colour, the invisible line that connects him to people like Clay Smith III and distinguishes him from people like Ramon Valdez is not nearly as secure as he imagines. At one of Smith's cocktail parties, Morell is made aware that his status is not a right but a privilege, something bestowed on him by others rather than earned by his own actions. After an argument between Morell and the host has turned ugly, Smith rounds on his former friend and spits, 'You fucking Cubans are all the same' (p. 226), and in doing so, confirms not just the existence but also the depth of exactly the kind of racial-ethnic schism which, as immigrant 'success' stories, Morell and other Cuban-Americans had once sought to dismiss as fiction.

Brief mention should also be made of Michael Nava's intriguing series of crime novels featuring Henry Rios, a lawyer of Mexican extraction, also located in Los Angeles. Arguably the best of these is *The Hidden Law*, in which Rios is called upon to investigate the death of a Chicano senator and in doing so opens up tensions and sometimes violent conflicts not just within the Latino community but also among different factions of Mexican immigrants. All, too, are interesting from the viewpoint of Rios' continuing struggle to assert his homosexuality in the face of hostility from both inside and outside his own neighbourhood, community and family. In some ways, Rios is too good to be true, someone whose humour, integrity and moral virtuosity remains in tact despite the vitriolic discrimination he faces and the often inhumane barbarity he is witness to as a legal defendant. Of course whether his homosexuality qualifies him as 'too good to be true' depends, to some extent, on one's point of view, but within the context of the novels, it functions to further disrupt the kind of cohesive group identity that politicians like the murdered Agustin Pena are keen to talk up, if only for reasons of personal advancement.

Rios lives, on and off, with Josh, an Anglo who is HIV-positive and, during *The Hidden Law*, finds his condition worsens. Apart from giving the books an added human dimension, their relationship, between a Chicano and white man, offends not just homophobics and whites but also Chicano 'activists' like college lecturer Tommy Ochoa, who in a veiled reference to his partner and career, accuses Rios of 'writing off [his] heritage'.[59] Still, Ochoa's remarks are misguided because they fail to acknowledge the extent to which diversity and also disunity is an inevitable feature of the Mexican-American community in Los Angeles – rich against poor, middle class against working class, straight against gay, the recently arrived against the long established. In Ochoa's eyes, Rios has sold out his ancestry in order to embrace the fruits (excuse the pun) of the United States, but as we learn in *The Hidden Law* he is simply trying to come to terms with the legacy of an alcoholic, abusive father. Furthermore, Henry comes to understand his father's action not simply in individual terms but rather as part of a larger cultural phenomenon of Chicano patriarchs venting their fury at their perceived marginalisation at the hands of white bosses on their wives and children.[60] In fact this is where the ambitions of Nava's novel Abella's *The Killing of the Saints* overlap because just when it appears that the cultural terrain has become so fragmented that it is practically unreadable, one is greeted by insights that point both to the existence and significance of what Dyson calls an 'enabling solidarity' – the idea in *The Hidden Law* that connections exist between Chicanos if only on the grounds that patterns of behaviour and cultural norms are replicated over generations – and the very real presence of a system built upon relations of racial-ethnic domination and subordination whose underlying logic has always, and continues, to privilege those of white European descent.

Colliding Worlds and the Native American Search for Order: Tony Hillerman, Carol laFavor

The increasingly fraught collision between the bloated, rotten civilisation transported to the New World from Europe and the spiritually inclined, apparently harmonious one descended from the various Native American tribes already settled through the American continent is a characteristic feature of the work of Tony Hillerman and Carol laFavor. If the crime and violence that Hillerman's two tribal police detectives, Joe Leaphorn and Jim Chee, are called upon to investigate emanate from the self-serving, neo-colonial ambitions of white businessmen, mafiosi, politicians and even cultural anthropologists, then the manner in which these ruptures are dealt with owes as much to a Navajo-derived need to return the world to a state of harmony or 'hozhzo' as to either the ratiocinative methods of traditional detectives or the action-orientated approach of their hard-boiled cousins. Part of the Slow Talking clan and a trained shaman, Chee's outlook as a tribal police officer owes much to his belief and indeed participation in Navajo traditions, rituals and practices. Able to see that all living matter has two forms – 'the form of the yei and . . . the outer form we see'[61] Chee's vision affords him an advantage over white police detectives who, particularly in their dealings with other Native Americans, tend to assume guilt where it does not exist. Hillerman's other detective, Joe Leaphorn is more sceptical and as an archetypal rationalist rejects traditional Navajo witchcraft beliefs, but his investigative methodology, too, is shaped and informed by his cultural heritage. 'He used [a map of Indian land] in his endless hunt for patterns, sequences, order', Hillerman writes in *Coyote Waits*, 'something that would bring a semblance of Navajo hozhzo to the chaos of crime and violence' (p. 150).

This particular frame of reference opens up Hillerman's crime fiction to a number of generically subversive possibilities, not least the problematisation of rational thought as the touchstone of investigative practice. Disappointingly, though, Hillerman tends to close off such possibilities, at least in so far as incidents and potential transgressions which appear to have no rational basis are usually revealed to be attempts by aspiring white conspirators to conceal their culpability by exploiting particular Navajo mythologies. Hence the death of a tribal policeman who has strayed into an area haunted by witches in *Coyote Waits* is traced back to the desperate actions of an antiquities collector or the apparent violence wrought on the Reservation's population by a Navajo wolf in *The Blessing Way* ultimately implicates a crew of mafiosi who are using the Reservation's proximity to a US military base to illegally procure weapons. Furthermore his detectives' search for harmony or 'hozhzo' tends to function as a more general palliative, particularly where relations between the Navajo and white population are concerned. Which is not to suggest that Hillerman entirely avoids exploring the impact of white cultural imperialism or the legacy of state-sanctioned genocide, just that these issues never become central to his narratives or their resolution. Unlike Welch's *The Death of Jim Loney* (1988) where the damaging effects of living in ghetto-like isolation and adopting white-derived demeaning identities are openly acknowledged, or James Lee Burke's *Black Cherry Blues* (1989) where institutional rather than individual malpractice lies at the heart of an attempt to steal mineral extraction rights from Montana's Native Americans, Hillerman's tendency to focus on the 'micro' rather than the 'macro' ends up obfuscating the state-sanctioned, racially determined foundations to social, political and economic inequalities.

Carol laFavor is certainly more vigorous about exposing the complicity of state-sanctioned institutions in damaging and subjugating the Objibwa population on the Red Earth Reservation in northern Minnesota. Her second novel, *Evil Dead Center* (1997), features a conspiracy between the Red Earth Social Service agency and a local politician-cum-foster father to forcibly procure Ojibwa children to appear in crudely made pornographic films. Indeed this particular crime, for laFavor, is part of a much larger problem whereby Native American children, despite the apparent protections offered by the Indian Child Welfare Act, are forcibly removed from their Reservation homes on spurious grounds and relocated with white families, thereby separating them from their families and culture and inflicting on them untold damage. laFavor's idyllic portrait of family life, at least that of her Ojibwa protagonist Renee LaRoche, is a utopian antidote to this particular example of white cultural imperialism. LaRoche, a lesbian, lives in comfortable harmony on the Reservation with her Anglo partner Samantha and her daughter Jenny, and close by her aunt and grandmother, whose wisdom and spiritual knowledge attests to important cultural differences between her own Ojibwa culture and that of the white-dominated Minnesotan population. As she informs LaRoche, 'They came to this land and forget their original instructions. We haven't forgotten. The spirits, who live in every grove of trees, every turn in the river, every lakeshore of the north country, whisper to us not to forget'.[62]

Like Hillerman, laFavor avoids oversimplifying divisions, so that a 'good' Native American population is locked into inexorable conflict with a 'bad' white one. Her first novel, *Along the Journey River* (1996), exposes the corrupt practices of tribal chief Jed Morriseau, while *Evil Dead Center* implicates a number of Ojibwa men in the pornography ring. Like Hillerman, too, laFavor skilfully opens up tensions within the tribe itself. LaRoche is not an officially sanctioned officer with the tribal police, in part because her previous involvement in the politically radical American Indian Movement has made her distrustful of institutional agencies. The fact that LaRoche works, even on an informal basis, for the tribal police, however, potentially alienates her from former partners like Caroline Beltrain, an activist with the Movement being sought by the tribal police and FBI in connection with the bombing of a government building. LaRoche works closely with head of the tribal police, Bulieau Hobey, but in trusting him so much risks her relationship with Beltrain. Moreover as a lesbian, she is only too aware of the fascist implications of her official role and seeks both to emphasise her agency as a freelance, someone 'trying to save the world' (p. 54), and acknowledge the difficulties of having to keep a 'foot in each world' (p. 25).

laFavor may open up these tensions but she also closes them off so ruthlessly that *Evil Dead Center* at least mutates into a less interesting, more straightforward crime novel. Hobey, the model patriarch, and Beltrain, the political activist, become friends, and to sweeten the pill, Hobey persuades the FBI to drop their charges against her. Beltrain and LaRoche remain friends, despite initial tensions, and between them expose and capture Floyd Neuterbide, the pornography ringleader whose guilt is prefigured by the not-so-subtle references to framed photographs of Rush Limbaugh and Ronald Reagan on his wall. Order, or in Navajo-speak 'hozhzo', is restored and one ends up with the impression that LaRoche has sacrificed nothing and yet gained everything by her involvement in the investigative process. One also senses that whatever happened to her, she would be able to pick herself up off the floor, dust herself off and start afresh, not unaffected but undamaged by what she has seen and done.

'Is this my assimilation, so many years in the making?': Chang-Rae Lee's Native Speaker

It would be fair to say that much of this book has been characterised by the meeting and uneasy conflation of two not altogether seamless methodological styles. On the one hand, its logic has been underwritten by an awareness, not always successfully articulated, of the multiplicity of meanings, an awareness that the critic or for that matter the author are not the sole guarantor of meaning, that meanings can also be constructed at the level of readership and that as a result, to put it bluntly, one person's nirvana can be another's purgatory. On the other hand, however, it would be a dishonest critic who failed to acknowledge that some books, some texts, some cultural artifacts are not necessarily 'better' than others – for such a word is too vague or too satiated with subjective connotations – but are certainly more innovative, challenging and therefore interesting than others. Who could deny, after all, that they do not have a sneaking preference for, in this case, crime novels that do not merely meet and satisfy their expectations but challenge them, that compel them though aesthetic or political or thematic innovation make them look at the genre and the world in fresh, illuminating ways? So to quote Sinatra, as we face the final curtain, it is perhaps appropriate or fitting to end the book by focusing on Chang-Rae Lee's *Native Speaker* (1995) and in a flourish of daring academic panache, stepping off the fence, if only for a moment, to state right at the outset that Lee's spectacularly innovative, startlingly fresh novel does all of this and more.

It is perhaps also appropriate to re-ask a question posed right at the start of the book; namely, to what extent do crime novels, as part of that larger beast known collectively as popular culture, simply reaffirm existing, culturally dominant ways of looking at and thinking about the world? Because while one such way is undoubtedly satiated in the logic of white, male, heterosexual bias, it would perhaps be fair to say that an alternative and increasingly 'dominant' way of conceiving of and understanding the world, at least within the academy, is through the tropes of race, ethnicity, gender and class. To this end, loci of power are both easy and less to identify, and while relations of domination and subordination do end up privileging certain groups and individuals at the expense of others, they are never fixed or unchanging. The question that we perhaps need to pose, then, at least in relation to the contemporary American crime novel, is not simply whether or how particular examples 're-affirm existing, culturally dominant ways of looking at and thinking about the world' but rather how and to what extent particular crime novelists (whatever their race, ethnicity, class or gender) exploit the complexities and ambiguities of the form to challenge or problematise both a residual white, male, heterosexual elitism and an emerging doctrine of 'political correctness' whereby the 'good' white, male, heterosexual detective is merely replaced by the 'good' non-white, female, gay detective.

The question of character is crucial. A type of crime fiction from Chandler through to Sara Parestsky and arguably writers like Carol laFavor and Michael Nava has been predicated on the implicit assumption that the essentially 'good' character of the detective can if not overcome then at least counterbalance the moral emptiness and degeneracy inherent in contemporary American society, and emerge at the end of each novel not exactly unscathed but fundamentally unaltered by what he or she has seen and done. Comparing this particular variant of the hard-boiled detective with Jake Barnes, the irrevocably 'damaged' protagonist of Ernest Hemingway's *The Sun* Also Rises, John G. Cawelti argues:

> In the end the hard-boiled detective story represents an escape from the naturalistic consciousness of determinism and meaningless death . . . Jake Barnes's insight and integrity, his freedom and false values, were forced upon him by his wound. He is as much a victim of the world as voluntary rebel. The hard-boiled detective has a few scratches, but no deep wounds spoil his function as fantasy hero. He is the man who has been able to say the hell with it, and yet to retain the world's most important benefits – self-esteem, popularity and respect.[63]

True enough, maybe, in relation to figures like Chandler's Phillip Marlowe, but could one apply this assessment to all hard-boiled detectives? To Dashiell Hammett's the Continental Op or Jim Thompson's Lou Ford? Because it is a fundamental assumption of this book that, perhaps evolving out of Hammett or Thompson's creations, there has been a growing interest in the type of crime fiction in which the detective or surrogate cannot simply brush off his or her 'few scratches' and unproblematically retain his or her 'self-esteem, popularity and respect'. Rather, he or she finds that the tensions caused by seeking to retain a degree of agency and yet having to operate within a larger system with usually antithetical ambitions, and the very nature of having to deal with crime, not merely 'crime' as a generic convention or plot device but as a tangible, messy, disruptive entity or force, seeing and having to cope with its effects, end up inflicting real damage – actual and psychological. Of course there are variations of this particular idea or model and it would be wrong to suggest that, say, Ellroy's protagonists are affected or damaged in the same way or even to the same extent as Himes' Coffin Ed and Grave Digger. Much of the book, to this end, has considered the different ways in which crime writers have transposed the kind of already problematised paradigm described above on to the contested, fractured terrain of cultural 'difference'; how being African-American or Chicano or female or working class or gay or a mixture of all these, and having to enforce or at least work towards restoring a *status quo* implicitly founded upon one's subordination, can have distressing consequences. Still, if a preference has been shown, it has been shown towards the kind of crime novel which foregrounds and explores these consequences – novels like Lee's *Native Speaker* whereby the figure of the detective and the conventions of the genre are transformed, brought into fresh, original configurations that acknowledge, implicitly or otherwise, the confusing, ambiguous and corrosive elements of crime and detection.

Set in contemporary New York City, *Native Speaker* tells the story of Henry Park, a second-generation Korean immigrant who is not exactly a detective but an undercover operative working for a covert surveillance agency that collects information for clients like multinational corporations or foreign governments on individuals working against their vested interests, 'Typically the subject was a well-to-do immigrant supporting some potential insurgency in his old land, or else funding a fledgling trade union or radical student organisation'.[64] Despite a claim to neutrality that recalls Sam Spade's legendary snarl at the end of Hammett's *The Maltese Falcon* – so that Spade's 'I stick my neck out for no one', becomes Park's 'We pledged allegiance to no government' (p. 15) – it is almost impossible, for the reader and later for Park himself, not to see the fingerprints of a loosely connected, albeit fractured power elite peppered all over the directives that the investigators receive via Dennis Hoagland, the agency's faceless but ruthless dispatcher-cum-boss.

Peter Messent's claim that 'the police procedural . . . seems to be supplanting the private-eye novel as "realistic" crime fiction . . . [whereby] a fantasy of extra-systemic freedom and authenticity gives way to a more problematic vision of individual detectives operating through systemic procedures'[65] is, in part, borne out by the trajectory of this book and its interest in the tensions produced by the uneasy conflation of individual agency and institutional authority. *Native Speaker* is not a police procedural, as such, but in so far as Lee characterises Park as 'amiable' and with liberal sympathies, and yet simultaneously implicates him in the hegemonic ambitions of an unseen power elite, he seems to be only too aware of the dramatic possibilities implicit in this conflation. Any thoughts that Hoagland's organisation, replete with its impressively multi-ethnic collection of investigators, is a billboard poster for a celebratory multiculturalism are rendered untenable by the revelation that Koreans or Japanese or Filipinos are preferred simply because they stand a better chance of being able to elicit information from their compatriots. Ethnic bonding is but a strategic ruse, as Park discovers soon after his induction. Watching another investigator, Pete Ichibata, 'take apart' a Chinese dissident responsible for organising anti-Beijing protests outside the UN, Park acknowledges being 'thrilled' by the success of their mission – in detective speak, a job well done – but with some unease, seems dimly aware that their 'success' has, in effect, 'doomed' the student's girlfriend back home in China. As another agent surmises, 'A bad thing can happen in the world. We do what we're paid for and then who can tell what it means?' (p. 41).

Park shields his wife, Lelia, and also himself, from the more unpleasant aspects of his job by conceiving of it in professional, neutral terms. Traversing the margins of preferred anonymity and heeding his boss' advice to 'just stay in the background . . . [be] unapparent and flat' (p. 40), Park's coolly methodical approach manifests itself most visibly in the apparently objective style of his report writing. 'I am to be a clean writer, of the most reasonable eye, and present the subject in question like some sentient machine of transcription. I will know nothing of the craft of argument or narrative or drama. Nothing of beauty or art' (p. 189). Still, Park's ability to remain so detached is tested and found wanting, first of all in his dealings with a Filipino psychologist who manages to probe his implacable surface to reveal the schizophrenic nature of his ambitions and sympathies, and then with a Korean-American politician and aspiring Mayoral candidate, John Kwang. Having joined Kwang's grass-roots organisation and taken his place alongside legions of not just Korean but also Japanese, Indian, Vietnamese, Haitian, Colombian and Nigerian volunteers, Park finds it increasingly difficult to dispatch potentially incriminating reports to his boss not least because he can see the value in Kwang's work and comes to genuinely like and respect him.

The depth and extent of his conflicted loyalties, to Kwang and his function as 'detective' (or at least detached observer), slowly and silently tear him apart, shattering his pretence of objective detachment and forcing him into the damaging position whereby he must betray people who have come to trust and depend on him, and in doing so, betray himself. Fearing what Hoagland might do should he quit the organisation in mid-assignment, Park reluctantly hands him a list featuring the names of recently arrived immigrants who have contributed to a 'ggbh' or non-profit-making money club set up by Kwang in order to redistribute funds to members in greatest need. The list is then passed on to the Immigration and Naturalization Service who identify three dozen families on it as illegals, thereby condemning them to the fate of deportation and ruining Kwang's political ambitions in the process. 'My ugly immigrant's truth', as Park later acknowledges, 'is that I have exploited my own and those others who can be exploited. This forever is my burden to bear . . . Here is my American education' (p. 297).

For this failure, this damage, is an inevitable consequence not just of his conflicted status as a detective but also as an immigrant, as 'Korean' and 'American'. Indeed, throughout the novel, Lee skilfully brings these two subjects – immigrant and detective – and their attendant cultural baggage into fresh, illuminating configurations, both in order to explore the problematic nature of identity and undermine the apparently natural association between whiteness and detection. On the one hand, whereas folklore and tradition would have us believe that the most visible and effective detectives were always white, Hoagland, Park's boss, is adamant that their very visibility renders them unsuitable to do the job:

> He bemoaned the fact that Americans generally made the worst spies. Mostly he meant whites. Even with methodical training they were inclined to run off at the mouth, make unnecessary displays of themselves . . . They felt this subcutaneous aching to let everyone know they were a spook, they couldn't help it, it was like some charge or vanity of the culture. (p. 161)

Yet the very fact that non-whites are suitable, at least according to Hoagland, on the grounds on their invisibility, is not for Park at least a cause for celebration. Stalking the anonymous margins has conspired to rob Park of his sense of self, who he is. Lelia, his wife, is not even sure, and as their marriage begins to crumble, admits, 'I realised one day that I didn't know the first thing about what was going on inside your head' (p. 117). Being a detective and being an immigrant, to this extent, are joined because to succeed as either requires sacrifice – sacrificing one's 'vanity' in order to achieve invisibility and sacrificing one's immigrant identity in order to blend into the mainstream. 'Success' is thus bitter-sweet and Park's acknowledgement of his effectiveness as an investigator and his ability to fit in – 'It appears I can go anywhere I wish' – is immediately followed by the achingly poignant rhetoric question, 'Is this my assimilation, so many years in the making? Is this the long-sought sweetness?' (p. 188).

This is perhaps why his connection to Kwang runs so deep, because Kwang offers him a chance to reassess himself in the light of a broader socio-political project intent not just on emphasising the 'positive' aspects of Korean ancestry and culture but also on forging links between Korean immigrants and those from Southeast Asia, India, China and

Japan, Central America and the Caribbean. Park's perception of Kwang, initially, is that of a skilful, 'consummate' politician, a barbed compliment that suggests slipperiness, manipulation and superficiality, and while this is an impression that he never quite manages to let go of, he is forced through what he sees and hears (as a detective but increasingly as a convert) to reassess its basic negative slant.

At the heart of Kwang's project appears to be not a cynical ploy to curry favour with minority groups in order to further his own political standing but a genuine desire to bind people from different cultures and ethnic-racial groups together in his own image of family and community – an image which in its most elemental version had 'nothing to do with blood' (p. 136). As Park later acknowledges, 'I know he never sought to be an ethnic politician. He didn't want them to vote for him solely because he was colored or Asian. He knew he'd never win anything that way. There aren't enough of you' (p. 302). Cast into a political system still dominated by an 'old syntax', in terms that barely acknowledge the extent of social and cultural transformation ushered in by successive waves of 'new' immigrants from Asia and Latin America, Kwang's ambitions are best articulated in the speech he makes to an audience of disgruntled blacks, Hispanics and Koreans, responding to the growing boycott by black customers of Korean-owned grocery stores following a series of incendiary encounters. 'That is not a black problem or a brown and yellow problem, that is not a problem of our peoples, that is not even ultimately a problem of mistrust or our ignorance', he tells the crowd, 'Let us think it is the problem of a self-hate . . . The problem is our acceptance of what we loathe and fear in ourselves' (pp. 140–1). In other words, as Charles Taylor argues, the issue of 'misrecognition', of being misrecognised by others and then transforming that distorted image into self-image, is crucial,[66] even or rather particularly if that distorted image is not exactly demeaning. 'When others construct you favorably, it's easy to let them keep at it, even if they start going off in ways that aren't immediately comfortable or right', Kwang tells Park, 'This is the challenge for us Asians in America' (p. 180).

Kwang's response to this problem is two-fold. He is quick to emphasise areas of common interest between blacks and Koreans – that 'what we have in common, the sadness and pain and injustice, will always be stronger than our differences' (p. 142) – but within a broader context which acknowledges how distinctive social and cultural forces have shaped their experiences (and relative 'successes' or 'failures') differently. Yet growing out of this concern over misrecognition, Kwang also argues that what needs to be tackled, at least in the public sphere is a prevailing (white) fear of difference and how this fear is seized upon and magnified by politicians and the media in order to further their own nativist agendas. As he remarks:

But the more racial strife they can report, the more the public questions what good any of this diversity brings. The underlying sense of what's presented these days is that this country has difference that ails rather than strengthens and enriches. You can see what can happen from this, how the public may begin viewing anything outside mainstream experience and culture to be threatening or dangerous. (p. 256)

It is here, finally, that the form and content of *Native Speaker* come together – and beautifully. Formally, Lee interprets the generic structure of the crime novel in its most radical configuration, to position his detective both as self-determining individualist and subjugated, state-sponsored henchman, and to open up the subsequent tension in order to both problematise the idea of the detective as guarantor of knowledge and meaning, and reinforce the damaging, corrosive impact of his or her involvement in a situation whose full implications only become apparent during the course of the investigation. Thematically, this revelation is so powerfully realised because Park's betrayal of Kwang (by giving up the names on Kwang's 'money-club' list to Hoagland and the INS) not only shatters any remaining doubts over his agency or lack of, but also induces a media-frenzy of 'negative' coverage for Kwang and thus brings about exactly what Kwang, and latterly Park too, have struggled so valiantly to stem; fear of difference influencing the political agenda and impacting upon the ability of non-white immigrants to define themselves. Success as a detective equals cultural annihilation as an immigrant. A bitter pill to swallow. But Lee cleverly sweetens it in the novel's concluding chapter without recourse to sentimentality or subterfuge. Because Park leaves the organisation and rescues his marriage, choosing instead to help Lelia, his wife, with the language classes she gives to non-English speaking children, and thus transforming himself from a 'false speaker of language' (p. 5) at the start of the novel, at least in so far as he cannot recognise what is distinctive about himself, voice and ancestry, into someone who is able to appreciate and even celebrate the diversity implicit in the visual and cultural landscape of New York City and in the richly evocative languages of Lelia's pupils. Thus *Native Speaker* concludes, '[Lelia] calls out each one as best she can, taking care of every last pitch and accent, and I hear her speaking a dozen lovely and native languages, calling all the difficult names of who we are' (p. 324).

Conclusions: Towards a Multicultural America?

Chang-Rae Lee's *Native Speaker* brings into focus what has always been a significant feature of American life; the sharp dichotomy between a nominal acceptance of diversity in all its guises – America, after all, has traditionally prided itself on its status as a 'nation of immigrants' – and a virulent anxiety that diversity begets fragmentation and dilutes the distinctive character of the nation, or at least the nation as conceived in white, European imaginations. Such anxieties have always characterised American life and from time to time, act as catalyst for more widespread, sustained attacks, not just on blacks and other non-white communities but at various times on women, gays, lesbians, Jews and the working class. Lee suggests that the nature and depth of current racially conceived anti-immigrant sentiment does not bode well for America's future and one cannot help but feel that as public optimism about the benefits of living in a diverse, multicultural society continues to abate and Americans retreat further into their own ethnic and racial groups, less afraid to voice their resentments and fears, their guilt and anger, further unrest seems depressingly inevitable.

Yet Lee's vision, and that of other crime writers discussed in this book, notably Abella, Kellerman, Mosley, Sallis and Phillips, is not resolutely apocalyptic and draws back from the politicised posturing of neo-conservative doom-mongers like Arthur Schlesinger Jr who talk about the Balkanisation of America and gaze longingly back at a largely mythic American past where unity of purpose and indeed character prevailed. Nor, though, is their vision excessively upbeat, a Disney-style celebration of diversity that flattens out cultural difference and overlooks the fact that different individuals and groups have not always co-existed in conditions of harmony and mutual respect. Writing in what I have defined as a 'popular-unpopular' genre (one with 'popular' appeal at least in so far as the basic parameters of the genre are, in Klein's words, 'well-known, widely accepted and easily accessible',[67] but whose protagonist is often confused, conflicted, violent, unsympathetic, or selfish, whose conception of 'morality' and 'justice' is deeply problematic) these writers have not shied away from showing the often bitter, irreconcilable differences that exist between, and significantly also among, particular groups, or been afraid to explore the way in which social power and its consolidation in the hands of a few has twisted and damaged people's lives, even in the case of the detective who in previous incarnations might well have shrugged off such difficulties with a slug of bourbon and a shrug of the shoulders.

These detectives are unable to transcend their circumstances, the materiality of their lives, in the same way as their generic predecessors or at least more overtly heroic figures like Chander's Phillip Marlowe or Ross Macdonald's Lew Archer. Yet damage does not necessarily correspond with defeat, and knowledge about 'the way things are' with nihilism. Not entirely estranged from their populist roots, these figures are made from sterner stuff and seen through their eyes, the world they inhabit, America on the cusp of a new century, is neither a utopian nor distopian one. Relations of domination and subordination may well be a fact of life but they do not necessarily preclude negotiation, dialogue and interaction. The contours of identity are clearly visible and yet elusively fluid. The contemporary American crime novel may not be what bell hooks describes as 'radical postmodernist practice' or that which calls attention to the 'shared, sensibilities which cross the boundaries of class, gender, race' and which could 'be fertile ground for the construction of empathy'[68] because the revolutionary possibilities inherent in the detective's anti-establishment mindset are often blunted or closed off by their implication in the hegemonic ambitions of their paymasters or the dominant culture. Still, multicultural detectives and multicultural crime fictions offer some hope that new relations between and among groups can be forged; straight, white, male traditions are in the process of being reconstituted while emerging African-American, female, gay, lesbian, Latino and Asian voices threaten old hierarchies and converse with one another, suspicious but also hopeful. America, as Nancy Abelmann and John Lie assert in their book *Blue Dreams* (1995), is irredeemably multicultural, 'frustrating the efforts of European-American suburbanites, African-American nationalists, and Korean American ethnic purists alike to find a place of their own'.[69] Whether a consensus can be constructed that deals with these frustrations, one not based on hierarchical domination of black over white, male over female, straight over gay, European over non-European, remains to be seen but the various, not always uniform messages put forward by those American crime writers discussed in this volume seem to suggest that such a task is not entirely hopeless.

Notes

1. Kwame Anthony Appiah, 'Race', in Frank Lentricchia and Thomas McLaughlin (eds), *Critical Terms for Literary Study* (Chicago, IL and London: University of Chicago Press, 1987), p. 277.
2. Howard Wincant, 'Dictatorship, Democracy, and Difference: The Historical Construction of Racial Identity', in Michael Peter Smith and Joe R. Feagin (eds), *The Bubbling Cauldron: Race, Ethnicity and the Urban Crisis* (Minneapolis, MN: University of Minnesota Press, 1995), p. 31.
3. Arthur Schlesinger Jr, 'The Cult of Ethnicity, Good and Bad', Time Magazine, 8 July 1992, p. 52.
4. See Lawrence Fuchs, *The Ethnic Kaleidoscope: Race, Ethnicity and*

Civic Culture (Hanover, NH: University of New England Press, 1990).

5. Michael Peter Smith and Joe R. Feagin, 'Putting "Race" in Its Place', in Smith and Feagin (eds), *The Bubbling Cauldron: Race, Ethnicity and the Urban Crisis*, p. 6.

6. Alluding to the status of black Americans without explicitly naming them, Article I, Section 2 of the US Constitution declared, 'Representatives and direct taxes shall be apportioned among the several States which may be included within this Union, according to their respective number, *which shall be determined by adding to the whole number of free persons, including those bound to service for a term of years and excluding Indians not taxed, three-fifths of all other persons*'.

7. See Ian Haney-Lopez, *White by Law: The Legal Construction of Race* (New York: New York University Press, 1996); extracts reprinted in Jon Gjerde (ed.), *Major Problems in American Immigration and Ethnic History* (full details below).

8. See Ian Haney-Lopez, 'The Evolution of Legal Constructions of Whiteness', in Gjerde (ed.), *Major Problems in American Immigration and Ethnic History* (New York: Houghton Mifflin, 1998), p. 300.

9. Haney-Lopez, *Major Problems in American Immigration and Ethnic History*, p. 302.

10. 'Thind vs. United States: "The United States Supreme Court Clarifies the Meaning of 'White', 1923", in Gjerde, *Major Problems in American Immigration and Ethnic History*, p. 290.

11. Haney-Lopez, *Major Problems in American Immigration and Ethnic History*, p. 305.

12. 'Thind vs. United States', in Gjerde, *Major Problems in American Immigration and Ethnic History*, p. 290.

13. William Peterson, 'Concepts of Ethnicity', in Stephen Thernstrom (ed.), *The Harvard Encyclopedia of American Ethnic Groups* (Cambridge, MA: Harvard University Press, 1980), pp. 235–6.

14. See Werner Sollors, *Beyond Ethnicity: Consent and Descent in American Culture* (Oxford and New York: Oxford University Press, 1986), p. 36.

15. E. San Juan Jr, *Racial Formations/Critical Transformations: Articulations of Power in Ethnic and Racial Studies in the United States* (London and New Jersey: Humanities Press, 1992), p. 5. Also see Michael Omi and Howard Wincant, *Racial Formation in the United States: From the 1960s to the 1990s* (London and New York: Routledge, 1994).

16. Manning Marable, *Beyond Black and White: Transforming African-*

American Politics (London and New York: Verso, 1995), p. 124.

17. See Roger Rouse in Smith and Feagin, *The Bubbling Cauldron*, pp. 17–18.
18. Smith and Feagin, *The Bubbling Cauldron*, p. 23.
19. Marable, *Beyond Black and White*, p. 124
20. Cornel West, 'Introduction', in Michael Lerner and Cornel West, *Jews and Blacks: A Dialogue on Race, Religion and Culture in America* (New York: Plume, 1996), p. 2.
21. Ibid., p. 2.
22. David Theo Goldberg, *Racial Subjects: Writing on Race in America* (London and New York: Routledge, 1997), p. 130.
23. Goldberg, *Racial Subjects*, p. 132.
24. Mary C. Waters, *Ethnic Options: Choosing Identities in America* (Berkeley, CA: University of California Press, 1990), p. 157.
25. Michael Lerner in Michael Lerner and Cornel West, *Jews and Blacks: A Dialogue on Race, Religion and Culture in America*, p. 67.
26. Ibid., p. 67.
27. Even the use of names – American Jew or Jewish-American – is significant. David Theo Goldberg writes: 'Common usage speaks more readily in terms of "American Jews" than of "Jewish-Americans", revealing more like American Indians than . . . Italian-American . . . This suggests that Jewishness transcends Americanness, ethnic belonging subsumes national identity rather than vice versa', *Racial Subjects*, p. 138.
28. Leslie Fiedler, *Waiting for the End* (London: Jonathan Cape, 1965), p. 70.
29. *The Ritual Bath* (1986), *Sacred and Profane* (1987), *Milk and Honey* (1990), *Day of Atonement* (1991), *False Prophet* (1992), *Grievous Sin* (1993), *Sanctuary* (1994), *Justice* (1995), *Prayers for the Dead* (1996), *Serpent's Tooth* (1997) and *Jupiter's Bones* (1999).
30. Dennis Porter, *The Pursuit of Crime: Art and Ideology in Detective Fiction* (New Haven: Yale University Press, 1981), pp. 171–2.
31. Faye Kellerman, *Day of Atonement* (London: Headline, 1991), p. 250.
32. Faye Kellerman, *Serpent's Tooth* (London: Headline, 1997), p. 158.
33. Diana Arbin Ben-Merre, 'Murdering Traditional Assumptions: The Jewish-American Mystery', in Jerome H. Delameter and Ruth Prigozy (eds), *The Detective in Film, Fiction and Television* (Westport, CT: Greenwood, 1998), p. 63.
34. Ibid., p. 63.
35. Ibid., p. 65.
36. See Kinky Friedman, 'Musical Chairs', in *More Kinky Friedman* (London: Faber & Faber, 1993), p. 202.

37. Kinky Friedman, 'Frequent Flyer', in *More Kinky Friedman* (London: Faber & Faber, 1993), p. 100.

38. For example, in *Frequent Flyer* we are told how 'good German doctors would inject air, water, gasoline, or toxic chemicals into the veins of children' (p. 61).

39. Friedman, 'Frequent Flyer', p. 129.

40. *Marilyn the Wild* (1974), *Blues Eyes* (1975), *The Education of Patrick Silver* (1976), *Secret Isaac* (1978), *The Good Policeman* (1990) and *Maria's Girls* (1993).

41. Jerome Charyn, *The Education of Patrick Silver* (first published 1976) (London: Bloomsbury, 1992), p. 13.

42. Jerome Charyn, *The Good Policeman* (London: Bloomsbury, 1990), p. 70.

43. Charyn, *The Education of Patrick Silver*, p. 20.

44. Ibid., p. 97.

45. Charyn, *The Good Policeman*, p. 153.

46. Charyn, *The Education of Patrick Silver*, p. 10 and p. 33.

47. Mike Woolf, 'Exploding the Genre: The Crime Fiction of Jerome Charyn', in Brian Docherty (ed.), *American Crime Fiction* (London: Macmillan, 1988), p. 133.

48. Ibid., p. 142.

49. Ibid., p. 134.

50. Jerome Charyn, *Metropolis: New York as Myth, Marketplace and Magic Land* (London: Abacus, 1986), p. 267.

51. 'Race', here, is defined as a concept 'which signifies and symbolises social conflicts and interests by referring to different types of human bodies' (Omi and Wincant, *Racial Formations in the United States*, p. 55).

52. Linda Chavez, *Out of the Barrio: Towards a New Politics of Hispanic Assimilation* (London and New York: HarperCollins, 1991), p. 6.

53. Smith and Feagin, *The Bubbling Cauldron*, pp. 8–9.

54. Goldberg, *Racial Subjects*, p. 65.

55. Ibid., p. 66.

56. Alex Abella, *The Killing of the Saints* (London: Serpent's Tail, 1992), p. 5.

57. A name given to Cubans jailbirds and political enemies who were released from prison in 1980 on the condition that they left Cuba for the US from the port of Mariel.

58. Porter, *The Pursuit of Crime*, p. 245.

59. Michael Nava, *The Hidden Law* (New York: Ballantine, 1992), p. 86.

60. As Nava writes:

Outside in the larger world, where they labored under the contemptuous eye of Anglo bosses, the fathers were social and political ciphers. No wonder, then, that in the families they tolerated no dissent from their wives and children. And they drank. (p. 169)

61. Tony Hillerman, *Coyote Waits* (New York: HarperCollins, 1991), p. 232.
62. Carol laFavor, *Evil Dead Center* (first published 1997) (London: The Women's Press, 1998), p. 32.
63. John G. Cawelti, *Adventure, Mystery, Romance: Formula Stories as Art and Popular Culture* (Chicago, IL: University of Chicago Press, 1976), p. 161.
64. Chang-Rae Lee, *Native Speaker* (first published 1995) (London: Granta, 1998), p. 16.
65. Peter Messent, 'From Private Eye to Police Procedural: The Logic of Contemporary Crime Fiction', in Messent (ed.), *Criminal Proceedings: The Contemporary American Crime Novel* (London: Pluto, 1997), p. 12.
66. See Charles Taylor and Amy Gutman (eds), *Multiculturalism and 'The Politics of Recognition'* (Princeton, NJ: Princeton University Press, 1992), pp. 25–6.
67. Kathleen G. Klein (ed.), 'Introduction', *Diversity and Detective Fiction* (Bowling Green: The Popular Press, 1999), p. 1.
68. bell hooks, *Yearning: Race, Gender and Cultural Politics* (London: Turnaround, 1991), p. 27.
69. Nancy Abelmann and John Lie, *Blue Dreams: Korean Americans and the Los Angeles Riots* (London and Cambridge, MA: Harvard University Press, 1995), p. 191.

Index